STUDIES IN GROUP BEHAVIOR

STUDIES IN
GROUP BEHAVIOR

EDITED BY

GRACE LONGWELL COYLE

ASSOCIATE PROFESSOR, SCHOOL OF
APPLIED SOCIAL SCIENCES
WESTERN RESERVE UNIVERSITY

HARPER & BROTHERS PUBLISHERS

NEW YORK AND LONDON

1937

CONTENTS

PREFACE

This book contains case studies of five groups which were developed as a part of the program of a social settlement in a foreign section of an American city. They are, we believe, fairly representative illustrations of what is now commonly termed group work. Similar group activities with an educational or recreational purpose are carried on in community centers, Y.M. and Y.W.C.A.'s, Y.M. and Y.W.H.A.'s, the Boy and Girl Scouts, public schools, churches, trade unions, and other organizations.

Such activities are being increasingly scrutinized by those engaged in leading them in the attempt to see more clearly what they might accomplish and how more effective leadership might be developed. With the fact of increasing leisure and the ever-present tendency to use much of it in group activities of some sort, these questions have become increasingly urgent. This case material is presented, therefore, in the hope that it will contribute to a critical analysis of group leadership generally and to a steady improvement in the quality of such leadership.

These records were written by students in the School of Applied Social Sciences of Western Reserve University. The School as a part of its training of social workers for various leisure time agencies requires each of its students to keep such a record of one of the groups with which he works. This method of record keeping was developed during several years of experimentation by Wilber I. Newstetter, the director of the Group Work Course at the School of Applied Social Sciences, and Clara A. Kaiser, at that time also of the faculty of the School and research director of the University Neighborhood Centers, the laboratory settlement of which these groups were a part. The material of the book, therefore, is essentially their product. I wish also to acknowledge my indebtedness to the following students who wrote the records here used: Eleanore Diskin, Virginia Ebert, Lois Kennedy, Eleanor McKay, Thomas McCullough, Emma Schauer, and Harry Serotkin.

In addition, I am indebted to various members of the faculty of the School and to several committees of social workers in Cleveland who have used one of the records for discussion and in so doing have helped by their criticisms to improve its method of presentation.

The records as here given have been cut and summarized by the editor in the interests of brevity and clearness. Such cutting inevitably betrays a bias but the editor has attempted to offset some of the dangers involved by stating in each case the main lines according to which the cutting has been determined.

These five groups are all organized as clubs, and with the exception of the women's group, they consist of so-called "natural groups," that is, small congenial groups of children or young people based on a gang impulse rather than united around some single common interest. This type of group is the predominant one in many settlements and in some of the other leisure time agencies. Of this kind of group, we believe, the following records are typical. The editor recognizes, however, that this is not by any means the only form of group used in various organizations and having educational value. Interest groups such as dramatic clubs, craft groups, or discussion groups; larger clubs formed by the agency or drawn from a wide area, have also an essential place in any well rounded agency program. The use of groups of only one sex also does not imply any preference for such groups on the part of the editor. It happens, however, that records are at this time available chiefly for this type of group. In issuing these records, therefore, we wish to make clear that they are regarded by us as only a partial illustration of the types of groups which can and should be utilized.

As research data we recognize that this material cannot stand the severe test of scientific accuracy. In the first place, the original data were collected by students often in their first year at the School. Although all these students were college graduates with a background of study in the social sciences and although some of them had had previous experience as group leaders, none of them had been trained for the difficult task of observation of social phenomena. They suffered from the lack of objective measuring instruments for recording these intricate social processes. Moreover the comparatively undeveloped state of the study of groups has meant that there were not always accepted or well defined concepts available for the description of the situations observed.

Yet with all these limitations we believe this material has considerable value for group leaders in many organizations and for the social scientist interested in the study of group relations.

For the professional group worker, for volunteer group leaders in social work and elsewhere, and for those training group workers, we believe this material can be of value by the concrete pictures it presents of many common problems. All case material suffers somewhat from the fact that each situation is unique. But these are, we believe, representative enough of many voluntary groups so that group leaders of many kinds will find much here that is comparable to their own experiences. It is our hope that the material presented may serve to stimulate among group leaders discussion of the objectives, methods and results of such group activities.

For the social scientist and for others interested in understanding our modern community, such case studies afford a picture, however imperfectly portrayed, of group relationships viewed from within. It is out of such rough pictures that the concepts for more refined description can be developed and the tools for observation and recording worked out. Here under a microscope, however imperfect the present lens, we see the intimate life of a group, the interactions of individuals, the exercise of leadership, the development of socialized attitudes. Here also we can see the antisocial effects of our community life producing delinquency here, frustration there, sapping initiative with unemployment, undermining health with low wages and anxiety. Here, too, we see the acculturation of the foreign community in process, the conflict between new and old authorities, the developing of our new generation of citizens as they become aware of the industrial conditions, political alignments, and social pressures of a typical American city.

It takes an imaginative insight into social reality to see in this petty squabble between a supercilious American and her Polish neighbors the process of cultural assimilation; in this recalcitrant youth caught stealing a light bulb from the club room, the effect of the depression on the rising generation; in this discussion of wages and vocational opportunities in a club meeting, the increasing awakening of the workers to their problems. Yet it is of these concrete and apparently trivial incidents that life consists and it is from such situations that our large sociological generalizations gain their reality. It is here in what William James called the "molecular processes" of our society that through countless minute decisions, through innumerable intangible pressures, the great currents of history take their course.

All of us as members of the community need to understand the

concrete reality of human situations such as those here depicted
if we are going either to analyze them fruitfully or to participate
in creating for ourselves coordinated and fruitful social relations.
This is the stuff of life. We must make of it what we can.

GRACE L. COYLE

Cleveland, Ohio
January, 1937

STUDIES IN GROUP BEHAVIOR

I

THE GROUP LEADER AND HIS FUNCTION

IN THE records that follow, we see a group leader participating
with his group in a great variety of situations. His presence
in the group undoubtedly affects its behavior in certain ways. It
is assumed by the organization of which these groups are a part
that the experience of group membership can be made more
fruitful for those participating by the assistance of a group
leader, not one of themselves. It is largely through this leader
that the organization or social agency fulfills its educational and
recreational function.

THE OBJECTIVES OF THE GROUP LEADER

What is this group leader trying to do with his group? Why
is he there? What is his function in the group? This will vary
with every agency and every leader. In regard to the purpose of
such groups it is possible to discern three main objectives governing these efforts. Such groups provide, in the first place, an
opportunity for developing social attitudes and the ability to
adjust to others in mutually enriching ways. Here in the club
is a school in human relationships. Leader and led, the cooperative and the recalcitrant, the autocrat and the democrat, all have
their opportunity in this setting to try themselves out and to discover which kind of relationship will yield them the greatest
satisfactions and which will bring the most effective results for
the group. Within the social agency this "natural" process is
observed and at points controlled by the group leader. His function is to affect it in ways which he believes will lead to the growth
of socially desirable attitudes and to experience in mutually developing relationships.

Secondly, in addition to such experience in social adjustment
to one's fellows these groups provide opportunity for the development of new interests, the broadening of knowledge and the
acquiring of new skills. Like the progressive educator, the group
worker must begin with existing interests, but building upon

them he may, if he has the skill, lead his group into enriching new experiences, into higher degrees of useful skills, into new realms of knowledge, or into the wider ranges of social responsibility.

In the third place, the group can provide training and experience in community living and in active participation in community affairs. These groups exist within a network of social relationships involving the parish church, the nationality society, the school, the political party, the labor movement. As the members mature they must find their way into some part in this intricate web of the community. These groups within a social agency afford an opportunity for them to learn cooperative effort for common ends. In community service, in legislative activity, in the creation of public opinion, in a great variety of situations, the members can discover how to participate in the economic, social and political currents about them.

All these groups have potential value as laboratories of human relationships, as opportunities for education in the pursuit of interests, and as training schools for community living in a democracy. Whether they realize these values will depend partly on what the members bring to the group experience, partly on the group leader's skill in making the most of what he has. In the records that follow we see the group leaders attempting to turn these aims into actualities.

THE BASIS OF EVALUATION

How should such efforts be evaluated? In order to judge the success of these groups or of the leader's methods in working with them it is necessary to see them against the background of certain criteria. In the hope of clarifying the evaluation of this material and at some risk perhaps of appearing to be didactic, the editor has attempted to set down here some criteria for group leadership in groups of this kind. This is done in the expectation that such criteria will need constant rethinking in the light of future developments.

THE RELATION OF LEADER AND GROUP

An analysis of the records reveals several areas in which evaluation of the leaders' methods is needed. The first is the leader's relation with the group. The establishment of an effective relationship between the leader and his group will have several aspects including the acceptance of the leader by the group, the definite contribution he may make to the group's activities, his function in relation to the mores or current values of the community, and his own integrity in the relationship.

In establishing an effective relationship, no leader can be successful who cannot win a place with his group so that they welcome his presence and are open to suggestions from him. Like any member coming into a group he must gain acceptance with them. This does not mean that he will seek to build up an intense personal loyalty to himself. He will at times be the object of hostility as well as of affection. He must learn to accept as inevitable the fluctuation of feeling from the group and to build a steady, diffused and cordial relationship out of mutual respect and common interests.[1]

In order to develop such a relationship, a leader will need to have something positive and definite to contribute to the group's life. Depending on his own interests, skills or knowledge he can contribute to the activities in ways which will enrich the group's experience and make him a vital part of it. He will not, of course, hold the center of the stage nor dominate the group's planning, but his relationship will be the sounder for any effective assistance in specific ways that he can render to the group's activities. The richer, more varied and more mature his experience, the more valuable a resource he may be for the group.

The leader is also a bearer of certain social values. In all the social agencies using group activities there is an assumption that the group will conform to certain socially acceptable behavior and that one function of the group is to conserve and strengthen the socially constructive forces of the community, however they may be defined. The leader is the representative of these standards within the group.[2] The group usually expects him to be, within

[1] An interesting parallel can be drawn here to the place of the educator as distinguished from the psycho-analyst described in Dr. Susan Isaacs' book, "The Social Development of Young Children." Dr. Isaacs points out that (page 410) the analyst has to accept and uncover the hate as well as the love of children. The educator on the other hand, while she will meet some negative feeling inevitably, is successful only if on the whole she can develop a positive reaction to herself.

[2] Here again Dr. Isaacs contributes an interesting contrast. The analyst she says must allow himself to represent anything which the child requires in working out his unconscious impulses but the educator must assume the representation of the super-ego, that is, the part of the child which urges him toward the good as he conceives it. The position of the group leader similarly

limits, the upholder of such standards. He will gain their respect not by becoming neutral, not by withdrawing from this responsibility but by so representing those values that they appear inherently attractive. This does not mean that he is priggish or dogmatic in his standards nor that he will attempt to coerce the group to an acceptance of his values. His own integrity, however, may require that he let his values be known at appropriate points. More essential, is the necessity of his incarnating such values in a way which makes them convincing. The group leader, like the teacher and parent, will function most effectively when he adequately represents the values in which the members can believe and when he is sufficiently secure himself to assert his authority when necessary.

The leader will need to maintain his own integrity. He will avoid any element of manipulation in his relation to the group. The control of the group for educational ends perhaps not conceived by it easily leads to a conception of the leader's function as benevolent manipulation. In certain groups where immaturity makes it impossible for the members to understand fully all that is involved, the leader will inevitably act upon certain premises which he cannot share with them. To the extent to which it is feasible, he will need to integrate his purposes with theirs, and to avoid all indirection in his dealings with them. This does not necessitate agreement, but it does involve a kind of frankness and mutuality which arise from a relationship based on respect and confidence.

In the relationship of the leader to his group, therefore, the editor would propose to the reader that he ask the following questions:

1. Does the leader establish and maintain an effective relationship with his group?
2. What positive contribution does he make to its activities?
3. Does he adequately and convincingly represent significant and constructive values?
4. Does he preserve a sincere relation to his group?

THE RELATION OF THE LEADER TO INDIVIDUALS

In addition to his relation to the group as a whole, the leader will have certain relations with individual members. Some of

is in part to symbolize the super-ego and strengthen the forces making for acceptance of higher values.

these will be administrative relationships for the carrying on of the group, some will be counseling relationships arising out of the need of the members.

Leaders will need to have in most cases a relationship to group officials in which plans are discussed, difficulties cleared up, and assistance given on methods of leadership. The leader has the opportunity as he works with a club president or committee chairman to aid in the effective management of the group and also to help the official to an understanding of how to handle difficult individuals, how to encourage initiative from the group, how to distribute responsibility, how to coordinate efforts. This training in leadership will need to be adapted not only to the needs of the group, but to the particular psychological needs of the indigenous leader.

In addition to such relationship many group leaders will have a counseling relationship with individuals. Most leaders are not trained case workers nor counselors. Inevitably, however, they will have to deal with certain personal problems of the members of the group. The leader should be sensitive to the symptoms of personal need evident in the group and should be accessible to those who wish his assistance as a counselor. Often, he will need to know and understand the family situation of his members. Under certain circumstances the leader may find that the members need to use him to a degree as a parent substitute. In both younger and older groups there are likely to be situations in which individuals are looking for support and authority and others in which they are wanting encouragement to go on to new experience. The leader will need to recognize that in his position as leader he is occasionally looked to for help in meeting one or other of these needs. He must accept the responsibility for meeting the need for support without becoming involved in the relationship in such a way that he cannot assist the individual to the development of a healthy independence.

While he should be sufficiently trained in the understanding of individual behavior so that he can be of service to the members when they turn to him, he must recognize when the member is in need of more expert help than he can provide. Leaders in some instances cannot avoid confidences which involve highly charged emotional experience but they should avoid trying to treat such problems. Where such situations arise leaders will need to get expert assistance from case workers or psychiatrists, as the serious-

ness of the situation may demand. In some cases, the group leader
may be the person to continue the relationship acting under the
guidance of a case worker or psychiatrist. In other cases, the member should be referred to someone adequately equipped to deal
directly with the problem. The group leader will, therefore, need
to be so accessible that he can provide the assistance to individuals
of which he is capable, and so wise that he will know when to
direct the member to more expert guidance than he is equipped to
offer.

The reader of the records that follow will therefore wish to
ask:

1. Does the leader have sufficient contact with the indigenous leaders of the group to assist them where necessary in the management of the group's affairs?
2. Is the leader sensitive to the personal needs of members
   of the group? Does he handle such situations wisely?
   Does he know how and where to refer the situations
   which he cannot handle?

In addition to establishing a satisfactory relation to the group
and to individuals the leader's methods must be evaluated in terms
of his handling of certain aspects of the group's life. For consideration of this material, the editor wishes to propose criteria
in four areas: a. the handling of social interactions, b. the problems of group control, c. the making of program, d. the handling
of group feeling. Others which might be used in other situations
such as those relating to the defining of membership policies, to
group structure or to the adequacy of group thinking are less
appropriate here because of the types of groups recorded.

THE HANDLING OF SOCIAL INTERACTIONS

Among the objectives held by leaders for such groups is the
training in social relationships on an increasingly mature level
and expressive of the higher forms of human intercourse. This
includes in practice the handling of quarreling and factionalism,
the management of conflicts between sub-groups, the creation of
cooperative attitudes, the balancing of the dominant and submissive tendencies in individuals—all the intricate interplay of personality by which basic impulses are expressing themselves, attitudes are being formed and personality created.

Adequate consideration of criteria in this realm would require a library on psychology, psychiatry and sociology. The editor can present here only some of the simpler elements for such an evaluation.

The development of mutual good will and cooperation is of prime importance in such groups. It is obvious that one of their functions is the creation of a friendly setting in which people can draw encouragement and security from the expressed good will of their fellows. The ability to make and keep friends on a mutually developing level, and the capacity to work easily and without unnecessary friction with others, should be promoted by experience in the group. The degrees of intimacy between the members of the group will vary widely, but the interaction in the group will need to be permeated by a degree of mutual respect and understanding if it is to provide experience in the developing of socialized attitudes.

Even where such attitudes are common, however, groups will now and then manifest hostilities, sometimes against each other, sometimes against the leader or another group. The leader will need to recognize this as inevitable and in some situations perhaps desirable. A distinction should be made between superficial and occasional disagreements and long-standing feuds involving highly emotional states. The former are to be expected in most groups and may serve a useful purpose in harmlessly eliminating emotional tensions. In some cases they can be handled in such a way as to result in an eventual integration on a deeper level with enhanced mutual understanding. In other cases this type of quarreling can be eased by competitive sports in which the hostility is harmlessly directed against another group under controlled conditions, thereby creating greater unity within the group. In some cases, the need for expressing aggression is turned against some ancient entrenched social evil, like a racial antagonism and so provides the dynamic for needed social change. If the leader recognizes the tendency to develop such feelings as a common factor in all human relationships he can often render them relatively harmless in their effects and sometimes help those concerned to direct them to constructive purposes. Where the leader finds that he is dealing with deep-rooted, highly emotional hostilities, the situation is more difficult. In certain situations where a feud threatens to split the group and where no integration is feasible, the group may be forced in the interests of unity to eliminate the trouble-makers. In some cases such feuds will be rooted in the serious emotional problems of individuals who are in need of expert individual service, which the leader may help them to find.

The leader will need to recognize also that individuals are in search of different satisfactions from the group. Some are looking for a chance to dominate, some for a leader to submit to, some for a satisfying use of newly developing powers, some for adventure, some for recognition. The group experience should provide as far as possible opportunity for meeting these needs of its members by such a variety of situations as will give scope to their various desires in ways constructive for the group as a whole. The leader with the present limited facilities in most agencies cannot know enough about all the members to be aware of all these needs and no group could meet them all in any case. But in so far as possible the leader should attempt to help individuals find scope for themselves along the lines of their particular needs and interests, keeping in mind the common needs of the group. This can often be accomplished through the administration of the group and the type of program adopted. Opportunities for leadership through committees, for participation at certain points, for recognition of special abilities, for the winning of a secure place by outstanding achievement for the group, are often afforded for some in the course of the group activities. Others perhaps can reach a satisfactory group adjustment best by being relieved of the need to compete and encouraged to pursue their own interests along lines appropriate to their unique concerns. The leader needs to be so aware of the individuals involved and of the social interactions between them that as far as possible the needs are met by suitable opportunities.

The reader will therefore wish to be on the lookout for the ways in which the interactions within the group are affecting individuals. He will therefore ask

1. Is the group permeated with sufficient good will and mutual understanding to create group cohesion and to provide an encouragingly secure environment for individual growth?

2. Are the hostilities and conflicts handled in such a way as to relieve individual tensions without injury to the group and to direct the feeling where possible to useful ends?

3. To what extent are individuals able to find within the interweaving of social interactions opportunities which meet their particular needs?

THE PROBLEMS OF GROUP CONTROL

In addition to handling the interactions between members the leader must deal with problems of group management and control. With younger children this takes the familiar form of discipline problems. As the groups become more self-governing it involves questions of participation, the use of indigenous leadership, and the administration of the group's affairs.

It is assumed in most groups that as the group develops it should become increasingly self-directing. The control of a group by itself can be promoted by the adoption of activities sufficiently absorbing to enlist genuine interest in their accomplishment. Where such can be found the group will learn through its own desire for successful accomplishment to force its recalcitrant members into line when necessary. In so far as possible the leader's authority should be held in reserve and the control attained by the intrinsic pull of the activities.

In situations where the group is needing to have the leader assume responsibility for them, he can use that opportunity to establish a non-authoritative, creative approach with only sufficient control evident to provide the security needed and with encouragement to independence given at appropriate points. In certain groups the members are happier and more secure if they are conscious of a firm but kindly control to be relied upon when needed. As the group develops, the planning and control of activities should be shifted into its hands as quickly as it is able to assume them. In groups where a greater degree of self-government has already been developed, the leader's rôle is that of assistant to the indigenous leaders in administering the affairs of the club.

One of the chief problems of self-governing groups is the development of participation. Sound group government, like large-scale democracy, rests upon wide and interested participation. A group run by a few is probably not providing much opportunity for growth for the others, for it is encouraging passivity on the one hand and domination on the other. The leader will, therefore, try to draw as large a proportion as possible into the active planning of the group's affairs and to see that the activities planned are those that will enlist the interest of all.

A further problem often arises in connection with the adequate selection of leadership. One of the problems of democracies, small and great, is in the selection of leaders who are equipped to carry out the will of the group. Group control is adequate only where the group is successful in selecting for its officials qualified persons. A sound group government will result where the electorate develops judgment in picking its officials in accordance with the work to be done and their ability to do it. The kind of group leadership being developed is very important for the group. In the control of the group various types of leaders will appear. Dictators, demagogues, weak or crooked officials, will occasionally be found in such groups. For the purposes of group work it is assumed that the type of leader which is being encouraged should be of the "group builder" variety.[3] This type of leader seeks to help the group to its own self-expression rather than making it a tool of his own personality. He organizes and deputizes, develops and integrates interests, and encourages the group to creative expression and increasing self-maintenance. The group leader seeks to develop this type of attitude among the officers of his group as well as to use this method himself in dealing with it.

Finally all group government must rest upon the creation of power out of common effort. In all groups power is required in order to unite individuals to carry out the agreed-upon enterprises of the group. Where activities rest on vital interests and participation is widespread, the power to carry through endeavors will rise spontaneously out of the situation. Authority will rest on the necessity for getting things done in which all are vitally concerned. Where program is superimposed or leadership is autocratic, the power to carry through endeavors rests on fear or loyalty, or on extrinsic rewards and punishments. Strong group administration consists in so directing the group that the power to do will rise from the groups' interests and enlist all freely and spontaneously.[4]

The reader therefore will wish to scrutinize the group's methods of control asking:

1. Is the group as self-governing and self-directing as its stage of development makes possible?
2. Is participation in the group's control widespread, interested, and intelligent?
3. Is the group showing itself capable of selecting leaders equipped to manage its affairs?

[3] Busch, Henry M. *Leadership in Group Work.* Page 120 ff.
[4] This is what Miss Mary Follette has called in another situation leadership based on "power with," not "power over." Metcalf, H. C., Editor, *Business Leadership,* New York, 1931, Chapters 4 and 16.

4. Is the type of leadership encouraged by the group experience constructive and creative?

5. Does the power to carry through an enterprise arise inherently out of the common concern for its accomplishment?

THE MAKING OF PROGRAM

The problems faced by a leader in helping his group to determine its program will include the location of its vital interests, the encouragement of creativity and progression and the adequate handling of various subjects or types of activities.

If the members of the group are to get significant educational value from their experience, their activities must be rooted in vital interests. The leader, therefore, will need to help the group to locate its common interests out of which program can be developed. Complete agreement will of course be unlikely, so that provision will need to be made for some differentiation to meet the particular interests of individuals or sub-groups. This is sometimes provided through division into sub-groups, or by taking various interests in turn. The best results usually come about when a common project can be located which requires a variety of skills and abilities and so provides for differentiated effort coordinated to a common end.

Having discovered the vital interests, the group will move forward only if the program is managed in such a way that they themselves have the experience of creating it. Planning, originating, experimenting, creating, can be significant experiences for the group members. Moreover, the program needs to show progression so that as the group continues it is able to accomplish larger projects demanding more ability and advanced thinking. If programs differ only in their variety but remain on the same level, the group is likely to get stale. As one leader put it, "We start where they are and end where they were." Activities requiring more skill, discussions demanding more knowledge, projects requiring more elaborate planning should be developed as the group matures. The leader will need to encourage both creativity and progression in order to make the program yield its best results.

Vital and significant content adequately presented is essential to a valuable group experience. The program of such leisure time groups tends to include largely sports and games, the arts, such as dramatics, music and crafts, discussion of various subjects, and projects which combine these interests. In many cases the prime reason for the group's existence is the pleasure of companionship. The educational purpose is incidental. At the same time, the interests which appear often provide an opportunity for significant learning if these are well handled. Many such groups suffer from superficial and trivial programs poorly presented by inadequate leaders or teachers.

When, for example, discussions arise, as they frequently do, on vocational questions, on international affairs, on sex education, or similar subjects, the leader has the opportunity to see that the group gets an adequate introduction to the question. The same need for high standards is found in relation to the handling of the various arts and in the area of the sports. If as in many cases the leader is not equipped to handle the matter himself, he can see that an expert is brought in, that books are made available or other experience provided. Since the only inducement to learning lies in the intrinsic interest aroused, this requires teaching skill of a high quality. These groups provide in many ways unusual opportunities for teaching along the lines advocated by progressive education. If the program can arise in vital interest, develop creatively and result in adequate teaching adapted to the needs of the participants, the group experience may make a vital contribution to the growth of its members.

What questions then will the reader put in regard to program in these groups? He may ask:

1. Are these activities rooted in vital interests and is provision made for the variety of interests in the group?
2. Does the program encourage initiative and creativity from its participants?
3. Is the program developing so that new learning on advancing levels is taking place?
4. Are the subjects or projects handled so as to give a sound and adequate understanding adapted to the needs of the members?

THE HANDLING OF GROUP FEELING

Every group has its ebb and flow of morale, its need for expression of attachment to itself, its group pride in achievement and discouragement in failure. Conflicts may split the unity of the group, success unite it, or outside criticism shatter it. The leader is always dealing with the subtle tone or esprit de corps which permeates the group.

The cohesion and continuance of any group is dependent upon the maintenance of this esprit de corps. While fluctuations are to be expected a strong and developing group will show a fairly even level of morale which will hold its less interested members in line. A group with a vitally interested core and an indifferent fringe is not likely to maintain its cohesion under difficulties. In a strong group, participation in attachment to the group will be widespread.

Groups will wish to express their sense of belonging in various ways. Such expressions often take the form of badges of membership, club songs, banners, or ceremonies. Esprit de corps expresses itself also in cohesion in the midst of other groups, in pride in its collective achievements and in competition with other groups. Such expression is natural and essential to the continuance of the group. It has value also to individuals in enlarging the scope of their emotional attachments. It is important, however, that it be attached to objects which are developing to the individuals concerned and socially useful. The leader needs to recognize the power of such group attachment in its hold over individuals and its importance for the group. He will need to help the group to find expressions for this devotion which are appropriate to their needs and which at the same time lead to larger and socially desirable loyalties. In regard to group feeling, therefore, the reader may wish to inquire:

1. Does the group show a healthy esprit de corps which is both fairly steady and well distributed?
2. Has the group developed methods of expressing its group feeling? Do these expressions provide an enlarging experience for individuals? Do they support the cohesion of the group? Do they aid its relation to other groups?

THE RELATION OF THE GROUP TO THE COMMUNITY

In addition to these criteria which deal with the internal processes of the group, the results of such group experience must be tested in the larger setting of the community. In this area we are confronted with questions of the relation of this group to other groups, of its effect on community relationships, of its contribution to active and intelligent citizenship.

Such groups are liable to become ingrown or to concern them-

selves too much with their own status. Group membership in
some cases may be encouraging a narrow, self-centered attitude.
The group leader, therefore, will seek opportunity for his group
to make contacts with other similar groups under circumstances
which will encourage mutual understanding and cooperation.
Inter-group activities between boys and girls are especially needed
during adolescence in order to establish easy and satisfactory relationships. Activities between groups of various nationalities or
races may serve also to widen contacts and to create better community relations. Inter-group activities may also be used to provide
recognition of group achievement, to stimulate ingrowing groups
and to supply experience in larger and more complex projects
than a single group could undertake.

In addition to relations with similar organized groups, such
groups have a relation to the large social groupings of the community. Most organizations are built up not only in relation to
personal congeniality; they also reflect community lines of nationality, race, occupation, sex, or religious affiliation. Groups
within the agencies will often act to strengthen nationality loyalties, to build up occupational consciousness, to encourage sex
segregation, or to support religious affiliation. Whether such results are considered desirable will depend on the philosophy of the
agency. Some organizations, for example, set out to foster nationality cultures and do so by organizing on nationality lines.
Some encourage an interest in economic questions by developing
organizations on occupational bases. Some aim to encourage better relations between the sexes and so organize boys and girls
together. Some set out to break down nationality or racial barriers
by mixed groups. Even in the case of the so-called "natural" group
which comes into the agency already organized it is likely that some
social factor such as nationality or occupation may be present. Each
individual will inevitably make certain alignments to various
groups as he grows up in the community. The agency and the
leader, therefore, will need to recognize how this particular group
may react on the interrelations of the neighborhood. The evaluation of the results will depend in each case on the equilibrium of
social forces within each community and also on the judgment
of those concerned as to which forces should be strengthened and
which broken down.

Social conflicts between such large groups may be inevitable at
points, but the way such conflicts are handled will determine
whether they result in destruction and chaos or in new and better

social institutions. Small groups such as these, if they learn how to handle conflicts within their group and between similar groups, may make a contribution to the constructive handling of social conflict not on the basis of coercion and violence, but in terms of intelligent integration and social insight.

In addition, such groups can encourage active participation in the community. As group members approach maturity and the responsibilities of citizenship, these groups can often provide encouragement to intelligent and active participation in community affairs. This may often need to begin in some project near at hand, like leading a younger boys' club. It can expand, however, into local political and economic issues. A developing group, therefore, is one which includes a widening interest in community affairs which encourages discussion of them and participation in them as opportunity offers. In relation to the community, therefore, the reader will need to ask

1. Has the group had contacts with other similar groups? Have these resulted in wider sympathies, increased understanding and an ability to cooperate with other groups?
2. How is this group affecting community relations? Is it reinforcing social factors which are constructive in the community? Is it breaking down useless or harmful barriers?
3. Is this group taking an active part in community affairs? Is its participation founded on intelligent understanding? Is it motivated by a vital interest in the social good as the group understands it? Will such activities contribute to an active and public spirited participation in the local political, social, and economic issues of the community?

These then the editor would offer as some of the criteria against which to test the records that follow. They will fall short of these criteria at many points. If, however, the criticism of these typical situations will lead to a sharper defining of objectives, a more considered development of criteria and eventually a better practice of the art of group leadership, the book will have fulfilled its function.

II

THE GAY GIRLS: A STUDY IN SOCIAL INTERACTION

THE Gay Girls Club is a group of about twelve girls who have known each other since childhood. At the time this record opens the girls range in age from eighteen to twenty.

All the girls are Slovenian by descent and are members of a closely knit Slovenian community. They are graduates of the parochial school and are active in the parish church. Their neighborhood borders upon a large community of Poles but there is little social contact between them and very little with the surrounding American community.

All of these girls are at work in worsted or garment factories, in the local telephone exchange or in other jobs of a similar kind. With the exception of one or two, most of them work in factories within the neighorhood.

The club was organized in the spring of 1929, through the efforts of Paula, its first president. They were influenced in starting their club by the example of a similar club of Polish girls, slightly older, also meeting at the Community House.

During the first year the club activities consist chiefly of simple crafts and parties. An attempt is made to go to the downtown Y. W. C. A. for swimming and dancing but this is opposed by Father Dubich, the Slovenian priest of St. John's Church, and so is dropped with regret by the girls. The group distinguishes itself in the community by its successful good times, its high morale and its support of Community House activities. Both within the Slovenian parish and in the House it is recognized as an outstanding group.

During the three years recorded here, the second, third and fourth of the club's life, the club engages in a miscellaneous collection of activities in which recreation and light education predominate. The chief value of the club lies in the satisfaction and security of a congenial group, closely bound together, not only by personal friendship, but by similar cultural traditions within the Slovenian community.

From the viewpoint of the group worker this group record has value as a study in social interactions of two kinds: the interplay of personality within the group and the relation of this group to its encompassing community. In the relationships, especially of Paula and Olga, the outstanding members of the group and in the group's reaction to them it is possible to see something of the structure and process of such small congenial groups. While the record is not full enough to reveal all the significance of the relationship, it is possible to understand something of the meaning of such groups to the participants. How do such relationships meet their needs? What do they learn from such experience? How do the needs of individuals and of groups supplement each other? Out of these mutual needs the club is created, and as these inter-relationships work themselves out, it serves its purpose.

This group is of interest also as an illustration of the process of cultural assimilation. Here a group of second generation Americans is working out its relation to the established authorities of family and of church and to the newer stimuli of jobs and recreation in an American city. It is seldom that one can see into a nationality community through the eyes of such a group and catch in the act the process of adaptation of old and new, of foreign and American customs and values.

DRAMATIS PERSONAE

Paula—the first president of the club and its outstanding member, a mender in the library, attractive, well dressed, vivacious, alert, full of initiative, one of a large family and the pride of her parents.

Sophie—a telephone operator with better pay than the other girls, well dressed and vivacious, friend to Paula, rather lacking in initiative and perseverance.

Olga—daughter of a prominent member of the Slovenian community, large, awkward, moody, often sullen and unresponsive but with an ability to get a following.

Rose—follower of Olga, quiet, acquiescent, drab in appearance.

Anica—follower of Olga, chief support of a family in which the father drinks and the mother has "spells" of intermittent insanity; pleasant but not outstanding.

Stella—oldest in a family which is receiving relief and in which there is constant quarreling between father and mother; charming, quiet, popular.

Yulka—unstable, vivacious, good looking, one of a family which has seen better days, sometimes the life of the party, at other times sulky and touchy.

Mara—frank, attractive, lively, sympathetic, an adept at smoothing ruffled feelings, a good singer, a pillar of the club.

Angela—small, slender and very blonde, quiet but self-composed.

Mimi—attractive, able, full of initiative and cheerful in spite of the fact that her family is on relief and her own opportunities severely restricted.

Bertha—clever, graceful, charming with a slangy way of expressing herself, and a flair for singing and dancing.

Josephine—quiet, amiable, not outstanding.

Wanda, Bernice and Bettie—temporary members for a few months.

FIRST YEAR

The Gay Girls open their second year which is the first year of this record with twelve members all of whom are carried over from the first year.

Bertha, the president, joined during the middle of the first year and took no outstanding part at first in club affairs. In her early contacts with the club she was prominent largely because she was entertaining but as time went on she developed marked leadership capacity. Although she showed decided improvement during the first year she still does not have much confidence in herself. She is inclined to be dominated by Mara. Her status in the group has developed partly through her capacity to be vivacious and enthusiastic. Paula, the first president and natural leader of the group, continues to be its outstanding figure.

The Leader of this club is acting also as the head of a new community center, one of several small units which are being developed by the Community House at this time. The Gay Girls are very much interested in the new center and are helpful to the Leader in paving the way for her with other groups, introducing her and helping in the development of the whole program at the center.

October 1, 1930

The first meeting of the year was held in the new quarters; ten girls were present. The Leader proposed that they take as a project the "fixing up" of the new house. Tie-dying, it was suggested, might be used to make table covers and wall hangings. This suggestion was greeted with the greatest enthusiasm. Immediately a large number of suggestions were made for various ways in which the appearance of the house could be improved. They suggested making candleholders and baskets, framing pictures, and making other decorations. Olga and Rose did not join in the enthusiastic response.

A suggestion from the Leader that in other similar community centers operated by the Community House there were women's clubs, led to a burst of further proposals for developing the center. "Gee, I got it," Paula said, "Olga's and Mara's mothers (she also named others whom the Leader does not remember) belong to a club at the school and I bet I could get them to meet here.

Gee, that would be swell!" Paula further added that she knew several women who would like to join a club and asked if she could call on them with the Leader. Both Paula and Stella said they would like to take clubs of younger girls in the new center.

> **Note:** This enthusiastic support of a project involving collective rather than individual effort in the line of crafts or sewing represents a change in interest from the previous year. The interest of a few in starting a women's club and in leading other clubs is further indication of a new capacity for community leadership. How can the Leader take advantage of these developing interests? How can this experience be extended from the few leaders to larger numbers?

The group also discussed the "rating" of the club in the neighborhood:

"Paula talked about various things they had done during the past summer and remarked that they had been too busy to do much as a club. 'Everybody's asking when I pass 'em on the street, "Ain't there a club no more?" ' The Leader said, 'The club is pretty well known, isn't it?' Paula then told the Leader how the club 'rated' in the neighborhood, without, however, bragging about it. 'Father Dubich sticks up for us all over, that's why people feel like they do about us.' She said that at church banquets if the club does not sit together he always remarks about it. 'And, gee do ya know what? He wants our pictures for the Slovenian paper! Ain't that swell!' she laughed. 'As a club?' the leader asked, and she emphatically repeated, 'As a club, and that's not all; he wants the pictures in the church year book.' "

> **Note:** This is interesting proof of the solidarity which the club has with the parish and of its place in the Slovenian community. Does it also indicate any dangers to the club either in its freedom to develop interests outside the parish or in the development of too much self-importance? Can anything be done to safeguard it at these points?

In the conduct of the first meeting, Paula with some difficulty extricated herself from her usual position of leader and handed the business over to Bertha, the new president. Bertha's inexperience as president made her very ineffective at first in grasping the situation. Difficulties also arose over a time of meeting. Yulka displayed her occasional pouting mood and when everyone else had finally agreed on Thursday, Olga upset the equilibrium by saying, "I ain't coming Thursday." When asked why, she said she just didn't want to. A vote finally decided it for Wednesday which Yulka took as a personal insult since that was the night she could not come. The meeting deteriorated into a squabble. The Leader allowed this to continue hoping they would make their own peace but finally had to act as mediator.

Note: Olga and Yulka both appear here in their characteristic rôles, Olga acting as a deterrent to action and an irritant, and Yulka as a spoiled child. The final vote allows Olga to impose her will upon the group. What should the Leader do in this situation? Should she make any attempt to understand the basis for Olga's behavior by personal contact with her?

October 8, 1930

This meeting saw the beginning of the project of furnishing the house. Tie-dying of materials for curtains was started. Everyone participated immediately except Rose and Olga who were finally drawn into it also after some persuasion.

Yulka who had said she could not come on this night of the week put in her appearance and rather self-consciously rejoined the group promising the Leader to come after this. The meeting ended with enthusiasm over what the group had accomplished.

October 10, 1930

In the interval between meetings the Leader had dinner with Paula and made the following plans for developing a women's club:

"Paula said, 'They just sit at meetings; they'd love to have us come up.' She added that 'we' would get something 'swell' to do for the first time in the way of handcraft and then they would just 'love it.' When asked whether it would be better for Paula to talk to the individual women in the club about it alone, she said, 'Oh, they'd just love it if you'd ask them too, they'd be so pleased.' Paula suddenly said, 'Gee, they can't all talk English, they couldn't talk to you, but I'll tell you what—we will translate for you!'

"She then told the Leader that 'lots of the Gay Girls have young married sisters who are "lively" and would probably like to join a club. I'll see them myself,' she said."

The following excerpt is also illuminating as to Paula's relation to the club and her opinion of Olga and Yulka:

"Paula told the Leader a great deal about the club itself and she again went into detail about the club's 'rating' in the neighborhood. She said that their parents and sisters always asked about it. 'And, you know what? That club at the school (the women's club already mentioned) said that any time we want them to help in something—they'll be right here.' She spoke of the 'stand-in' the girls had with the Sisters at St. John's School.

"She also said that she had considered 'quitting' the club because of Yulka and Josephine. Yulka, it seems, had tried to make trouble for Paula last summer because she thought that Paula was trying to take her boy friend away from her. Yulka had Josephine on her side and the two of them had talked about Paula, and among other things had said she 'tried to run everything.' It came to a showdown when the rest of the club went to Yulka's house about it, and Yulka was shown to be a 'liar.' 'The girls are still kind of sore at her for it,' Paula said, 'that's why they wouldn't change the club night for the two of them.' Paula added that Yulka is spoiled at home and often does not tell the truth about things. 'And Josephine isn't so nice as we used to think either—she's been talking about the whole club.'

"Olga, according to Paula, was one of the most 'loyal' members. The Leader told her that she often did not quite understand Olga. Whereat Paula said, 'She's a wonderful girl but she's just kind of funny, and we just let her alone then.' Paula recalled the time last year when Olga had disrupted a club meeting by saying that Paula had talked about her. 'She called me up next day and apologized and said, "I didn't mean it, I just had to cry because I had a toothache and I was ashamed so I blowed it on you." Olga likes to act as if she's mad at you—she likes to be coaxed.' "

Note: Is the Leader wise in making this contact with Paula and planning with her? Her remarks throw a new light on the real meaning of the conflict over the meeting time and also on the personalities of Yulka and Olga. Should the Leader have more such confidential interviews with Paula?

October 15, 1930

In addition to various minor matters of business, such as decorations for a coming dance and plans for swimming at the Clybourn bath house, the club made plans for enlisting their older sisters and other friends in a club, setting a date a month ahead for a first meeting.

The following account by the Leader gives a picture of the group:

"The girls talked so much and were so full of 'pep' and enthusiasm that it is rather difficult to attempt to give a picture of them: Paula, to whom all the girls turn for leadership; Bertha, slangy, with a way of expressing herself all her own; Mara, very loud and good-natured; with the others, with the exception of Olga and Rose, saying plenty. Olga and Rose were enthusiastic even though they said very little, for once readily agreeing with the others in their plans.

"Occurrences at this meeting demonstrated more than ever that Paula is the natural leader of the group. They turn to her for everything but she does not always do everything for them as they want her to. When she does not initiate activities, however, they usually do nothing. The group is unusually cooperative."

Note: Paula's abilities as a leader continue to keep her in a predominant position even though she is no longer president. Can this be avoided in such "natural" groups? Is it desirable? How could Paula use her abilities more effectively?

October 17, 1930

Between meetings the girls, with the exception of Bertha and Mara, attended the Senior Club Dance at the Community House. The Leader reports it as follows:

"They were dressed 'fit to kill' as one of them expressed it, and as usual enthusiastically labeled the dance as 'swell.' Paula came up to the Leader once and said, 'Gee, I never had such a swell time yet in my life.' In between dances the girls always sat together and when refreshments were served, they with some of the boys sat at the same table. They were strenuously 'rushed' by the boys, with the exception of Olga and Rose who always danced with girls."

Note: This cohesion of the club in the midst of a dance is an interesting evidence of its importance to the girls. Why do they tend to bunch together in the midst of a large group? The lack of popularity of Olga and Rose with the boys is also significant in explaining their difficulties of adjustment elsewhere. Note, however, Paula's popularity in this setting as well as with girls.

October 23, 1930

The meeting on October twenty-third was devoted to continuing the decorating projects by making lamp shades, and to baking a cake. This latter project was undertaken by Olga and was very successful. The Leader took pains to praise her in every way possible for this, with the result that she became very talkative and participated in everything. Yulka and Josephine who attend night school on Wednesday dropped out of the club temporarily at this point.

Note: This reaction of Olga's to praise seems to be characteristic. Is this a clue to the method of helping her to participate more fully?

November 5, 1930

On November fifth plans were completed concerning the new club of older women. Most of the time was occupied with work on lampshades and pictures for the house. The Leader commented on Olga's cooperative attitude and participation as decidedly an improvement over her usual behavior.

November 5–12, 1930

During the week the Leader and Paula called in the neighborhood on women who might be interested in the proposed club.

November 12, 1930

The program consisted of making candy but as often happened conversation circulated freely. The following excerpts are illuminating:

"When they returned, Mara and Stella were making taffy in the kitchen while the others were sitting around chatting in the front room. They were discussing the matter of the Y. W. C. A. Mara told the girls that she had been so enthusiastic when she got home from swimming the year before that her father had gone to see Father Dubich about his forbidding the girls to go. 'He's afraid we'll fall in love with somebody else down there,'

Mara said. 'Naw, he's just scared we'll get their religion,' this from Bertha. 'Anyway, what difference does it make? He says we can't go and that's all there is to it,' retorted Angela. That seemed to settle the matter."

Note: The recurrence of the discussion of this question suggests some dissatisfaction with the outcome of the previous incident but not enough to cause a break with established authority in their community. What part, if any, should the Leader take in such a discussion? Could she have turned this to account by raising any questions about other opportunities available outside their own community?

The Leader explains her plan for this as follows:
"The Leader always tried to further discussion to the extent of stimulating their own thinking and raising questions, feeling that gradual growth was much to be preferred to upsetting their equilibrium. Any 'break' would have meant the girls would be forbidden Community House connections because of the reaction of the priest. The slower process of thinking things through for themselves therefore seemed preferable."

The following account of the discussion of a proposed dance also throws some light on their close relation to the parish:
"Paula finally asked Bertha if they might not have a business meeting. The girls trooped into the front room, some still pulling taffy, others still eating it. They discussed the dance which they would like to give at St. John's. Plans for it were booming more than ever. The question of an orchestra was brought up, Paula suggesting that they ought to have at least fifty dollars for the orchestra. 'Aw, let's have Rudy Vallee and be done!' Bertha yelled. Finally someone suggested that Father Dubich and Father Nesich (another priest at St. John's) would have to be given complimentary tickets. Rose objected, 'Aw, we don't want them; they'll spoil our fun.'

"After considerable argument among the girls, the Leader ventured to say that she did not think Father Dubich would spoil their fun but rather would enjoy seeing them having a good time. 'He's so interested in us and asks about us all the time. It would be a shame not to invite him,' Paula added. 'Aw, let's invite Hoover and be done with it,' Rose objected again. 'Aw, who'd want Hoover around anyway,' from Bertha. They spent almost an hour on the subject of the dance and whenever another matter was brought up, they invariably returned to it. Even Olga and

Rose were so enthusiastic about it that they offered numerous suggestions."

Plans were considered also to get a club picture taken and arrangements were made for a program of crafts at the next meeting when the women's group was to meet for the first time.

The Leader also talked to Stella and Paula about taking clubs of younger girls, and joining a course for training volunteers which the Community House was offering.

Note: The policy of the Community House in using its older club members as club leaders for younger groups is first referred to here. It has increasing importance for several members of the club, in providing them with a new and developing experience and, in time, in affecting their handling of the problems of their own club.

November 19, 1930

This was as Paula said their "big night" when the women's club which they had been working to organize was to meet. Refreshments were brought. Paula and Mara had planned some entertainment in the way of a "dance number" and singing. Olga was ill and so did not come, but Anica appeared without her. The women arrived in small groups until finally eight had come. In spite of their preparations the girls at first were at a loss as to how to entertain them until the Leader suggested getting out the crafts they were working on, at that time the painting of jars. The women accepted this activity with interest and with the help of the girls seemed to enjoy it thoroughly. After an hour and a half the refreshments were served.

At this point Josephine and Yulka appeared. They had had no part in the plans for the women's club and sneeringly asked the Leader who the women were, what they were doing there and whether they were going to be here with this club. The Leader explained the situation but evidently the idea did not arouse any enthusiasm in them.

The end of the evening was devoted to games led by Paula, and to singing and dancing. Bertha and Mara sang Slovenian songs which the women enjoyed very much. Plans were completed for the dance which they expect to give in January, and for having the club picture taken.

Note: This occasion is interesting as showing the ability of the girls to plan and carry out a social event with great success. Their effort to recruit the women's club, the careful planning of the evening and their success finally in putting on games and entertainment are evidences of an increased interest in something outside their own group and also of a growing social assurance. The negative response of Yulka to the plan, the Leader suggests, is due not only to having been out of the planning but also to the fact that the presence of the women diverted attention from her return and so did not give her the center of the stage as she wished. What is the constructive way of handling such tactics as these characteristic of Yulka at this point?

The much discussed club picture was taken the following Sunday. The Leader was especially invited to come so as to be included.

November 26, 1930

The program continued with crafts. The women's group was organized as a club with its own leader and continued thereafter as a separate organization.

The proofs of the club picture arrived. It had been the cause of some dissension, first because two girls who had not been coming to club came back to be in the picture, and also because there was difficulty in agreeing on the proof, everyone tending to pick out the one particularly flattering to herself. Father Dubich had asked for a "cut" and it was finally decided to give him one of the pictures instead.

The Leader comments on the increasing responsibility carried by Bertha and Mara and their development in leadership. Paula brought floral designs from the library for their painting but hesitated to show them, evidently feeling that she should not take too much leadership. In discussing the dance, the girls looked to Paula chiefly for advice. She gave it and then tactfully referred decisions to Bertha.

Note: The balance of power between a former and more experienced leader like Paula and a newly developing one like Bertha is shown all through these weeks. Paula realizes the necessity for stepping into the background and not continuing to assume first place, if Bertha is to be allowed to take her job as president. How can the Leader best assist in this process?

How can Paula's abilities be used without preventing the development of Bertha's?

In the intervening week, the Leader saw Paula and Stella several times in connection with their younger girls' clubs. They had joined the group of volunteers and were taking a great interest and pride in their clubs.

The Leader commented that Paula was extremely busy and was out nearly every night. She had spent four nights the previous week at the Community House. The Leader tried to talk with her about the danger of her doing too much but she replied with great enthusiasm, "I just love it! I just love it!"

Note: What is the Leader's responsibility, if any, for the heavy schedule of group activities assumed by Paula? Is there any harm in it? Is it in any case entirely the responsibility of Paula herself? What relationship should the Leader attempt to develop with Paula in regard to the planning of her avocational interests?

December 10, 1930–January 4, 1931

The next few meetings were taken up with finishing up the jars and planning the dance. The following gives a glimpse of Paula's methods and the Leader's comments on them:

"Paula finally arrived and then things began to happen. She had a list of about fifteen items to go over for the dance. 'Did youse bring the posters?' she asked Mara, who shook her head negatively. 'Oh, ya horse!' Paula burst out. Then a few minutes later: 'How about the tickets?' There were more shakes of the head. 'Youse horses, you make me sick!' The girls did not appear to mind especially, so the discussion continued and many details were settled under Paula's direction. Sometimes, however, when she tried to get them to express an opinion on some detail of the dance they were inclined just to say, 'Sure, it suits me,' to both alternatives.

"The girls got nowhere in their discussion or in anything else until Paula arrived—when the dust began to fly and the girls listened. They seem like a ship without a rudder in her absence —no initiative nor anything to talk about. They are too easily satisfied usually and it is small wonder that Paula became exasperated with them. Perhaps if she assumed less responsibility they would assume more."

Note: Here we see Paula in action. Could the Leader help her at all in developing her methods of leadership?

Two incidents showing community attitudes occurred during these weeks. The women's club developed some difficulty because of a conflict over two Polish women whom the majority of the club (being Slovenian) did not wish to include. The Gay Girls were consulted as to how to handle the situation. Their first advice was to tell the Polish women they "don't want 'em," but they finally retracted this idea and concluded it was best to do nothing about it. Paula said, "I didn't used to like the Polish either but I like lots of 'em now since I know 'em."

A further change in attitude was shown in connection with an Open House which was being planned at the Community House. At the Leader's suggestion another club, the Bluebirds, was invited to join the Gay Girls in putting on an entertainment. When they arrived on January seventh only one or two of the girls knew each other and a rather awkward moment followed. Several of the Gay Girls continued to play games and ignored their visitors until the Leader urged them to be better hostesses. Finally games and refreshments were started and then discussion followed about the program for the Open House. At first there were few suggestions. Then a Bluebird said, "We could sing in Polish," and a Gay Girl said, "And we could sing in Slovenian." A joint program was then arranged on this basis to the apparent satisfaction of everyone.

Note: These two incidents indicate the social distance between the two nationality groups in the neighborhood and also something of the way the distance is decreased by contact through the Community House. Does this suggest what more could be accomplished on such community attitudes?

January 1931

During the following month the Gay Girls went through a crisis as a group. This was precipitated by several factors. For some time four of the ten girls had been irregular in attendance: Yulka, Josephine, Olga and Rose. They had made periodic exits and entrances, had threatened to leave, had then returned and in many ways had shown instability in their relation to the group. This was particularly important at this point because the dance which was for them a big undertaking was about to come off.

News of the instability within had leaked out so that various members reported that they had been told the Gay Girls were going to pieces. To cap the climax Father Dubich had written to Paula rebuking them for not attending a Sodality meeting which was their first responsibility. One of the girls was inclined to snicker over the rebuke but the rest took it seriously since it threatened their outstanding position in the parish.

The six remaining members—always the most active and reliable—considered the situation very seriously. The question was whether to drop the recalcitrants before the dance or afterwards. The record states the dilemma presented:

" 'They told me it was a heck of a time to kick 'em out just before a dance,' Angela said, 'but I thought like this.' She then proceeded to say that the constitution stated that too many absences without a good excuse 'means you're out and whether it's good for our dance or not we got to uphold the constitution.' The others agreed and Mara added that if the club had waited to 'kick them out' after the dance they would have said, 'See, you only want us when we can be useful.' Paula told Olga that she and Rose were not technically out but that they would have one more chance. They would, however, have to start as new members. 'She was just kind of snooty,' Paula said, 'and they didn't come this time so they're out too.' So that was that, and the club now has only six members."

Olga and Rose felt much abused on hearing of the decision and insisted they had not been absent three times in succession. Upon looking up the record it was found they were right so they were finally reinstated after the dance.

Due to the tenacity of the remaining six the dance went through very successfully, all the arrangements were carried out efficiently, the girls acted as hostesses with great success and the large number who came apparently enjoyed themselves. A balance of seventy-five dollars was made for the treasury. All the ex-members of the Gay Girls attended and it appeared to the Leader that they were very sorry they no longer belonged.

After the dance the club morale rose again. Their reputation in the neighborhood had been redeemed and they had proved that they could carry through a project without their recalcitrant members. To improve their spirits still further they had a second letter from Father Dubich.

"Its tone was the direct opposite of the previous letter and began: 'My dear Gay Girls.' He said that he was happy that they were so well employed both in their club and in their sodality and that he felt sure that so long as they were engaged in such activities no harm could come to them. The whole thing was very complimentary to the club. The comments of the girls were very interesting at this point. 'He ain't mad anymore.' 'Yeah, he must have liked our dance. Everybody said it's the first one like it they ever had there.' 'He must still like us, our picture is still in his office.' At this point Paula tilted her tam at a still more cocky angle and read the letter aloud, distorting every sentence to such an extent that she made the whole thing sound very un-complimentary to the club. 'That's so youse won't get swelled heads,' she finished."

Note: Such fluctuations in group spirit are characteristic of any group. What are the factors in this situation which make the come-back possible? Were the girls right in their decision to drop the unstable members before the dance? What can the Leader do in periods of low morale like this? Olga here almost loses her foothold in the group and regains it with difficulty. Evidently the group satisfies some important need of hers even though she cannot bring herself to accept it with enthusiasm. Should the Leader have taken this occasion to talk with Olga to try to discover how a more satisfactory group adjustment might be made?

Another significant incident occurred during this period. Paula had attended an inter-settlement dance which she reported to the club on January twenty-eighth as follows:

" 'Oh, I must tell you about the inter-settlement dance I went to last night,' Paula said. She then proceeded to tell them about the 'cute' colored people who were there and how at first 'there was just like a wall between the white and colored people.' Then she and three members of the Collegiates (a boys' club) 'made up to rob the colored fellows' and this seemed to break down the barriers until in the end 'everybody mixed like water.' When someone rather incredulously wanted to know if she had danced with the colored boys, she said, 'No, I finally couldn't get up the nerve. I just couldn't.' She then gave them an imitation of how 'cute' they danced and said that next time she did not think that she would be afraid to ask them to dance.

"The Leader took this opportunity to tell the girls about the Washington Settlement (for Negroes) and asked them if they would like to visit it some day and perhaps see a play at the Congo

Theatre in connection with it. 'Would we? Just give us a chance,' came from Bertha. From this and other comments the Leader gathered that they were really quite interested."

Note: This incident again shows Paula as the most adventurous and the most independent of the group. Her contacts are gradually widening to take in not only other clubs in the Community House but other settlements. As a result her education in human relations is including other races as well as other nationalities. It is through her experience and interpretation that the rest of the group get contact with new ideas. How should the Leader follow up this incident? Does it have leads for future discussion or for trips?

The weeks following the dance were very full of activities outside the club. The group participated in the Open House as planned by providing part of the entertainment. Olga came and brought her mother which was an unusual sign of cooperation. The club also participated, at the invitation of Olga's mother, in an informal program at the Slovenian Hall, put on by the P. T. A. of the parochial school, at which they took the leadership in the games.

February 11, 1931

This meeting was significant for two incidents. The money produced by the dance had raised a problem. Was it to be spent on some club affair or divided among the girls? Ten dollars were voted to Father Dubich for the church. The Leader had proposed a trip to a city ninety miles away to visit a settlement there where a former staff member known to the group was working. This was enthusiastically accepted by Paula and a few others. Two of the girls, Angela especially, wanted to have it divided among them. The final decision was postponed until more information was at hand about the possible trip.

Yulka meanwhile was making efforts to get back into the club. These varied from inviting them to a dance she was giving and boasting that she and Josephine planned to start a club of ten boys and ten girls, to asking directly to be taken back. Her approaches were received differently by the various members of the club, Paula and Mimi inclining to be lenient and Angela and Bertha holding out against any favors to them. The resulting discussions showed some strain between the two subgroups but resulted in her not being accepted.

During the week following, the Leader talked with Paula about attending the Bryn Mawr Summer School for Women Workers in Industry. She was very much interested but doubtful whether she could make arrangements at home and at work. She filled out the application.

February 25–April 1, 1931

The meetings during this time were occupied largely by craft work on the jars and by planning various stunts in which the club was to take part in the Community House and in connection with the church. The interest in crafts seemed to be on the wane.

Note: The craft program throughout this year, after the club completed the decorating project, consisted of making vases by painting glass jars. No great skill was involved evidently and not much learning of artistic value. Could this interest in crafts have been handled more adequately and a higher standard of work encouraged?

The Leader comments that since her return Olga has been joining in more actively without urging and has not lapsed into sullenness nearly so frequently.

Paula meanwhile had applied to the local Bryn Mawr Committee for admittance to the summer school. Her comment on her experience in going to a meeting of the committee was as follows:

"She told the Leader that there were eight or nine other girls there, all of whom talked about books they had read except Paula herself. 'They're all so different, those girls,' she said, 'all interested in Russia and industrial stuff and none of 'em in social work or psychology.' She added that she thought she, too, could read the same 'stuff.' 'Gee, if I kin only go; if I kin only go.'"

The Leader discovered on March nineteenth that the money from the dance had been divided among the members. This was done without official action in any business meeting but seems to have been agreed to outside of club meeting.

The Leader's suggestion for a collective use for it by a trip had been at first well received but she had not been able to follow it up immediately with definite plans. The interest therefore dropped and those who wanted it divided were able to convince the others.

Note: Could the Leader have managed this situation better? Should she have had several definite suggestions ready so that the group could act while the iron was hot? Is there any disadvantage in having the money divided among the individuals?

Bertha, at the Leader's suggestion, took on a younger club and attended the volunteers' meetings along with Paula and Stella. Mara who was Bertha's particular friend refused to join the volunteers. The two following conversations indicate a new step in Bertha's thinking:

"Bertha wanted to know whether a leader was considered a regular teacher or not, so the Leader told about the whole setup of the Community House. Bertha was surprised to learn that group leaders needed as much if not more training than regular school teachers and did not understand what there would be to study about. This was also explained to her, the Leader emphasizing the study of people's actions and reactions in certain situations. Bertha was greatly interested, saying she had never thought of any of these things before. The Leader brought in the fact that this type of work was 'fun' and said that Stella and Paula greatly enjoyed leading their clubs, hinting that perhaps Bertha, too, might be interested. She burst out with 'Gee, I'd just love it. So many times I walked past on Friday night when they were having club but I was afraid to come in.' The Leader suggested that she visit the clubs on Friday night if she wished and she enthusiastically said that she would come."

"The Leader later had another illuminating conversation with Bertha. When asked where Mara was, she said, 'Oh, she didn't wanna come.' The Leader expressed surprise at her coming without her, upon which Bertha said, 'Well, I might as well tell ya.' She then told how since she had talked to the Leader on Wednesday she had been thinking that she did not stand on her own feet enough and that Mara 'bossed' her too much but she stated emphatically, 'She ain't gonna boss me any more.' She added that she was going to divide her time between doing what she had been doing on Friday night and going with Mara and that through her experience in leading a club she hoped to become more independent. The Leader later learned from Paula that Bertha had also told her all this on Friday night, after asking Paula to go for a walk with her. 'She asked me to tell her more about my club too—and I did,' Paula added."

Note: The development of Bertha during this year is an interesting instance of learning by doing. When she was first elected she was very awkward about leading club meetings. The Leader comments on her increasing social adjustment to the group and capacity to lead. Now she is able to use her new learning in another group of younger girls and to become more objective as to the process of leading. Her own decision to become independent of Mara is also an evidence of a change. Should the Leader attempt to get more understanding of her in order to assist her in these situations?

April 1931

During April the agency began rehearsals for an operetta. Several of the Gay Girls tried out for it and five were accepted. (Olga and Rose refused to try out.) Bertha had the leading rôle. Much time was occupied also in rehearsals for the stunt to be given in the Slovenian Hall for which the club made itself new dresses.

On one occasion some discussion arose over the fact that one of the girls had gone to a dance with a boy instead of coming to club. The girls were very indignant at this and Angela said it was clearly understood that no dates were to interfere with club. To which Olga retorted, "Yeah, if you had a chance, you'd go too."

Note: This is one of the few references to "dates" in the record, although there is plenty of evidence that most of the girls are popular at dances and go to a good many. A majority of the girls dated all through the year. However, club night was one on which, by common understanding, dates were usually forgotten. Also dating seemed to take place, on the whole, more individually. Girls worked in different places and had friends whom all of them did not know.

Paula received word, much to her delight, that she had been accepted for the Bryn Mawr Summer School.

May 2, 1931

The girls went to camp for a week-end along with other senior groups. Everyone but Rose and Stella went. Bertha and Paula in particular did their share of entertaining the crowd with singing and dancing. Olga proved to be as enthusiastic as the others.

During this time rehearsals for the operetta continued and through these the girls got acquainted with the Hudsons, a club of boys. Paula told the Leader that she and Stella made dates with some of the Hudsons at a party. "Gee, I like 'em," she said. Rehearsals interfered with regular club meetings. The operetta was finally given the middle of May.

May 20, 1931

This was the next to the last meeting of the year. Plans were discussed for another camp week-end for Decoration Day. It was proposed by Stella to invite the Hudsons to the last meeting of the club. Evidently the enthusiasm for them was not shared by all so the idea was finally given up.

On May twenty-third Paula found she could not go to Bryn Mawr after all because her father was only working one day a week and might be laid off at any time. The Leader reported that in a visit to Paula's home, she felt the whole family looked undernourished.

The Leader and Paula talked over the money required and found that by saving a dollar and eighty-eight cents a week she could pay back the loan she would have to make to go to the school. They also discussed what she could do if she could not attend summer school; she felt better when she realized that she could still go next year and that she could attend a shorter Workers' Institute which was to be held nearby, for two weeks. She said that she had attended two sessions of the Preparatory Classes and "the girls are so different from any I know now, I love it!"

Several days later the Leader records:

"The library decided that the financial responsibility of a loan was too much for her to assume. The Leader asked her if she thought it was and she said 'no.' The Leader told her that if she wanted to assume it, she thought that the Community House would back her. Paula then again decided to go and upon asking her mother found that she, too, approved. However, the next morning she called the Leader on the telephone and told her that the final decision was 'no.' It seemed that her mother had to pay a hundred and seventy-five dollars on a mortgage in the near future and she was so anxious to have Paula go to summer school that she had not mentioned it. Apparently Paula had overheard her mother and father talking about it and had then decided that she should not go."

Note: Could anything else have been done to make Paula's going possible? Is this the wisest decision?

May 25, 1931

This was the last club meeting of the year. It consisted chiefly of games and refreshments which were combined with the women's club referred to earlier. Officers were elected for the next year: Stella, president; Angela, secretary and treasurer.

During the summer a Workers' Institute, a two weeks workers' education project, was to be held nearby. It was a community affair but the Industrial Secretary at the Y. W. C. A. had an influential part in it and was receiving registrations. The Gay Girls were told about this and several of them, especially Paula, wanted to go. The record then reports:

"Almost immediately Paula said to the Leader, 'I want to tell you something.' She then told her that on Sunday, in church, Father Dubich had told all parents to refuse to let their children have anything to do with the Y. W. C. A. and that since the registration slips to the Workers' Institute were to be sent to the Y. W. C. A., she was skeptical as to whether they could go. The Leader told them that the Y. W. C. A., as such, would have almost nothing to do with the place and that in her opinion they would not be violating anything. They asked the Leader what they should do but she let them make their own decision.

"Paula, Mara and Bertha decided that they would go if they had an opportunity. Mara stated that she could see nothing wrong with it and that she was living up to her religion as she interpreted it.

"Angela and Rose, however, insisted that they would have to ask Father Dubich. 'Oh, then I know we can't go,' Mara said. The Leader asked if it would not be possible to interpret the situation to him. 'Oh, you can't tell him anything,' Mara said, 'he's too narrow-minded.' She then cited the example of another Slovenian church where the whole sodality attended the Y. W. C. A. in a body. Rose and Angela took exception to what Mara said and a battle was then on between Rose and Angela on one side and Bertha and Mara on the other. Bertha flared up, saying that Father Dubich forbade the young people to do anything anywhere else and wanted them to stay in their own neighborhood. 'And then, what kin they do? Nuttin! Youse wanna know why

St. John's kids are so dumb—yes, dumb—I said dumb?' She followed the same line of argument that they were not allowed to go outside the neighborhood for anything, and yet nothing was provided in the neighborhood itself for them. Mara then heatedly chimed in with, 'Yeah, all the fellows in our neighborhood are bums—my brother Mike, too. All they do is drink. The priest says, "Don't do this, don't do that," what is there for 'em to do?' This lasted for almost an hour, Bertha and Mara finally getting to the point where they were shouting. Meanwhile Rose and Angela would chime in with, 'Oh, don't say that. I don't see how you kin say that, Mara.' Their defense was that Father Dubich said that he had to answer for them and therefore had to advise them. Paula sat with head downcast during most of the discussion, saying nothing. Once she said to the Leader, 'Every time I get a break, it's gone, just like this!' and she snapped her finger. She also said that Father Dubich would probably 'blame' her for everything—'he always does,' she added. In the end, Rose and Angela were still planning to go to Father Dubich while the other three were determined to go to the Workers' Institute without consulting him."

The Leader did not express an opinion on the matter under discussion but let the girls see that it was something they had to decide for themselves, since it would be a very poor policy for her to become involved in any conflict with the church.

Note: This discussion shows the conflict of second generation girls very clearly. What position should the Leader take on this? It is through her that knowledge of opportunities outside the community is brought in. Is that a part of her function even if it precipitates the conflict?

June 3, 1931

"Paula, on her way to work, was waiting for a car, and upon seeing the Leader hurried across the street with, 'I want to ask you something.' She said that she had to go to Father Dubich about something else and so had asked him about the Institute. He had told her that a Y. W. C. A. worker would be there and that therefore she should not go. 'What should I do, go or not?' The Leader talked it over with her but told her that the decision would have to rest with her. She said that she had thought she would send in an application and not say anything but that Father

Dubich was going to try to get a camp for them for the same
two weeks' period."

June and July, 1931

Paula, Bertha and Mara sent in applications for the Workers'
Institute but did not follow them up. On July seventh the Leader
talked over the situation with each of the girls. Paula said that
Father Dubich had heard she was planning to attend the Institute
and had called her in and forbidden her to go in spite of her
explanations of the purpose of the Workers' Institute. However,
Paula said that she would go down to the Y. W. C. A. to a special
meeting July eighth to learn more about it—if the other girls
would go. The Leader offered to talk to Father Dubich or to ask
the Y. W. C. A. secretary who was director of the Workers'
Institute to talk to him but Paula preferred to have no one speak
to him about it for fear that he would think the girls complained
to outsiders about church affairs. Mara was eager to go to the
meeting and said she thought Bertha would want to go too. When
the meeting time came, all of the girls had decided that it was
no use pretending they could do something that Father Dubich
had forbidden, so they did not attend the meeting. Paula was
very much perplexed and worried over the whole situation. All
of the girls were keenly disappointed not to be able to go.

Note: The reaction of the club to this prohibition was much
more violent than in the situation the previous year. The struggle for independence and for contacts outside their nationality
community is very evident here.

The Leader made an appointment for Miss D.,[1] as director of
the Workers' Institute, rather than in the capacity of an Industrial
Secretary of the Y. W. C. A., to see Father Dubich on July six-
teenth. She explained the purpose of the Institute and asked him
to be one of the special speakers Tuesday, July twenty-first. He
accepted.

In his speech at the Workers' Institute Father Dubich traced
the evils of unemployment as they affect the home. He mentioned
that the lack of income meant that children went to work earlier
and were thereby hindered in their education. The fact that they

[1] Throughout these records the form Miss or Mr., followed by an initial is
used to indicate a professional social worker or group leader.

were wage earners made them feel independent, which led them
to defy parental control and even to become lawbreakers. He
ended by stressing the fact that the hope of the future was in
workers' education and commended highly the work being done at
the Workers' Institute. At the Institute he met other Slovenian
girls not from his parish and was greeted by them with great
cordiality.

Note: The method of Miss D. in her attempts to change Father
Dubich's attitude is interesting here. He became not only open
minded in his attitude toward such community projects as the
Workers' Institute but was evidently quite liberal in his economic views. His contact with the Institute and with the Y. W.
C. A. resulted in a gradual liberalizing of his attitude toward
such opportunities for his parishioners.

ANNUAL SUMMARY 1930-1931

The Leader's evaluation of the progress of the club for the
year may be summarized as follows:

The club has maintained this year its strong sense of loyalty
and its ability to carry responsibility as a group. It has developed
a new and valuable interest in the affairs of the community and
a desire to play some part in their improvement. Initiative is increasingly shown and more independence in thinking for themselves is evident. A growing interest in further education appears
in most of the group. They participate well in inter-club activity.

They show some deficiencies in that not all the group enter
into the community activities with equal enthusiasm. This is producing signs of a difference in interests which comes into conflict
with the strong group loyalty which holds them together. They
have a tendency to exclusiveness which is limiting their membership to a small group. They have lost four members this year
and added no new ones. The Leader still feels that they show
some tendency to depend on authority and to be held back by a
conservatism which restricts them unnecessarily at certain points.

In the light of the criteria suggested in the introductory chapter
it may be well to consider the following questions especially about
this year's record:

1. Is the Leader developing her relation to individuals sufficiently? Should she have helped Bertha more in assuming her
responsibilities as president? Should she have made more personal

contacts, especially with Olga or Yulka? Does she handle her contacts with Paula wisely?

2. Does the process of social interaction within the group produce valuable results? Is the conflict over the expulsion of the unstable members well managed? Could an integration of differences here have saved the loss of those members? Is the club providing enough variety of opportunity to meet the needs of its members?

3. In regard to group control what type of indigenous leadership is the group developing?

4. Is the program providing opportunity for initiative and development? Could it encourage higher standards of work in the crafts?

5. How is the group learning to participate in the community? What effect does the project of the older women's club have on this? What effect does the relation to the church have on such participation?

SECOND YEAR

The Gay Girls begin their third year, the second of this record, with Stella as president and Angela as secretary. Stella is also acting as President of the House Council. She is not a very forceful officer and does not naturally assume leadership in the group. She has had the reputation in previous years of being stubborn but she is inclined also to be a "yes man" when it is to her advantage. Stella is rather self-sufficient, dresses well and knows her own good points. She has always been especially successful in contacts with other clubs and seems to enjoy being prominent in inter-club affairs. She has had a club of younger girls the previous year but she does not continue it this year.

Angela has played no very active part in club affairs until this year. She is a great friend of Paula's and follows her lead in most matters. She also has had a reputation for stubbornness but it does not seem to be very much in evidence this year. Angela is developing an interest in being a volunteer and is given responsibility for a younger girls' club.

October 7, 1931

October seventh saw six Gay Girls collected for their first meeting. The evening was taken up largely with planning for the next few meetings. This included a discussion of whether the club should make new club dresses, plans for swimming and gym at one of the Bath Houses, a hike and a week-end at the Y. W. C. A. cabin. This last proposal elicited great enthusiasm and the Leader was requested to go ahead and secure the cabin.

October 14, 1931

This meeting was uneventful except for the following stunt which showed the hilarity of the girls so common in Gay Girls' gatherings:

"After a while the Leader went into the room where Mara and Bertha were singing hoping that the rest of the group would drift in naturally. Suddenly, the Leader heard a shriek and turning found Paula very obviously a bride, with someone's sewing being used as a veil, and Angela the groom, with a beret on one ear. They were put in chairs in one room and several others sat beside them. Mara and Bertha stood in the other room and sang to them. Paula sobbed in a loud voice. Suddenly, Rose picked up a newspaper, crushed it and twisted one end to make it look like a bouquet, stopped the singing and rushed over to give it to Paula. Angela tore an edge from the paper, saying she wanted a flower from the bride's bouquet for her buttonhole. The singing began again. Paula wept so loudly that the choir had to stop and tell her to cry more quietly. Finally at the end of the song someone took the 'veil' from Paula's head. Mimi picked up a pillow, rushed to the groom and danced with him. He put the pillow on the floor in front of the bride who knelt down and they gave a demonstration of an extremely 'soulful' kiss. In fact it was so 'soulful' that they lost their balance and fell. Several people rushed to the rescue and helped them to their feet. The pillow was thrown on a chair and all joined in the Slovenian Polka.

"After a few minutes everyone was so worn out from laughing and jumping that when Mara said, 'Oh, let's sit down and have our meeting,' they all agreed immediately.

"Plans were made for a hike and a movie party during the next week."

October 28–November 11, 1931

The next several meetings were occupied largely in games, particularly bridge which several wanted to learn to play. Plans for other events outside of the club, especially for the week-end trip to camp were also discussed.

A new member was proposed but the suggestion was not well received. As one of them said, "I don't mind because she's Polish but I just don't want anybody else in the club." Paula had a friend also Polish whom she would like to have proposed but after the reception of this suggestion, she felt it was not wise to bring it up.

Note: Although the girls have come to the point of denying that the Polish factor is important, it is doubtful whether it is actually eliminated in their minds. Their close relation to the parish and to the other Slovenian organizations also makes it more difficult for them to accept girls of other nationalities. Is there any danger in this tendency to restrict membership to their own crowd and their own nationality? Should they be encouraged to enlarge the club?

Discussion of club dresses arose again and consumed much time. The expense, however, was a serious handicap to several of the girls. It was finally decided to knit scarfs and caps, both because it would cost less and because they wanted to learn to knit.

During this period a strained relation developed between Olga and Bertha. Olga continued her usual tactics of indifference or opposition but Bertha adopted a policy of not giving in to them as the others do. The contrast between her response to Olga and Paula's reaction is indicated in the following:

"After all the plans for the week-end had been made, Olga decided she would not go. Bertha picked her up almost immediately and said, 'Oh, yes you will, you can't kid me. You just want to be coaxed.' Paula stepped in quickly and said, 'Sure you're coming Olga, you just gotta come.'"

November 14–15, 1931

This was the week-end that the Gay Girls went to camp. The following gives a graphic account:

"There were many exclamations of surprise and pleasure when the cabin was reached. As soon as the Leader opened the door they all rushed in. It was rather dreary and stuffy. Mara said, 'Let's open some windows and get some air in here.' They deposited their wraps and bundles in the bedroom. Stella asked, 'Could we have a fire?' Paula looked around and said, 'Come on, kids, we gotta get some wood if we want a fire.' Stella and Olga stayed and helped lay the fire with the wood that was already there.

"After supper the whole group gathered around the fire and sang songs for some time. A few at a time they changed into pajamas and finally Angela asked to play 'Bridge.' They decided to play something everyone could play together. 'Pig' was chosen. After several hilarious games, they wrestled a bit and then put on a little chorus act.[2] Bertha and Mara suggested going to bed to conserve the wood for morning. They said they wanted to get up about six-thirty so that they would be sure to get to church on time at ten-thirty o'clock. Before she went to bed, Olga piled a bed and some chairs in front of the door because it had no lock and she was afraid to sleep with the doors unlocked.

"Stella, Angela and the Leader talked for a while in front

[2] Compare this with the evening entertainment on the Hudsons' week-end, page 116.

of the fire while it burned down. The only thing of interest which
came from this was their enthusiasm for the volunteer leaders'
training course. The group went to bed at ten o'clock but talked
and sang till two the next morning. Mara and Bertha were especially hilarious.

"In the morning most of the girls set off for church. Paula,
Angela, Olga, Bertha and Mara came back about eleven-thirty
saying that they had had to walk almost the whole way there
before a woman picked them up but a woman in church saw
them come in and brought them back afterwards. They had breakfast at once. Each took turns making the pancakes. Just after
they finished eating and began to prepare dinner, Stella and Rose
came looking very tired and dejected. They had had to walk both
ways.

"The girls that had stayed at the cabin had gathered a lot
more wood and they began to build fires immediately at the
Leader's suggestion. All took certain responsibilities for dinner
and soon everything was ready. The station wagon came to take
the blankets and dishes just a few minutes after dinner was over.
All helped to clear the place and see that it was left in order.
It was not till nearly five o'clock that they were ready to start
back."

The Leader comments that the week-end seemed to have little
value except pure recreation. However, she also quotes conversation with individuals as follows:

"There was almost no water left and no one wanted to go for
it. Bertha, Mara and the Leader finally went. They told the Leader,
upon being asked, that Olga and Rose had had a fight about
something. Mara said that Olga was used to getting her own
way too much. 'Everybody spoils her, especially Paula.' Bertha
added, 'Yes, that's true. That's why I told her she just wanted
to be coaxed the other night at the meeting.'

"While walking up the road, the Leader had a chance to talk
with Paula a bit about the meetings for volunteer leaders. She
was most enthusiastic and said 'I'd like that. We need to learn
things too.' Paula asked if it would be possible for the Leader to
get the names and addresses of the girls who went to Bryn Mawr
Summer School. She wanted to write to them to find out what
happened there. She talked about some of the books which she
had read and how interesting they were. The Leader asked her
if she thought any of the other girls would be interested in reading
some of the books. She said she thought they would and promised

to bring the reading list to club. 'We could read them and then talk about them at our meetings, couldn't we? Some of the books were on politics, and do you know what? I'm going to be able to vote for president next year. I'm so excited I can hardly wait.' The Leader suggested that the group might all want to find out about the government and politics. Paula answered, 'Gee, maybe they would, I'd *love* to.' "

Note: Is the Leader right in expecting more of this week-end trip? What more might have happened which would have been more valuable? How could the Leader have brought this about? The comment of Bertha on Olga's behavior shows a definite re-action which may serve as a corrective to her methods of getting her own way. What is the Leader's place in this process by which the group is beginning to discipline Olga? Paula's en-thusiasm for learning and her interest in public questions indi-cate again her divergence from the rest of the group and her greater ability. How can these be encouraged and developed in connection with this group? Or will Paula have to look outside the Gay Girls for a group interested in such matters? How can the Leader be of the greatest use to Paula in developing these interests?

December 2, 1931

Following her idea that the club program might be improved, the Leader attempted to introduce them to the question of budget-ing at the next meeting.

"The Leader showed to Bertha 'The Cost of Living of Wage Earning Women,' a pamphlet from the Women's Bureau of the United States Department of Labor saying that she (the Leader) had remembered a remark Bertha had made about paying board. Bertha and Mara became very much interested and took it across the room to look it over more carefully. Finally Olga became in-terested and the Leader suggested that they put it on the table that all might see it. Bertha said, 'Do you have a pencil so we could figure ours out.' She and Mara compared theirs and both agreed that they would rather give their pay to their mothers and get money as they needed it. Bertha and Mara said their mothers had talked to them about paying board but since they had not ever done it before they did not want to start it now. Bertha said she would not be able to get as many things if she used her

own money. She also said, 'I'd be so tight. I'd never spend anything myself.' Rose said she would like to figure how much she
could live on. She was quite careful about it. For the section
marked 'clothes' she put down the amount she had actually spent
during the past year—the large amounts, such as for dresses—and
divided it to be sure she was right.

"The consensus of opinion was that they would like to know
how much they really do spend. The Leader suggested a personal
account book, saying she was going to start keeping one herself.
Bertha said she would like to keep one too and asked questions
about what went in it. Then she said, 'Maybe after Christmas I'll
tell my mother I'd like to start paying board.' When Paula came
in she looked at the budget and said, 'Gee, I could live swell on
that. That's a lot of money.'"

Note: Is this a good move on the part of the Leader? What
might be learned from such material? How should the Leader
follow up the interest evidently aroused?

At the same meeting Paula, also acting on the impetus given
in the conversation at camp, brought a popular book in psychology
called "Behind your Front." The girls seized on this also and tried
to decide what "type" they were.

Note: Does this kind of stimulus to an interest in psychology,
necessarily very superficial, serve any useful purpose? If it
arises from one of the members as in this case, what should
the Leader do with the interest aroused?

December 16 and 23, 1931

The next two meetings were occupied with planning and putting on a Christmas party to which they invited another Slovenian
girls' club, the B. T. M.s. The party was a great success. As usual
Paula took charge of the games.

This occasion was the first in which mention was made of
Paula's connection with Stan Rovich, one of the boys in the
neighborhood. He is going to college and is organist in the church.

January 1932

January was very irregular in the Gay Girls' history. Outside
events crowded in on their time so that they only had one regular
meeting on January sixth.

In that meeting they were asked to participate in the Senior Dramatics Tournament run by the Community House. At first they were much interested. In the discussion they decided to take the parts of men themselves rather than to bring in another club of boys as Mara suggested. It was later decided not to enter at all.

Note: This decision not to bring in outsiders for a play is another indication of the close bond holding the group together. Should the Leader encourage this? Is it possible that such a closely knit group of girls is not desirable for girls at this age? How could the Leader gauge the values or dangers of such a situation?

The lectures being put on by the League for Industrial Democracy were discussed and the girls urged to get tickets. The following discussion indicates a new interest in the group:

"Paula said she would like to go to about four or five and Angela said she would like to go, too. All of the others, with the exception of Stella, expressed an interest in going to some of them. The Leader pointed out the advantages of a season ticket but no conclusion was reached. Rose said, 'I left one of these programs on the table at work and my boss found it. He asked me if that was the kind of thing I went to. I told him that I was going to some of them and he looked at them and pointed out the ones he thought would be the best.' The Leader suggested that Rose might encourage him to go by telling him of the meeting she attended.

"Paula asked what was meant by 'America in an Interdependent World.' This led to a discussion about the League of Nations. All of them thought that America was a member. The discussion was switched to ancient history about which the group knew a surprising amount. From there it shifted to Gandhi and a discussion of conditions in India. All this time Stella had taken no part in the discussion. She sat perfectly quiet until there was a break and then said, 'Well, we'd better get back to business. Does this club have a constitution?' There was a laugh and someone said, 'The House Council president is speaking.' "

Note: This discussion is the first reported in the club on any public question. It arose here casually and was evidently regarded by Stella as an interruption, not a part of the program. It therefore was terminated abruptly by Stella's bringing the club to order. Could the Leader make a recognized place for such discussions in the program? What preparation should she make if she attempts to do this?

Other events interrupted club meetings until February third. The first of these was a Slovenian wedding which the Leader attended. The other two Wednesdays were occupied by parties— one given by the Yodelers, a boys' club, and the other by the House Council. The following gives some glimpse of these latter occasions:

"Again Olga was the only one who did not dance with men. Toward the end of the evening Rose began to dance more with men and the rest of the girls, especially Angela and Paula, had one or two in tow all the time.

"There was no regular meeting since this was the night of the House Council party. The girls came in quite late and became popular immediately, especially so during the robbers' dances. Paula, especially, changed partners every few steps during some of the dances. During the program the club sang two songs, one of which was 'Down in the Valley.' Stan Rovich accompanied them and insisted upon jazzing the song. Angela began to giggle and that set them all off. The songs were not a huge success."

At the close of the last party, plans were made informally for the next meeting and Bertha asked "Could we talk about Mahatma Gandhi and others just like we did last time? We liked that." Everyone agreed.

Note: These glimpses are interesting in that they show the girls participating in mixed affairs and, with the exception of Olga, apparently making a good adjustment. What bearing does this have on the place of the club itself in their lives?

February 3, 1932

At the next regular meeting the plan made to discuss some public questions while they made baskets was attempted, with the following results:

"After they had all got started on their baskets, the Leader asked about the lectures which Paula and Angela were attending. They were not very articulate beyond the point of saying that they enjoyed them. Questions about the World War and Gandhi failed to bring any response. After a while the Leader asked if anyone had seen the book which she had brought. Stella replied, 'Oh yes, here it is on my chair. I want to read it some time, may I?' It was a copy of 'Mrs. Grundy is Dead,' a book on modern etiquette based on questionnaires sent out to young people. The Leader explained what the book was and read several questions quickly.

"Angela said, 'Oh, read some more.' Without any suggestions from the Leader they began to answer the questions as they were read. On some questions they agreed immediately, on others they did not. Bertha and Paula were inclined to be more liberal in their point of view than the rest. Sometimes they changed their minds after a bit of discussion. There were some very interesting opinions revealed. Rose was the only one who absolutely objected to smoking. The others all thought that it was all right if not done in public. Paula said, 'I'd never do it again. I did it once and got sick.' Evidently none of the girls had known that she had tried it but none of them showed any evidence of being shocked. The question, 'Do nice girls pet?' brought an immediate and emphatic 'no.' Then almost as quickly Bertha said, 'Well, I don't know,' and Paula, 'I think maybe they do sometimes.' Finally the Leader, discovering that it was a question of the technical difference between necking and petting, asked what, in their minds, was the difference. Mara and Angela tried to express it but could not. Angela turned to Paula and said, 'You tell her, Paula, you know how to say it.' Paula answered very seriously, 'A petter is a man with roving hands.' All nodded their heads in agreement and said that they would not pet with anyone but as Bertha said, 'I think it's all right to neck with your steady.'

"The discussion showed that they were well acquainted with the Women's Page in the newspaper. Rose especially quoted it several times, once when there was an argument as to where the man should walk in relation to the curb. Some of the girls began talking about some of the other books which they had read recently. Paula said that all of them would probably enjoy 'Charm' and 'The Psychology of Leadership.' Angela took the names of both down and said that she would like to read them. Bertha said that she had just got some new books on sex. The Leader asked the names but she did not know the exact title or the author. She said they had been given to her by a girl at work and that she had learned a lot of things she never knew before."

Note: This episode is an interesting illustration of the relation of expressed interests to activity. Although the previous discussions had stirred enough interest to promote a desire for its continuance, when the time came the mood had changed and it was not possible to pick up on a latent interest. The Leader's technique in having material there on etiquette and sex practices may have been of equal or greater significance. What preparations does the group leader need if she is going to lead such discussion? What more could she have done with this question than seems indicated here? What leads seem to be presented by the girls' interest in reading at this point? Should the Leader have let it go at this? Brought in a psychiatrist or psychiatric social worker at a later meeting? Followed up such a discussion by personal interviews as the occasion presented itself? Provided books on this subject? The Leader's comments on this meeting do not seem to show that she considered seriously how to follow up this interest in sex questions and in fact no further reference is made to the subject in the record.

February 10, 1932

The next meeting was uneventful and the morale was low, due evidently to the fatigue of several of the girls and the low spirits of Paula.

February 17, 1932

At the next meeting, however, the discussion of popular psychology and etiquette revived. The record describes the occasion as follows:

"The girls asked the Leader what books she had brought. She gave them the three: 'Behind Your Front' by James Oppenheim, 'Etiquette Junior' and 'Charm.'

"The Leader asked the group if they would like to take some of the personality tests in the book. They agreed readily and gathered around the table. The tests were to discover whether they were in general introvert or extravert. In general, the results were what the Leader expected: Angela, Paula, Stella and Mara were extraverts but Rose and Bertha, much to the Leader's surprise, were introverts. When they were about half through taking the test Olga came in. Everybody immediately asked her to join but she refused, saying that she wanted to work on her basket. She went into another room alone. She came in once for scissors and when the group was leaving came in again but that was all during the whole evening."

Note: Was the Leader wise in injecting this type of popular psychology? What value could come from such an experience? Olga's withdrawal from this is natural in view of her sense of inferiority in the group. Though she may have been playing up for attention as usual, it would seem quite likely that she would not like to expose herself to comparison by such tests. Was this method of handling her reaction wise under the circumstances?

"The interest in Bryn Mawr reappeared again. The Leader remembered some publicity from the Bryn Mawr Summer School which she had with her and asked if anyone was interested. Immediately Rose said, 'Oh, I'd like to go. Could I? Would I have to get off for more than two weeks?' When the Leader explained that it was two months Rose said immediately that it would be impossible for her even to think about it. Mara and Angela, however, said that they were very much interested and that they were sure they could get off that long. Mara especially said 'Oh, I'm sure my boss would let me go as long as I would learn something!'

"All this time Paula said nothing. After the group went out to get their coats the Leader asked Paula if she thought there was any hope of her going this year. At first she said, 'No, I don't think so,' then she suddenly burst forth with, 'But I want to go this year. Last year I thought that I could go for sure this year so I was satisfied to wait but now I don't want to wait any longer. I don't know what I'll be doing next year. I might be an old married woman by that time.' Rather jokingly the Leader asked if there was any chance of her being a married woman by next year and Paula said, 'No, but even so I don't want to wait. I want to go this year.' The Leader asked if there was any possibility at all. Paula said that her father worked a day now and then but that really she was the one that they depended on. Suddenly she said, 'I wonder if they would let my sister take my job for the summer. I think I'll ask tomorrow.' The Leader suggested that it might be wise to talk it over with the people at the library and Paula said, 'Oh, if I could only go.'"

March 2, 1932

The next meeting also was of no great significance except for the Leader's further comment that the girls seemed tired. This apparently was due partly to the fact that they went to Lenten services before work in the morning.

March 16, 1932

At the meeting the Gay Girls returned to their interest in hand-craft, this time to the making of what-nots out of light wood. This apparently proved to be of great interest and gave some chance for individual designing. The Leader noted that in a conversation with Paula following the meeting she said that she did not want the girls, with the exception of Angela, to know when she goes out with Stan, "because they kid me too much."

The following week was Holy Week and no meeting was held.

March 30, 1932

Four of the girls arrived and waited impatiently for Mara and Bertha. As they did not arrive there was some question as to whether to go after them. Finally the girls, accompanied by the Leader, started out without making any decision but by common unspoken consent turned into Mara's gate. The record describes the incident as follows:

"They went over and found Bertha, Mara and two friends there getting ready to go out. Bertha greeted the club with, 'My God, look who's here.' She invited them in and called Mara. It was not necessary for the Leader to say a word. Paula demanded, 'Why weren't you at the House?' Mara replied that she did not want to go to the House Council party and therefore did not go to club. 'What about the meeting?' questioned Stella. 'Oh, are you going to have a meeting,' Bertha asked. Angela said, 'Sure we're going to have a meeting.' Mara tried to change the subject by admiring Paula's coat. 'Keep your hands off me. Just don't even touch me. Fine Gay Girls you are, both of you.' This same sentiment was expressed by all the girls. The friends were very much embarrassed and wanted to leave. Mara and Bertha refused to hear to that. Finally they agreed to go to the House for a meeting but not to stay."

Note: On this occasion it is possible to see group discipline in its most obvious form. Loyalty to the group is enforced with a heavy hand by Paula. Even though the occasion is only the matter of attendance at a meeting, the resulting fear of group

disapproval is well taught by such an experience. Are such methods necessary and desirable in producing group solidarity?
What is the Leader's relation to such procedures?

During this period Mara assumed responsibility as a volunteer
for working with one of the playgrounds which was about to open.
The Leader also hoped to interest Olga in some form of volunteer work so that she would not feel omitted from the general interest in such activities shared by nearly all the club. Olga was
not interested.

At this time, too, a conflict appeared between the Gay Girls
and the B. T. M.s, another club which was making itself felt in
the neighborhood. The prestige of the Gay Girls was threatened
by this rival group. Paula attempted to meet the situation by promoting better relations through the joint party previously mentioned. This was not successful apparently since it now appeared
that the B. T. M.s "talked about the Gay Girls' actions even while
they were entertaining them."

Note: The play of the unseen public behind the record is very
evident in such hints of inter-group and community relations.
The status of the Gay Girls as a group is a definite asset to them
as individuals and any threat to it affects each member. This
accounts also for the strenuous measures taken to preserve its
solidarity and to prove its ability to do "big things" in the
neighborhood.

April 4, 1932

This meeting was occupied chiefly with handcraft and with the
discussion of a play the club had been asked to put on as a part of
a Slovenian entertainment. Toward the end of the meeting a new
proposal was made.

"All had gathered around the table with Mara and Paula on one
side of the Leader, Bertha on the other and Olga across the table.
While a friendly argument was going on between Angela and
Rose, Paula said in a low voice, 'Say, listen, you're not coming
back next year are you?' The Leader replied that she expected
to and asked why. Mara uttered a long drawn out, 'Oh, you'll
be our Leader then, won't you?' The Leader, still in the dark,
assured them that that did not necessarily follow, that they could
change if they wished or that they could meet without a Leader.
Mara answered quickly, 'Oh, no, that wasn't what we meant. We'd

never want to meet without a leader but we knew that you only stay two years and we were just saying Sunday morning that just when we get used to a person she leaves.'

"The reason finally came tumbling out, partly from one, partly from another. The group had met Sunday morning and evidently had had a grand talk session. The Yodelers had an idea which they passed along to the Gay Girls. There was a bungalow on the church grounds—The Madison house, as they call it—which they thought should be used as a community center. They would like to approach Father Dubich and ask him if they might use it for that purpose. The young people themselves would take care of the house and provide leadership for the clubs which would meet there. Paula said, 'We'd ask the B. T. M.s and the Gayhearts to help us too. There are some girls in those clubs that would make good leaders and besides the fathers of the B. T. M.s are directors of the church.' They realized that it would cost money to furnish it and so they were thinking of a harvest festival to raise money. 'We could make a lot of the things ourselves, too,' Paula added. Mara, Olga and Bertha were also very much excited about the plan but the other three, Stella, Rose and Angela did not look enthusiastic and Rose expressed herself as being decidedly against it. 'You're just trying to throw Mr. Madison out of his house,' she said. 'Well, if we do maybe he'll go home to his wife then,' Mara answered. 'He has a home in Bulkley. Why doesn't he live there? My father wouldn't do that.'

"The three dissenters went into the other room and tried new dance steps while the four favoring the plan stayed and talked. The Leader learned that Rose had not been in favor of the plan from the beginning but that Angela had been in favor of it Sunday. 'I guess she's talked to Rose since then,' Paula said. Stella had not been at the meeting and therefore did not know about it. She had been listening very attentively and had immediately taken sides with Rose.

"After talking for some time the Leader persuaded them to postpone seeing Father Dubich the next night and really take time to formulate plans so that they could sell the idea to him.

"Paula said, 'Well, what we'd really like to know is would you be willing to help us? We couldn't do it alone.' The Leader replied that she would be glad to do anything she could. Mara beamed and said, 'I told you she would. She's always willing to help us.' Paula made no answer to this; she merely smiled. Mara

went on, 'That's why we asked if you were coming back next
year because we wanted to know if you'd help us before we said
we'd do it.' Paula continued, 'We'd need someone to help our
leaders. They don't know anything about leading clubs. We'd
have to have some training for them.'

"Stella, Rose and Angela came back into the room and Rose
immediately began to accuse them of running Mr. Madison out
of his home. Mara grew excited and replied that two of his sons
were Yodelers and that if they were in favor of it, why should
the Gay Girls worry about it. Rose answered in a surprised voice,
'Oh, do they know about it?' The Leader tried to play the rôle
of peacemaker and suggested that it might be wise to have Mr.
Madison live there since the house would be safer if someone were
in it all night. This suggestion seemed to appease the three and
Stella said, 'All right. I guess I'm in favor.' Angela and Rose,
however, were still a bit skeptical.

"This was the first time that the Leader ever noticed Olga's
taking the initiative in any situation. She smiled and seemed to
have a very good time singing and later in the evening became
actually enthusiastic about the plan to use the Madison house for
a community center. Her eyes sparkled and she stated definitely
'I think we should do it.'

"It seemed to the Leader that the Yodelers did not want to take
the responsibility themselves since they asked the Gay Girls to
present the idea to Father Dubich. The plan seemed feasible to
the Leader if they could get enough neighborhood people behind
them and did not try to initiate too many activities in the very
beginning. They should not be allowed to rush into this without
realizing what a large undertaking it was and how much effort it
would take to keep it going."

Note: This proposal is an interesting outgrowth of the club's
project of furnishing one of the houses connected with the Community House the previous year and of their experience in
leading groups. They are now projecting into the parish community methods which the Community House has taught them.
This is an interesting illustration of the process of cultural
assimilation between the American and Slovenian communities
through the efforts of a group of the younger generation. The
place of the Leader as indicated here is significant. Is this a
legitimate part of her function as leader? How much should the
group now be able to carry independently of such assistance?

April 8, 1932

An informal meeting of part of the club was held four days later.

The Leader reported that Miss W., Mr. D. and other staff members at the agency were very much interested and were willing to help in the development of the community center at St. John's. They had suggested that a committee be made up of Gay Girls, Yodelers, B. T. M.s, and Gayhearts to make plans to present to Father Dubich. The girls all agreed and Paula said, "How many should we have on the committee?" The Leader suggested two or three from each club. Mara said, "Let's put Olga on it. She's really interested and this is the first time she's ever shown any interest in anything. Let's give her a chance. You and Olga go to the meeting, Paula." Paula asked if there was anyone else who would rather go. "I'd just as soon let someone else go." However, no one else volunteered and Paula said she would go.

Note: The conscious treatment of Olga by the group and the attempt to force her into a position of leadership are interesting here. Is this likely to have the desired effect?

Before leaving, Paula told the Leader she would again have to withdraw from applying to the Bryn Mawr Summer School because of economic conditions at home. This is the end, as far as the record shows, of Paula's attempt to go to Bryn Mawr.

April 9, 1932

The next night, the Yodelers gave a Minstrel Show at the Slovenian Hall to which the Leader was invited by the group. This was the occasion of further development of the community center project.

After the show was over, the Leader explained to Paula that she was not staying very long and asked her if she would find out whether the other clubs wished to participate in a meeting concerning the community center. After some discussion, two or three girls went to one of the B. T. M.s and some to the Gayhearts. In a few minutes they came back saying that both groups were considering it. In a few minutes the B. T. M.s reported that they were not interested and the Gayhearts said there were too few of them to do anything and they would rather not. Stan Rovich came up just then and reported that there had been some difficulty between the Yodelers and Father Dubich. The Leader understood that there was a change in the price which was to have been charged for the Hall. Stan made several remarks to the effect that there really was not any use trying to do anything for the parish because it was not appreciated anyway, and that they were planning to give their next show some other place. The girls were all properly sympathetic and the Leader and Paula felt that there was no chance of a meeting since the others were not interested. The Leader left after a few minutes. Other records at the Community House indicate that several months before this proposal, Father Dubich had himself suggested the use of this Madison house for such purposes. There is no indication as to why he did not at this time agree to work with these clubs on it.

Note: So died this plan which might have given them the opportunity to use their knowledge of group leadership and to set up an indigenous community center. From the record it appears that dissension between the clubs, the rivalry with the B. T. M.s and difficulty between the Yodelers and the priest made it impossible. Should the agency or the Leader have attempted to push this enterprise further? How much was it due to fundamental differences between the older and younger generations in the Slovene community? Can this interest of the girls in community affairs find other outlets through the agency if not through the parish?

April 20, 1932

Club meetings the next weeks were uneventful. On April twentieth the Leader was invited to attend a Sodality meeting at the church. Her account of it again shows the Gay Girls playing a prominent part in the church affairs.

"The secretary began to call the roll. The girls were very noisy, talking in small groups all the time. Every now and then the secretary could no longer be heard; the president would get up and say, 'Now why don't you keep quiet! We have a lot to do tonight and I have some place to go after this is over.'

"The president asked who would read a letter written in Slovene. No one volunteered. Finally Stella, who had not been listening said, 'Here, I'll do it.' The Gay Girls began to laugh when the letter was given to Stella and she answered in a very embarrassed

tone, 'Oh, I didn't know it was written in Slovenian.' Finally one
of the girls agreed to read it. The letter concerned the canonization of a Slovene priest. The Sodality was being asked to contribute
money to the committee which was working for canonization.
The president asked several questions which evidently had been
answered in the letter since some of the girls said, 'Why didn't
you listen while the letter was being read?' She answered,
'Wouldn't have understood it anyway.' They finally decided to
contribute five dollars since that was what the mothers' club gave
and they did not want to be outdone.

"The president then passed out the Sodality paper and some
song sheets. Just then Father Dubich came in. After speaking to
the girls, he asked the president if she had arranged who was to
make the collections. She said, 'Oh, no, I was waiting till you
came for that.' He laughingly protested and picked up the sheets
which were being passed around. Looking at the Sodality paper
he remarked, 'I see you have a Socialist paper.' The girls all
laughed at this. Then he asked who were going to make collections
for flowers for the month of May. The Gay Girls kept saying
in low tones, 'Well, we're not going to make any.' He then began
to divide the parish into sections and asked who wanted to collect
on each street. The first street he asked about was Thirty-seventh.
None volunteered for a few minutes. Then Paula turned around,
looked at Stella and said, 'We'll do it, Father.' The same happened with the rest of the girls. The Gay Girls took the first three
streets in pairs. Mara, in volunteering, said, 'Bertha and I will
take Thirty-eighth, Father. Bertha isn't here but she'll take it.'
Most of the other girls had to be urged.

"The girls stayed and practiced their stunts for the church program Sunday night. None of them knew their parts and no definite
plans for rehearsals had been made beyond the dress rehearsal
Friday night which was required by Father Pronko, the second
priest at St. John's. In a few minutes the rehearsal was over and
Bertha and Stan Rovich joined the girls. Paula told Stan about
some books which she had got for him and some she had ordered
at the library. In telling him about the books she said, 'Oh, honest,
Stan, it has the funniest names in it and it's so dry. Do you know
what it's like? Just like an American history.' Stan laughed and
explained that it was mythology. Paula answered, 'If you have to
read books like that in college, then I don't want to go.' Bertha
and Mara said they were ready to go home and asked the Leader
if she were coming. Just about that time three other boys came

up to the group. After they were introduced to the Leader they all started out together."

Note: This episode shows the girls embedded in the Slovenian community and acting as pillars of the church. How is this related to their attempted revolt of the previous spring?

April 24, 1932

On April twenty-fourth the entertainment at the Slovenian Hall was put on. The Leader was present at the invitation of the girls.

"The Gay Girls' acts were always accepted with enthusiastic applause. Suddenly in the midst of the applause after one of the numbers there was a sound of booing in the back of the Hall. This occurred after each number but did not visibly disturb the girls. Many people stamped and clapped louder seemingly to drown out the booing.

"The Gay Girls were last on the program and the Leader went back stage immediately after their act. She made no mention of the booing but merely congratulated them on their success. Father Pronko came back stage, went directly to Olga, saying, 'Did those asses in the back bother you with their booing?' Olga replied that they did not.

"While talking, the Leader congratulated the girls on their stage presence and the fact that they had not got excited during the booing. Rose and Paula both looked surprised and said, 'I didn't even hear it.' Angela, however, admitted hearing it, saying, 'It was just that alley gang. One of the B. T. M.s goes with them; maybe that's why they did it.' "

The booing of their stunt was commented on at the next club meeting when they were discussing the putting on of another play for Mothers' Day at the church.

"Woven in with the above conversation," notes the Leader, "was a discussion of the 'booing' which had been done the previous Sunday. Bertha did not want to take part in any other performance because she was afraid that it would happen again. Some of the others seemed to agree with her. Mara said that Father Dubich had written about it in the paper and that the ones who had done it, the 'Oakwood Place gang' had come and apologized to Mara and Bertha. They said further that they did not believe that it was entirely the boys but that the Jesters, another girls' club, was connected with it.

"The girls admitted at this time that they had noticed and had been a bit concerned by the 'booing' Sunday—a thing which they had formerly refused to do. Mara was rather inclined to let it pass but Bertha was more stubborn and said that she was sure it would happen again. She also indicated that she had refused to accept their apology when they came to her."

Note: This is the first sign of actual hostility to the Gay Girls in the community. How much of this is due to the rise of other groups to prominence it is impossible to say. The earlier successes of the Gay Girls have made them spend less time in preparation for such affairs and they have become rather careless about them. Also the need to enforce club attendance, mentioned earlier, suggests a slight weakening of the group solidarity. It is possible that these weaknesses are evident to rival groups and that they now dare to express their disapproval in such forms.

May 1932

During the month of May there were several evidences of disorganization in the group. A general tendency to irresponsibility appeared. An appointment to play baseball at another agency was broken without notification. The election of officers became impossible since everyone refused office. Finally Rose was elected president and Bertha, secretary. The year closed with morale low. Paula after one controversy summed up the general feeling:

"A little later, after sitting quiet for several minutes, she glanced up at the girls and said in a rather disappointed tone, 'What a club we have. You know, I used to think we were pretty good but we never do anything any more. We never go any place together; we don't even keep our appointments. I wonder what people think of us. I guess they know what we are now.' The other girls tried to laugh it off, Angela saying, 'Well, we might as well let them know what we really are.' "

ANNUAL SUMMARY 1931–1932

In commenting on the year's activities the Leader sums up the club's accomplishments.

The club, she indicates, continues its live interest in the community and its loyalty to its own group. The interest in education, developed the previous year, continues with many of the group and a growing independence of thought is evident in their behavior. The experience in leading younger groups which several have had has developed an objectivity about group and individual behavior which is reflected in the way they handle their own internal problems, especially Olga. They wish to give everyone a chance at leadership and to have the group accomplish something definite each year.

On the other hand, the club continues its tendency to exclusiveness and shows a certain self-importance which makes them unpopular in the community. They are inclined to withdraw into themselves and refuse to take part in inter-club activities as they have formerly done. A rift between Olga, with her limited interests, and the rest of the group becomes evident this year.

In the light of the criteria, we might ask the following in regard to this year's record:

1. Should the Leader have developed her relationship to individuals, especially Paula and Olga?

2. How are the social relationships developing within the group? What sort of treatment should Olga have from the other girls? Are their present attitudes constructive for her?

3. Are the methods of group control evidenced here valuable for the group? Should the group coerce its members into attending meetings? What type of leadership does Stella develop during her term of office?

4. Is the program developed as fully as it could be? Should the Leader have provided more adequate handling of the questions raised in regard to psychology and sex? Could the group have been encouraged to go farther in the interests in international or economic affairs? Could the interest in crafts have been carried on into more developing experience? Were the evident interests developed as fully as they might have been?

5. In their relation to the community, could their interest in the proposed center have been carried further with help from the agency? Could the Leader have helped them to better their inter-group relations with other clubs in the neighborhood? How can their widened community interests find expression?

THIRD YEAR

The summer between the third and fourth years (the second and third of this record), of Gay Girls' history is noteworthy in two respects. The girls do less as a group during the summer than in previous years which the Leader believes is due to increasing diversity of interests among the members. Paula and Mara attend the Workers' Institute, a two-week school for industrial women conducted on a workers' education basis and emphasizing economics and industrial problems. This is the school which Father Dubich had forbidden them to attend the previous year. He had gone to the school the summer before to speak, had had some contacts with Miss D. of the Y. W. C. A. and this year did not oppose their attendance. Paula distinguishes herself at the Institute, is very popular with both faculty and students and is elected chairman of a continuing committee for the winter.

Rose has been elected president of the Gay Girls, partly on the principle of "giving everyone a chance." She is not an outstanding personality in the group and is usually dependent on some other person, either Paula or Angela. She has gained more confidence in herself through the club experience and does succeed in conducting the meetings with orderly procedure. She lacks the power to unite the group and "pep" them up.

Note: The election of this type of president this year is significant at a time when the club bond shows signs of weakening. Whether it is a cause of such weakening or the effect, it is impossible to say, but the result during this year is important in the solidarity of the group.

September 27, 1932

At the first meeting only one girl showed up so that the group did not get under way until the second meeting. The Leader reports the following conversation with Paula at her home:

"Paula came in the gate just as the Leader was talking to her little sister. After greetings were exchanged, the Leader asked Paula about her summer. She talked very excitedly about the Workers' Institute which she and Mara had attended. She told about the classes in English and economics especially. She said she was very glad she had not gone to Bryn Mawr this summer because she would never have known what it was all about.

"She would like to join an industrial club which meets at the 'Y' on Wednesday. She would have the advantages of limbering, swimming and discussions. The Leader urged her to do it.

"Paula had been ill during the summer and had consulted both her own doctor and the doctor at the Y. W. C. A."

October 5, 1932

Four girls appeared for this meeting: Paula, Stella, Angela and Rose. Another club came in and Paula jumped up to show them around. The Leader jokingly asked Paula if she were the official hostess. She laughed but Stella answered, "She likes to show off."

Note: This remark, while humorous, gives a hint of change in attitude toward Paula. Is this perhaps significant of the weakening of the club loyalty?

Most of the evening was spent in discussion of an etiquette book which one of the girls produced.

October 11, 1932

The Leader reports on a further conversation with Paula several weeks later:

"The question of Paula's health was brought up by the Leader. Paula talked freely and without urging. She said that she was afraid she might now have or might contract tuberculosis. The Leader discouraged this idea and tried to set before Paula the necessity for finding out what really ailed her, of following through the treatment and chiefly, of not worrying about herself so much. She agreed that that was necessary. The Leader realized that she has a great deal to overcome in that she is carrying the responsibility for the entire support of her family and is afraid that she is threatened with a serious illness.

"Talk then drifted to the two weeks at Workers' Institute. Paula spoke of her great admiration for Miss D., the head of the Institute. She and Mara used to sit at Miss D.'s table because of the stimulating conversation there. 'We always learned something new at each meal.'

"Just before leaving, the question of her health again was brought up. Paula said she thought that the rest of the girls would want to take gym but she was afraid she could not take it in her condition. The Leader assured her that exercise would probably not hurt her since she had no organic disease. Paula seemed a bit confused by the Leader's attitude since she had always before been very sympathetic. Paula, however, said that she would try the gym class and see how it affected her.

"The Leader asked about Stan Rovich. Paula replied that she and Stan had been doing a lot of reading together. 'I don't tell him when I don't understand things but I either go and look it up or else I get someone else to explain it to me. Oh, and do you know what? The other day I asked him what he thought of the Socialist party. He didn't say much—just sort of stalled around. About a week later he gave me a regular lecture on it. He'd gone and looked it up. It was so funny I had to laugh after he left.'"

Paula had been taken by Miss D. of the Y. W. C. A. to several specialists and there was no evidence of any discernible illness. Miss D. and the Leader therefore agreed to encourage Paula not to think so much of her physical state.

Note: Is this preoccupation with her health a sign of some more important disturbance? Is the Leader's decision to minimize her fears the best approach to this problem? What does her report of her relation with Stan indicate?

October 15, 1932

The Leader called on Paula and reports the following:

"She mentioned as an example of good times the Alumni dance she had been to the Saturday before. The Leader had been there and said to Paula, 'Stan wasn't there, was he?' Paula explained that he was in New York playing for some friends. This opened up the discussion about Stan and Paula's feeling for him and in this it was revealed that Stan's family did not approve of Paula, or so she thought. In fact, Stan's mother thought that Paula was silly and giggly. Paula finally admitted that that was back of her feeling of withdrawing from the neighborhood. It all seemed so hopeless and useless for her and she wanted to avoid every opportunity of having any one talk about her so that it might get back to Stan's family."

Note: What light does this throw on Paula's attitude toward her health or toward the club? What further could the Leader do under these circumstances?

October 17, 1932

On October seventeenth six of the group got together to make plans for the year. The problem of locating the meeting night possible for all arose as before. The question of the content of the program was also discussed. It was finally proposed that they change their meeting place to a community center a little out of the neighborhood in order to get gym and tap dancing.

October 26–December 12, 1932

The next six weeks saw an unsuccessful attempt to follow out this proposal. The plan included attendance at classes until nine-thirty and then a club meeting following. In practice it worked out that they could not all go in the same class because they wanted different activities occurring simultaneously. They did not finish their classes at the same time and the meeting was delayed. They were shifted from place to place and the time left for the meeting was too short to be worth while. Some girls complained of the distance from home and the expenses for classes. The auditorium program which they wanted to attend also turned out to be too expensive for some of them, especially Paula. As a result attendance dropped to four, the morale of the group was very low, and there was a general state of discouragement.

In the short club meetings which were held attempts were made by the Leader and by several of the girls to stimulate reading and discussion of books recommended by the Leader after consultation with the Readers' Adviser of the Library. This did not work out, however, as the girls did not get the books read in many cases and were not interested in discussing them. There was a noticeable lack of enthusiasm about all the proposals made for club activity. Plans were made for attendance at a Youth Forum—a discussion on public questions being held downtown. The group agreed to go but no one came on either night and no explanation was made of this absence.

Finally the Leader decided to stop all efforts to hold the group together and to allow it to lapse at least until after Christmas.

Note: The decline of the Gay Girls to a state of almost complete collapse appears to be due to a series of accidents about time and place of meetings and expenses. Actually, however, it would not have occurred if it were not the result of a definite decline of interest in the group. In other years such obstacles could have been surmounted by the enthusiasm of the group. What could the Leader do in this situation? Was her suggestion on program a wise one? Would something requiring more collective effort than reading have been a better creator of morale? Should the Leader attempt to find ways of reviving the group when it shows signs of falling apart?

During this period individuals have been developing in different ways. Bertha after being one of the mainstays of the club for several years had dropped out entirely. Her absence arose from the influence of her "boy friend."

"The Leader was told by Mara that Harry, Bertha's boy friend, told Bertha there were four things she must do before he would go out with her steady. She must stop walking around the streets, stop singing on the stage, stop singing with the Slovenian Singing Society and stay away from the Gay Girls. Bertha promised to do this for a period of two months. If after that time she felt that she did not wish to go on with him she said she would be ready for anything."

On January first, Bertha was to return to the Gay Girls. Later records show that Bertha continued to go with Harry but that he no longer disapproved of the Gay Girls. She also continued to sing on the stage and was active in the Slovenian Singing Society.

Note: It would be interesting to know why Harry made these requirements. Do they affect Bertha's reputation unfavorably, or is it merely a matter of the time required, or is there evidence of too much independence on her part? Bertha's return to the club after Christmas is proof evidently that she was able to change his opinion on these matters. The Leader's acquaintance with all this is at second hand. Should she have attempted to discuss with Bertha her dropping out?

Paula during this period was very discontented with the club program because she was very much interested in tap dancing but could not afford to attend the class at the Community Center. She was getting most of her satisfactions out of a class in economics and public speaking at the Y. W. C. A. which continued the interest she had developed at the Workers' Institute. She also was reading a good deal of both fiction and popular discussions of social questions. Even here, however, Paula was not up to her previous accomplishments. She never took much responsibility as chairman of the Workers' Institute committee and gradually lost interest in the classes.

> **Note:** What relation has the Leader to these interests of Paula's in affairs outside of the nationality community? Should she encourage them? To what extent is it desirable for Paula to shift her interests in this way? Does her shift in attitudes here indicate a more serious underlying problem? If so, how could it be met?

The following excerpt from a conversation during a club meeting gives another hint of a change in Paula:

"During a lull in the conversation Paula's voice carried further than she intended. She said, 'If I'm not married by the time I'm twenty-five I'm going to get sophisticated.' Everybody laughed. Paula was rather embarrassed and the Leader asked her what her idea of a sophisticated woman was. 'Oh, you know, one who smokes, and drives her own car and goes to men's apartments.' Angela challenged her. 'Where would you get a car?' Paula replied knowingly, 'If you do some of the things sophisticated women do you will get the others!' The meeting broke up with a chorus of, 'Oh, yeah?'"

During this time Paula continued to go with Stan Rovich with whom she had many interests in common. His father had died, however, and he was considering leaving college in order to support the family. Paula continued to be the chief support of her family as her father was unemployed practically all the time.

> **Note:** Does this outburst of Paula's indicate a discouragement about her chance of marriage under present circumstances? Could the Leader be of any use in this situation if she and Paula should discuss it?

The Leader also comments that Paula admitted she was tired of providing the ideas and enthusiasm for the group. She said she wanted a good time and would like to drop her rôle as leader.

> **Note:** Considering all these factors what should be the Leader's attitude toward Paula? How can she help her most effectively?

Father Dubich, through his contact with the Workers' Institute, seemed to have become more friendly with the Y. W. C. A. He spoke at a meeting of its Industrial Department during this

winter and evidently removed his prohibition against the attendance of his parishioners.

Note: This is an illustration of the changing attitude of authorities within the nationality community. What effect will this
have on the girls' conflict over outside contacts reported earlier?

January 9, 1933

After the holidays, the club began its regular meetings again
with considerable renewal of interest. At the first meeting, January ninth, the lowered reputation of the Gay Girls in the neighborhood was reported. Olga said she had heard several people
talking about the Gay Girls' club being dead. The Daisyettes (another Slovenian girls' club) had asked especially "and I told them
sure we were still meeting." Bertha added, "When they ask me
I tell them we belong to the secret service now and have our meetings in private." The mothers of some of the girls seemed to be
concerned because the Gay Girls have begun to break up.

This started reminiscences of all their past accomplishments
as a club and they went back to their early acquaintance as small
children playing about the railroad tracks and gullies.

Paula attempted in this meeting to draw them into a discussion
of future program by reminding them of their plan for reading
and discussion. This met with no response. The Leader then
brought up the question of a barter plan which was being started
by the agency and one of the staff of the agency came in to present
it. It was received with some interest but no great enthusiasm.

Note: The importance of the club in neighborhood life is noticeable here in the way its decline is commented upon. The
standing which membership in it had given them as individuals
is one of the factors which still acts to perpetuate it as a group.
It is significant of the present state of club morale, however,
that they turn to the past for reassurance rather than planning
any future achievements.

In spite of these evidences of decline their reputation in the
parish was still good. Another staff member from the Community
House records a conversation with one of the sisters at the parochial school in November in which she mentioned the Gay Girls
favorably. She said that the Gay Girls were becoming somewhat
self-conscious because they felt the people of the parish thought

of them as clowns. But she said that some people, and she among them, admired the Gay Girls and were sorry that they felt this way. Father Dubich also commented to the head of the Community House at about this time on the high regard he had for the Gay Girls and their contribution to the parish.

January 10, 1933

Early in January the Leader called again on Paula and reports as follows:

"The Leader called for a friendly visit with Paula, since she had not been at her home for some time. Stan Rovich was there when the Leader arrived, playing a game with Paula and smaller members of the family. These younger children left and the radio program including Leslie Howard in 'Smiling Through' occupied them for a time.

"After telling the story of Berkeley Square, Stan began to talk about school and psychology. He explained that he was a scholastic since Catholics were not allowed to believe in the modern psychology which denied the fact of 'universal ideas.' As he was leaving to go to rehearsal, he remarked, 'Forgive me for going off this way; I guess I do that most of the time.'

"Paula told the Leader she had much to tell her about Stan. She talked for some time on this subject and revealed that at present the two have planned not to go together except once a month. This was Paula's suggestion, since she explained to him just how she felt. She said she felt much better about it than she had for a long time and now whatever happened will be up to him."

Note: Paula has evidently been going through a crisis which may have accounted for her declining interest in group activities, her health and her generally lowered morale during these months. The group leader evidently is helpful to her as a person with whom she can talk things out. Does she require any more assistance than can be given in this way?

January 16, 1933

On this occasion Paula arrived ahead of the others and the Leader seized the occasion to talk over the situation with her. She reports:

"The Leader asked Paula if she might talk with her quite pro-
fessionally for a little while. She asked what Paula thought about
continuing the club, saying that it was her opinion that the girls
were no longer getting as much from the club as they had formerly. Paula smiled and said that she had felt the same way for
some time. The girls, she said, had developed different interests.
She, for instance, was interested in reading and further education,
but Olga was interested in church events to a much greater extent
than formerly. She felt that the girls were no longer interested in
continuing with regular club activities but that they just did not
want to admit it. As Paula said, 'We used to have a lot of fun
just running up the street chasing after each other, but we don't
want to do that any more. That shows that we have changed.'

"The Leader asked Paula about the club's reaction to being left
alone just before Christmas. Paula remarked, 'It was the best
thing you could have done to them. Some of the kids went over to
the Community Center the week after we decided not to meet.
When they didn't find you there they came back and asked me
where I thought you were. I told them that we had agreed not to
meet until after Christmas and they said they knew that but
thought you'd be there anyway. I told them it would be good for
them if you didn't meet with them at all any more. They didn't
like that but they took it from me.'

"The Leader encouraged Paula to talk about the girls in the
club. She began with Angela, saying that she was very much
disgusted with Angela for not trying to get a job. She said that
Angela's sister Jessie, 'Just worships the ground Angela walks
on and gives her everything.' Paula felt that as long as the sister
continued to do this Angela would not make any attempt to get
a job. When the Leader said that she felt that even after two
years she did not know Angela, Paula replied that she had been
going to her house for five years and was just now beginning to
understand her a little. Paula complained about Angela's lack of
security and confidence in herself. She said no matter how many
books she advised Angela to read and tried to discuss with her, all
she could ever get from her was, 'Oh, it was *so* good. I *liked* it.'

"She admired Mara a great deal. She said of her, 'I always
wanted her for my girl friend. She was always the smartest girl
in our class and she has a critical mind. I always liked to bring
books to her because she told me what she really thought of them.
The only thing is she's so religious—too religious. You have to be
so careful what you advise her to read. On Saturday I brought

her a book and she wouldn't go to Communion the next morning because she felt it was a sin to read it. I don't think it is and I even asked Father Pronko about it and he said it wasn't, so I don't see why she acts that way.'

"She went on to talk about other friends of hers—Ann, the girl who worked at the library and Stan. Ann, it seems, worked in the bindery department of the library when Paula started. She liked Paula and paid quite a bit of attention to her. 'I didn't like a lot of things she did, like smoking and going out on drinking parties, but when I told her this she told me that she understood my feeling about it but that she didn't want me to interfere with her life when she wasn't with me. She never took me to any of her parties although she used to take me other places quite a lot. I liked her because she told me things which really helped me. I could talk to her about everything. She stimulated me and encouraged me to read a lot. That's one thing about Angela; she doesn't talk about anything but neighborhood gossip and I don't know any of that. We aren't allowed to gossip at home. I don't remember more than twice in my life when my father told us something which he said was not to be repeated. I have the worst time trying to find something to talk about to Angela. That's one reason why I like Stan. He learns something at school and then comes and tells me about it. The only thing we can't talk about is Socialism. He happened to get a book which said that Socialism is a destroyer of Catholicism so he refuses to try to find out any more about it. We got kind of mad about it one night so we agreed not to talk about it at all any more.' "

Note: What clues are there here to Paula's emotional problems and to the help she needs in meeting them? What indications are there of the type of friends she wishes and needs? What kinds of avocational interests does she need? What could the Leader do to help her meet these problems?

The next few meetings were uneventful.

February 6, 1933

At this meeting the group was asked to fill out a questionnaire for a student's thesis, giving information on their work experience.

The Leader reports as follows:

"This led to a discussion of what each one did on her particular

job. Rose told of her factory in which more and more women
were doing the work that had formerly been done by men and
said that the men resented being shoved out in this way. Someone
mentioned a hat factory where Olga had worked a while and found
that thirty cents was paid for completed hats so that if a girl
made only one hat a day she would get only thirty cents. This
had happened to Rose's sister and she had refused to go back
a second day, even though her father urged her, saying that she
would get used to it. Olga said that one had to be very fast to
make any amount of money at all. The Leader then told of the
present situation of the garment workers where completed gar-
ments brought only the small sum of twenty-five or thirty cents
for each one. Paula said that seemed dreadfully unfair when the
shops sold them for five or six dollars.

"Paula mentioned a new book she was reading called 'The
Black Princess,' a story of Negro life. This led to a discussion of
the racial problem. The group talked first about what was thought
of the Negro in the South and commented on the fact that they
were very segregated, and yet men who owned plantations were
often very kind to the Negroes who had been in their families for
years. Olga said, 'It must be terribly hard for them to get an
education. I wonder what the first ones that started did. They
must have had to fight awfully hard.' The Leader suggested
Booker T. Washington's book 'Up from Slavery' for a picture
of the beginning of education for the Negro and also mentioned
the present Wilberforce College, in the state of Ohio, for Negroes.
Angela asked why there were more in the North now and this
brought out the fact that industry had brought them from the
South. Finally Olga said, 'Well, I know I shouldn't feel this way
and I know it isn't right but, nevertheless, I think the Negro
should have some special place where he can go and live with his
own people and develop there. Perhaps this would be in Africa,
almost any place.' Paula smiled at this but said nothing. The
Leader then told of her conversation with a Juvenile Court worker
who felt that the only hope for the Negro was education by segregation with their own race as teachers. Olga said, 'Well, that's
the way I feel. It seems to me now that the Negro doesn't have
any chance.' Conversation lagged after this and finally Paula
said, 'What do you want to do the next time?' Nobody answered,
so she turned to Olga and said, 'What do you want to do, Olga?'
and Olga failed to respond. After questioning as to interests, likes
and dislikes, Paula said, 'Well, I don't see what we can do. You

kids don't seem to want to do anything.' Then hanging her head, in a lower tone of voice she said, 'I suppose nobody wants to read.' Mara looked at her and smiled and then Paula began her tactics of drawing out the group all over again and finally she said that each one was to bring whatever she wanted to work on in the way of sewing or knitting. Also they decided that they would make graham cracker custard pie and Paula assigned each one what she should bring."

The Leader comments on this:

"As to the discussion which followed the questionnaire, the Leader felt that its success lay in the fact that it was very informal and spontaneous. However, it was marked by apathy on the part of Angela, Rose and Olga, while Mimi and Paula carried the burden of the discussion. However, the Leader felt that Olga and Rose had been more interested than they wished to indicate for the Leader out of the corner of her eye caught them sitting forward in their seats during the discussion of the Negro problem.

"On the whole, the techniques employed by Paula and Rose to get the group's cooperation were very interesting to the Leader. Certainly, in the case of Olga, Paula exercised all the principles of drawing out interests and likes and dislikes. The fact that the group has turned to cooking and sewing as an activity seemed to indicate that the hope of turning this group into a study group has almost gone. Paula intimated this to the Leader and said that she felt subjects could only be brought in indirectly through conversation and discussion during activities of the above-mentioned kind."

Note: This is one of the few occasions in the history of the club where their work experience becomes the basis for discussion. The inter-racial interest has appeared sporadically before. Would it have been possible to go on from these beginnings to a more advanced program including reading, trips and discussion? Could this be done if the meetings were more systematically planned or the material presented in a more interesting way?

The Leader in commenting on the work of the term at this point indicated that the major problem causing the disintegration of the club was the clear divergence of interests. On one side was Olga and her one, or sometimes two, friends. Olga seemed to lack interest in any kind of program except cooking or sewing, in

which she excelled, and yet she was extremely proud of being a
Gay Girl and defended the group against all criticism. Rose, her
particular friend, also acted as a deterrent to progress by her lack
of response to any proposal. The other four girls who were active
were ready for a program including discussions of various public
questions or work problems. They tended to drop, however, to the
lower levels of interest in order to maintain the solidarity of the
group.

Note: Can any solution be discovered for this conflict? The
chief bond during these months seems to be the pull of habitual
association and the prestige which each still gains from membership. Are these sufficient bases for group continuance?

February 13, 1933

The plan of doing sewing and cooking interspersed with informal discussion was tried out at the next meeting. Several of
the girls brought things to make, Olga again getting favorable
attention through an elaborate quilt. There was some teasing about
hope chests. Part of the group made a pie. While it was baking
and some were sewing, the Leader reverted to the previous discussion.

"The Leader said to Mimi, 'Do you still feel the same way
about the Negro that you did last week?' She smiled and said,
'No, I've grown soft-hearted. I feel sorry for him now. I don't
think it would be quite fair to put them off by themselves.' The
Leader said, 'You mean then that for their own good they perhaps
should be segregated but you think it's impossible?' 'Yes,' Mimi
replied, 'Something near that. It seems to me they would have
more chance to catch up with us by themselves but it's making
too much of a distinction.' Stella who was sitting next to the
Leader said, 'Well, couldn't they all be transported? How large
is the population in the United States?' The Leader replied that
she was not absolutely sure but thought it was somewhere near
seven million, and got up to get a book by Scott Nearing, 'Black
America,' which she thought might give the information. Stella
looked over the Leader's shoulder as she ran down the list of
chapters and said, 'Oh, that looks interesting,' and then turned
to someone else with a remark about her sewing. The Leader tried
to turn the conversation back to a discussion by saying, 'Do you
think it would be so practical to transport that many people?'

and Stella closed the subject by saying, 'I suppose not,' and let it go at that."

Note: Again the interest in Negro problems rose slightly but was soon shifted to more immediate concerns. This interest recurs more frequently than any other social question but each time it gets only superficial attention. Could the Leader have brought in material or resources which would have shifted this to a more adequate treatment of the question? What could she have used? The Leader suggested starting a discussion group outside the club for the four girls who are interested in that type of program. In fact, this never developed. Would this have been the best way of dealing with the diversity of interests?

February 27, 1933

At the next meeting nothing occurred except desultory conversation. It took place just when the banks were beginning to close before the Bank Holiday of March fourth. The group's reaction to this event is recorded as follows:

"Rose then turned to the Leader and said, 'Say what about the banks? Thank goodness I didn't have any money there.' The girls all then began telling stories about friends who had money in the banks and now had nothing to live on. Rose told of one man who had twenty-one hundred dollars saved and then added, 'Of course he doesn't need it now but it's just the idea of having that much and not being able to get it.' The Leader explained that there was another side to the question in that such a limitation meant that payrolls might not come through, although the papers assured people that everything possible would be done. The discussion also touched on what might happen if the whole credit system collapsed, as the Leader said many people predicted it might. Rose said, 'That would mean starting all over again with nothing, wouldn't it?' The Leader agreed and there was much joking about how funny that would be."

Note: Could the Leader have picked up on this situation if she had been prepared to discuss it? What leads were there here for further discussion?

March 6, 1933

By this time the national catastrophe to the banks had broken and was affecting many members of the group. In spite of the interest in a recent dance which they had all attended, the following discussion arose in the club meeting:

"The question of the banks came up and Stella said the Warner factory had closed down for a week. 'They had a big meeting and asked us if we were willing. They have plenty of orders and to spare, but they figure they'd lose money if they couldn't pay us the week's wages, so we just closed.' She thought it would be funny not going to work but a vacation would be nice too. At this point Rose and Olga came in and became much interested in the subject since they too had discussed it at their factory. Olga said her place had had a meeting, too, but had decided to run the next week without pay. She said only one girl had said she would not work and she had changed her mind when she saw she was the only one. 'Gee, I wouldn't have the nerve to say "no" and I don't think anyone else would either,' she explained.

"Stella began asking questions about the President's proclamation and the reason for it. The Leader explained that it was the only way in which the banks could be made safe, the only way in which confidence could be restored. Rose said her factory had been closed for two weeks and she had no idea when it would open. If the banks became safe, she wondered if that would make any difference. Angela asked how long the bank holiday of the President would last and the Leader said she did not know but she doubted if it would be over on Thursday, the appointed time. The group began telling stories of people having no money and how funny it was to buy things on credit. They mentioned the fact that movies were operating on a check basis.

"The Leader then told of the similar situation of 1907 when the banks had all closed and scrip had been issued. 'That was before we were born, wasn't it?' Angela asked. 'Oh, let's forget it,' Olga suggested, 'There's enough of that all day long.'"

Note: It is interesting here to see the way in which this event is reflected in a rising interest in current news. Could the Leader have carried this further?

Conversation then drifted to attempts to get jobs and the Leader reports:
"This led to Olga's and Rose's telling of their 'jobbing' days, which at one time lasted over a period of five or six months. The whole group got to laughing so hard at Olga's dry way of telling funny incidents that they almost fell off their chairs. 'I'm telling youse, I know every factory on Fifth and Michigan, and we've been in 'em all, ain't we, Rose?' and Rose nodded assent between

her giggles. Some of the incidents included: getting up at five every morning, walking almost all day, applying at a pants' factory where only men worked, being errand girl in a shirt factory for a day, stemming strawberries for a week, being taken to a hotel as a salesperson for hosiery and being offered fur coats and cars. Olga then went on to explain that she had never liked the Brocker Factory and described some of the 'dirty deals' that she got there. Stella defended it and said that Olga had merely been unlucky."

Note: This glimpse into Olga's working experience suggests that she might be interested in discussing work problems and even perhaps eventually some of the ways in which they might be remedied. Could the Leader have followed this up further?

At the end of the evening the next meeting of the club was discussed:

" 'Is there any use of our going on this way?' Angela inquired. The others hung their heads. The Leader asked what they could plan to do. Angela replied, 'Well, I think it's a waste of time for you to come here when we don't do anything but just sit around.' The Leader explained that she did not mind that, that she enjoyed coming to club, but that the time was wasted on their part. Going further, the Leader said that they had grown beyond the things they had formerly liked and had not brought the club up to themselves. Stella inquired, 'How can we do that? What would we do?' The Leader said that depended first on the sort of thing they wanted to do and then on building club activities around those things. The Leader said that perhaps what they wanted above all else was a good time, which was well and good in itself, but they should then proceed to have a good time which at present they were not doing. In fact they were not enjoying anything at present. 'Well, we'll think it over,' Angela promised at the end of the discussion, 'and we'll let you know whether we'll be meeting any more or not.' "

Note: The morale of the group here reaches its low point and disintegration as a group becomes imminent. Was the Leader's technique here the best one? Is there any value in attempting to continue the group? Has it served its purpose?

The Leader analyzes the situation as follows:
"Looking at the whole picture the Leader would say this. At the present time and the present crisis of things, when most of these girls are carrying more responsibilities than they have be-

fore, the club stands to them as the place where they can get away from all of it and therefore it should supply a certain good time which they do not get anywhere else. However, they feel that they are obligated because of their past history to do more than this and yet they do not know how to go about it. The very ones who have outside interests and activities which satisfy their needs are the ones that have always given impetus to the club and been able to mix 'fun and seriousness' in the right amounts. So, the ones who need the club the most are the ones who seemingly cannot go ahead on their own. If, in other words, they should catch a new motivation, a 'reason for being' the situation would be quite different."

For the next two weeks the meetings were omitted because they conflicted with other events in the neighborhood. Toward the end of this period the Leader dropped in to see Paula about the future of the club. Paula felt that some new plan was needed if the group was to be revived and proposed that the club start meeting at the St. John parish house instead of at the Community House. This plan grew out of the hope that from this transfer to the church might grow a project for a community center at the church like that proposed earlier. The Leader assured her that the Community House would cooperate with such a plan in any way possible.

Paula said the group was to meet Thursday night after singing society and the plans would be presented to the club then. She promised to notify the Leader about their decision.

Note: It is significant that Paula's idea of how to revive the club again takes the form of furnishing and running a club room in connection with the parochial school. It is evident that what she has learned at the Community House makes her anxious to use the same methods independently. In spite of the failure of a similar plan before she still clings to it as the one hope of rallying the group to new achievements. Is it likely that there is enough cohesion in the group at present to make it possible for them to carry through such an enterprise?

March 28, 1933

A week later the group met at the Community House to discuss the plan further.

"Conversation then drifted to what they had been doing lately and the Leader said, 'I'm all agog to hear all the latest news on

your plans.' Paula began, 'Well, we didn't get to have that meeting last week so really there isn't much more to be told. We
haven't talked it over a lot and some of the girls don't even know
the latest, that is, what has happened since the last time. I guess
I'll begin at the beginning. One night Mara and I were walking
by the parish house and she said, "Let's go in to see Father
Dubich." '

"Paula unfolded the plans very much as she had given them
to the Leader when she called a week before. She kept saying
every little while, 'Of course we've got to get the rest of the clubs
back of us or it won't be done. Also Father Dubich says we've
got to make out our plans very well before we start so we'll know
just what we're going to do and why. He says you can't sell things
on just the idea, it's got to be backed up with facts and plans.'

"She assured the group that Father Dubich would be very much
in favor of any such plan and that Sister Nella had come to the
girls and said she would be only too glad to help them in any
way to fix up the room.

"The subject then shifted back to what they could really do in
regard to fixing the club room as they would like it. Mara mentioned lamps and draperies and Angela felt that people in the
community could probably be interested in giving some furniture
to it, as well as those members of the clubs who might be using it.
Bertha spoke up saying that the Ferdinand's Funeral Home was
to be changed around and that she 'bet' the owner could be persuaded to give some of the furniture he no longer wanted.

"Next came the question as to how the various clubs were going
to be interested in this and Paula said, 'Father Dubich said not
to be discouraged if everyone didn't take fire immediately. It
always takes a while for an idea to soak in and we've just got
to keep hammering away.' Plans were made for presenting it to
the other groups in the parish.

"The Leader pointed out the difficulty they, as the Gay Girls,
would meet when originating anything like this, saying that there
had been jealousy and resentment of some of their activities. She
suggested that perhaps if they worked as individuals and not as
the Gay Girls they might get farther. They have the feeling of
unity now and they will know that is there whether they broadcast it or not and people will resent it if they put that forward.
Paula said that was a very good idea and that would be a thing
that would certainly have to be watched since there was quite a
bit of feeling against them.

"The group began to break up into smaller groups chattering about what they could do, so the Leader began to get the tea and cookies ready. Paula brought them back together again by saying to the Leader. 'We're going to need loads of help on all this and you're the one that's going to give it to us. After all, the Community House knows a great deal about all this that we don't, so we're going to have to call on you to help us out.'"

Note: The inter-group relations within the parish are very evident here. The difficulties of cooperation between clubs which made the previous plan impossible seem to be reappearing here. Does the evidence of jealousy and unpopularity indicate that the attitudes of the Gay Girls toward their own achievements might be responsible in part for their trouble in getting other groups to work with them? Could the leadership in the agency have helped this by more inter-group cooperation? Is the plan proposed one that is likely to be successful with the present state of Gay Girls' development?

April 20, 1933

Nearly a month later five of the girls met in the school where they were planning to make their community center. Another group was in the room, however, and so the evening was spent in casual conversation about their former schooldays, a possible camping trip and similar matters. No progress was made on the project and it was evident that it had been dropped. The group seemed to want to do nothing but enjoy themselves without effort.

Note: The fact that the plan adopted so enthusiastically at one meeting had been allowed to lapse almost without comment shows again the lowered state of club morale.

The club completed this year without any election of officers or plans for the summer.

ANNUAL SUMMARY 1932–1933

The final year of the Gay Girls shows the further development of the trends toward disintegration evident in the third year. Certain of the strong characteristics still remain, however.

The group still shows a loyalty to each other and a certain degree of cohesion as a group. The interest in further education and in public questions is present with a few but it is not sustained nor widespread enough to develop into a program. Certain individuals show marked development during the year but it is of a kind which tends to pull the group apart rather than to unite them.

The main causes of the disintegration so evident throughout this year seem to be an increasing divergence of interests between the members, the inability therefore to decide on any program satisfactory to all and the pressure of personal responsibilities due to the depression which reduces the interest available for the group. It is possible that the needs originally satisfied by the group are now being met in other ways.

On the basis of the criteria suggested, the reader may ask:

1. Does the Leader carry through her personal relationship to Paula to the place where it can contribute to the solution of her problems? Should she have sought more personal contact with Bertha, Olga or any of the others?

2. What could have been done with the club program to develop interests common to the group? to carry further the enlarging interests of a few? to provide for more adequate treatment of the interests which appear?

3. How can a lowered esprit de corps be revived under such circumstances? Is it possible or desirable? Has this group perhaps served its purpose so that no effort should be made to revive its failing spirits?

4. What could be done in regard to the community status of this group and its contribution to the Slovenian community? How could its relation to other groups have been improved? How can the widening community interests of its members find expression?

III

THE HUDSONS: A STUDY OF YOUTH IN ADVERSITY

THE Hudsons is a club of ten to fifteen young men ranging in age from twenty to twenty-two. They have grown up together on the streets and in school. Few of the members belong to any other group and much of their spare time when not at the Community House is spent in each others' houses or on the street.

All the group is American born but they come from various nationality backgrounds. Five are of Polish parentage. The other ten include boys of Serbian, German, Bohemian, Irish and American descent. This mixture of nationalities is the result of the proximity of several nationality groups within the area. Their membership in one club would also seem to indicate less consciousness of their traditional nationality background than is evident in the girls' group of the same age.

At the time the record opens five of the group are unemployed and the rest hold jobs as steel workers, finishers, diemakers, bakers, time keepers, shipping clerks and stock boys. Several of those employed are carrying the support of parents, brothers and sisters. Wages are low and work irregular. Very little opportunity is available for those unemployed to get jobs or for those at work to look forward to better pay or a chance for advancement.

Such limited resources produce a difficult situation for boys of this kind. Amusements are severely restricted. The possibility of marriage must be postponed. There is little to do that offers adventure or excitement in legitimate ways. But this group has not become a predatory gang. It is regarded as one of the more responsible groups of the neighborhood.

We can see here, however, the struggle of these young men to find outlets for their developing powers. Not all of them succeed in doing this constructively. The picture of the group's life makes vivid what late adolescence under such circumstances is meaning to growing youth.

The significance of this record for group work lies especially at three points. In the first place, it is valuable for the light it throws on the interests and activities of a group of average young men in a foreign neighborhood during a period of depression. For those that are unemployed the club activities occupy an important place in the use of their time. For all of them the club provides companionship and recreation during a period of extremely limited resources and family difficulties. In the second place, the record illustrates the growth of the interests of the group from a recreation program of a rather limited type to the development of several projects providing new experience, expanded interests and more mature community attitudes. In the third place, the record describes the conflict between the standards of the group in regard to gambling, drinking, stealing and sexual promiscuity and those of the Leader and the agency which he represents. The attempt to affect such standards is presumably one of the purposes of such agencies and the Leader is necessarily the representative of those standards. Here we see the conflict between standards as it arises in relation to club activities. If the Leader tries to enforce his standards too rigidly he loses rapport with the group. If he accepts their standards or allows them to go unquestioned he fails to carry out one of his functions as the carrier of the standards of the wider community. This record does not provide solutions to these problems but it supplies material for discussion of them.

DRAMATIS PERSONAE

Steve—the president and natural leader of the group, of Serbian parentage, unemployed most of the time, boisterous, self-important, able and energetic, tending to be dictatorial.

Tom—the son of Polish parents, the chief support of his two sisters and his widowed mother who is paranoic; an apprentice diemaker earning twenty dollars a week, cooperative, dependable, honest, with unusual ability and integrity.

Carl—the son of Polish parents, a shipping clerk, formerly an upholsterer and member of the union; sensible, likeable, even-tempered, athletic, formerly a frequenter of poolrooms.

Dave—the son of German parents, unemployed and no longer looking for work, waiting for something to turn up, boisterous at times, otherwise sensible and well-balanced.

Joe—the son of Bohemian parents, a timekeeper in a factory, sensitive, self-conscious, dependable and ambitious.

Larry—a happy-go-lucky boy of Irish parentage, out of work and not concerned about it, jovial, loyal, popular.

Charlie—a boy of Polish parentage, a laundry worker, the support of his family which is intermittently on relief; bashful and boisterous by turns.

Jim—a boy of Polish parentage, a worker in a bakery, the chief support of his family, quiet, loyal, enthusiastic, excelling in dramatics, singing and basketball, and much interested in girls.

Dick—the son of a patrolman, a stock boy by trade, a "wise-cracker" and a baseball player.

Jake—a boy of Polish descent, unemployed, dependable, willing but lacking in initiative.

Frank—a brother of Jim's, inactive the first year because employed at night.

Several other minor characters appear for short intervals.

FIRST YEAR

The first formal gathering of the club is recorded in its minutes as having occurred on the street in front of 1538 Beaumont Avenue on January twelfth, 1931. At that time four were present: Steve, Tom, Carl and Dave. Ballots were distributed and the following officers duly elected: Steve, president; Tom, secretary-treasurer; Carl, Sergeant-at-Arms; and Dave, chairman. The last mentioned office may seem rather superfluous but it served to provide eminence for an otherwise obscure member. Dues were set at fifty cents a month and meetings were to be held at the members' homes in rotation.

Between the original meeting, often referred to later with great emotion by those present, and its appearance in the agency in February 1931, the life of the group is veiled in obscurity. On the latter date it had an enrollment of five charter members which was soon enlarged to fifteen. Its founders state its purpose as follows: "Whereas, the need of some sort of entertainment or of organization to hold our friendship more closely, we, Steve, Dave, Carl, Joe and Tom have resolved to organize a club to fulfill our resolution. The purposes of this organization are as follows:

1. To exist for the purpose of making life more pleasant in the forms of good times.
2. To have an organization which will be known everywhere and known forever.
3. To aid our members educationally, morally, and physically.
4. To become friendly and make friends at all times, not only with our own members but with everyone who wishes to do so."

February 2, 1931

At this first meeting of the Hudsons in the agency the boys' worker introduced the Leader Mr. S. to his group and the record begins:

"This first meeting was occupied with the discussion of several matters of business. It was agreed, on Tom's suggestion, to keep a capital of fifty dollars in the treasury for emergencies. Dues were to be twenty-five cents a week, with the exception of party weeks when the members would have other expenses and so would be unable to pay dues."

The next item of business shows the dilemma of the Leader in regard to club standards.

"Final plans were made for a party at the home of one of the boys, for which each will contribute a dollar and fifty cents. It was agreed that nobody is to come without a 'jane.' No one is to plan on 'picking one up.' Steve emphasized the point that this party is to be a respectable party and there is to be no rowdiness. The Leader was not invited. Mention was made of drinks and someone apologized to the Leader by saying something like, 'Our Leader probably doesn't approve of this,' to which the Leader said nothing in reply."

At the close of the meeting:

"Steve asked the Leader what he thought of their meeting and how it was conducted. The Leader replied that he thought they had a mighty fine club and a mighty fine club spirit. He told Steve that the business was done very well. The Leader asked Steve what he could do for the club. Steve replied that they wanted the Leader to help in making up a program of recreation to include other things besides cards. The Leader suggested dramatics and gave an illustration of what he thought the fellows might like."

The Leader comments on Steve's management as follows:

"It would seem that Steve wants to leave every question up to the club but he always has his own idea which he tries to put over. The Leader is afraid Steve tries to run the club too much. He does more of the talking than a president should. He does not state the motions clearly and invariably gives his own interpretation of them before they are completed."

Note: We see here the conception which the group has of what the Leader is to do for them. He is to assist with recreation and suggest a new program. In coming into the agency they accept the presence of a Leader but they conceive of his function as accessory to their own plans. The Leader, on the other hand, sees his function already as involving the modification of Steve's method of leadership in the direction of a more democratic variety. Is this typical of the differences between the group's conception of the function of the Leader and his own objectives in leading the group? Is this difference inevitable or desirable?

February 16, 1931

The party having taken place in the interval, the next meeting had to deal with the results.

"The meeting was called to order and the first bit of business was concerned with the conduct of Jim and Jake at the party. Jake insulted the woman at whose house the party was held and Jim and Jake got into a fight on another occasion. Steve gave quite a long lecture on what their conduct would mean to the club's reputation. He even went so far as to picture headlines in the paper saying a Hudson had been hauled in for drunkenness. Joe called him on that point. This led to a discussion of the possibility of expelling Jim and Jake from the club. There was some difference of opinion here. Larry argued that 'While we are having our meetings and having our recreation here together and getting good out of it, those fellows are outside. They ought to get that good.' Tom then said, 'They were both drunk and were feeling good; all of us were. You can't blame them any more than ourselves.' Steve added, 'Drink affects people differently.' Tom remarked that Steve would have been drunk too if he had not had 'that other sex' with him. Finally Steve asked the Leader what he thought. The Leader said, 'I think Larry's idea is right for the present but I think there should be a dead line on the breaking of club standards.' The final decision was to allow the fellows to come back but to give them a lecture on their conduct. A vigilance committee of three was appointed by Steve, with Tom as chairman, and two other members to be chosen secretly by him. This committee is to have full power to expel a member for rowdy conduct. The Leader was unable to get the full facts of the quarrel between Jim and Jake. He was told, however, that Jake went home and got a gun. One of the fellows found out about it and relieved Jake of the gun, after which Jake apologized to the mother of the host for his conduct."

Note: This is a good instance of the attempt at the creation of standards by the group itself in which the influence of the club and, to some extent, the agency is evident. Was the Leader wise in his handling of the question as put to him?

The Leader comments on the situation as follows:
"Last week emphasis was put on the prohibition of 'rowdiness'

at this party. The Leader was interested in this because they deliberately made plans for the drinks. Everyone was quite well filled up and feeling irresponsible but this was not rowdiness. Getting into a fight as a result of drinking, however, was considered rowdiness. Someone brought out the idea that they not be allowed to get so much to drink. The Leader did not feel that the time was right for a discussion on drinking but as long as there is doubt in some minds as to advisability of drinking at a party, especially with this experience, there is a possibility of discussion in the future. The Leader does not think that much can be done about this drinking except in discussion and in the defining of club values on the question. It is not likely that a group such as this that has been brought up on wine and beer would rule it out. They might decide on something in regard to how far drinking should be carried. In connection with the drinking it is interesting to note the reliance of the club on force in obtaining obedience to the rules. The vigilance committee illustrates this. They depend on force and penalties rather than attacking the problem in a preventive way."

Note: Is this the wisest attitude for the Leader to adopt in this situation?

The meeting ended with the playing of pinochle and singing. The Leader's relation to the group is shown somewhat by the following:

"During the games and once before the meeting Tom said to the Leader 'Just feel at home.' He came around after the meeting and tried to explain that these fellows are different from the Leader's kind. He said, 'We do different things. We don't have opportunities to go places so we do other things.' He explained that the Leader should not feel out of place if they did things differently from what he was accustomed to. The Leader assured him that he felt perfectly at home and could see nothing so different from what he was used to. He said he thought the Hudsons were a mighty fine bunch of fellows."

February 23 and March 2, 1931

The next meetings were devoted chiefly to planning a pinochle tournament for the club and a week-end hike for the following week when the Leader had obtained for them the use of a shack.

March 7, 1931

The following gives an account of the week-end:

"They found mud and more mud at the camp and a few of the fellows grumbled about that because they had failed to bring any overshoes. But when they saw the shack the typical expression was, 'Boy, ain't this a swell place?'

"Steve took complete charge of cooking and the others waited patiently for supper although it was about six-thirty before it was ready. At supper a fork dropped on the floor and Steve said, 'We must be going to have company,' and there followed what the Leader believed were 'knowing' laughs. Nothing more was said about visitors until about eight o'clock when a shout was heard from across the creek. All ran out on the porch and began calling 'Joe,' 'Eddie,' and 'Walter,' and went down to the creek. Soon visitors and all were back in the shack and after a few preliminary greetings, Steve asked the Leader if he minded if they had a 'nice little game of sociable poker.' The Leader did not protest and within fifteen minutes after the visitors came the game was under way. Several times in the course of the evening, Tom turned to the Leader and said, 'You don't mind this, do you now?' and 'Now don't get us wrong,' but the game went on. Occasionally there was a little cussing and at these times Tom made such comments as, 'Watch yourself,' 'Watch your language.' The Leader said nothing. Later the Leader heard Tom use some of the words which he had called others for using.

"The play went on with little observable friction. After a couple of hours Tom dropped out. He said he was broke, although he could not have lost more than fifty cents. Later he went back into the game with the help of one of the others who made him a loan. Jake did not enter the game at all. He kept the victrola going and when asked why he did not play said, 'I've tried that stuff. You lose too much money.' Larry lost sixty cents and had to borrow car fare to go home the next day.

"At one o'clock the visitors went home and Steve decided there should be some food. At two o'clock everyone was in bed but Steve and Larry did not get to sleep until around six. The Leader did not stay awake to hear what was said. The last thing the Leader remembers hearing was a 'spooky' story. Dave had brought five quarts of beer along. As they started eating breakfast they brought it out and asked if the Leader objected to their drinking it. He said he thought it would be all right if they held it all right. (The Leader can certify that the beer was not bad for beer.)

"On the way home the conversation in the street car was about the 'hot women' they saw. Steve especially talked loudly. At these times Dave remained silent and looked bored. Joe asked Steve twice if he was trying to broadcast. Steve quieted down. The Leader remained silent or talked in a normal tone of voice."

The Leader comments on the week-end as follows:

"The group gets along remarkably well together. There seems to be a minimum amount of conflict. This is possibly because each one definitely recognizes the leaders of the group. The Leader was surprised to find that the poker game went so smoothly. There was a minimum amount of swearing and no conflict so far as he could see. It truly was a 'sociable' game of poker. The Leader questions if there was much evil effect from the game outside of the money aspect of it. None of the fellows can afford to lose any money. But money making was not the reason for playing. It was sport to them and they carried it on as a sport. It might be argued that they are being trained in gambling. It should be the job of the Leader to get them interested in other diversions.

"Evidently the poker game had been definitely planned for and the Leader was powerless to do anything about it, for they immediately went about the business of the evening. The Leader had hoped there would be an opportunity for some serious talk but the group had its plans set otherwise.

"In spite of the beer and poker the Leader feels that the trip was a success from the standpoint of good to the group. The outdoor experience was good and was appreciated by the fellows. Their expression of a desire to go back some time would tend to prove this. Some were skeptical before they went as to whether they would have a good time and they did find out that a camping trip could be a lot of fun even in winter."

Note: Here again the Leader finds himself rather ignored in the group's plans as they proceed with activities of which they do not expect him to approve. In fact they seem to look for more disapproval than he feels. What does this signify about their attitude toward the Leader or the agency or the activity itself? What should the Leader do in such circumstances? Could this camping trip have been more valuable to them?

March 9, 1931

The next meeting was occupied chiefly with pinochle and with an enthusiastic discussion of the previous week-end experience. The Leader plans to make some personal contact with Steve both in order to help him in his job as president and also in order to establish better rapport with the group.

March 16, 1931

The pinochle tournament continued haltingly because partners were often missing. The problem of the collection of dues became quite urgent.

"Steve asked what should be done about these fellows who were behind in dues. Larry said, 'You ought to appoint a committee to go and see them.' Steve then said he would do it but Larry came back with the remark, 'You try to do everything and say you'll do a lot of things and you don't do them. You better appoint a committee.'"

Note: This is the first time that Steve's leadership is seriously challenged. The pressure of the group for more democratic methods is evident. Can the Leader do anything to assist in developing Steve's leadership along more constructive lines? He comments as follows:

"The Leader feels that this meeting was somewhat of a crisis for the club. There seemed to be much objection to Steve's rule. The complaints were legitimate and natural. Larry's demand for more committees did have some effect on Steve although he did not take any action on it. Steve is too stubborn to act on such suggestions. The Leader purposely said nothing to Steve about these incidents after the meeting because he felt that Steve would probably be somewhat emotionally disturbed and not able to look at the problems calmly. The Leader believes the group gave Steve the finest kind of treatment for his case of swollen head and he plans to follow up this lead."

An invitation to a party at the Community House was announced by Steve.

"He was somewhat apologetic in saying there would be no dancing[1] nor drinking but he said he thought there would be a

[1] This was due to the fact that it was Lent.

good time. Most of the fellows expressed their intentions of going."

Note: The difference in the standards of an agency party and
one of their own outside the agency is here recognized. Could
the Leader have clarified here the reason for that difference and
perhaps interpreted the agency's position. Is this an opportunity
for explanation or is it better to have them experience a successful party of another sort first?

March 23, 1931

The experience with this party at the agency seems to have been
satisfactory.

Plans were made for a party with a girls' club—The Jolly
Jumpers—for which a date was tentatively set.

March 30, 1931

At this meeting the conflict in standards between members of
the group and between the Leader and some members becomes
very obvious.

"By seven-thirty all except Tom were at the meeting. The group
seemed to think in terms of gang stories and movies. The Leader
listened for about ten minutes and heard Larry tell how the First
National Bank at Twenty-third could be held up. His speech was
colored with gangland terms gleaned from 'The Last Parade'
movie. Others in the group told about stories they were reading in
newspapers and books which dealt with gang life. The Leader
asked the group, 'Seriously now, what do you think about the
racketeering business and gang life?' Larry immediately replied,
'That's the life. You may not live so long but you have to die
sooner or later and you may as well be rich while you live.' Steve
added that it is impossible to get out of gang life once you are in
and you will be shot sooner or later. Larry said something about
taking his own life if he should get cornered to which Joe replied,
'Anyone who would commit suicide is a coward.' This angle of
the discussion dropped and the Leader remarked that a person
dealing in crooked business like that could not possibly have any
peace of mind and be happy. All the money in the world could not
ease that constant fear a man has who does not know whether or
not he is going to draw the next breath. 'Security is necessary for

happiness and happiness is what we all want,' said the Leader. Larry remarked, 'I guess it's not until after your first man is killed that the racketeering business bothers you but after that it's not so much fun.' 'Don't kill anyone,' said Dave. Larry replied, 'If you had just pulled a job and were being pursued, would you let a policeman try to kill you and not shoot back? I sure wouldn't.'

"Throughout this discussion the rest of the group participated. Very few committed themselves for or against racketeering. The general trend of the talk was that it is all right if you can get away with it. Al Capone's name was brought up but he was not condemned. A few admired him because he was such a good leader that no one could get anything on him.

"Steve gave the discussion a new turn when he said, 'Well, I think a fellow is more happy if he tries to be satisfied with thirty-five or forty a week and not be so anxious to get easy money.' Carl added, 'And have a wife and some kids.' At this Steve laughed but Joe said, 'I couldn't be satisfied to get married on less than fifty dollars a week.' Carl added that the union scale of wages for married men called for fifty-five to sixty-five a week. Joe was asked by Steve how he was going to earn that fifty dollars a week. Steve pointed out that pick and shovel workers or ordinary laborers did not get that much. Joe claimed that office work was better and sought to prove it by saying, 'My boss gets a hundred dollars a week.' Carl replied, 'Yes, but he has a lot of responsibility. You can't expect that.' Joe remarked, 'Well, it will take some time.' Steve said, 'Factory labor always gets more than white collar labor.' Joe replied, 'Sure' and shrugged his shoulders. At this point Steve stopped the discussion by calling the meeting to order.

"Earlier in the evening when Dick came in, everyone noticed his black eye. He told the group that Saturday evening when he and several other fellows were walking along the street a gang of drunkards attacked them and since their number was greater, walloped Dick and his friends. He said, 'The bulls came along and broke up the fight. We all ran and didn't get caught.' Larry told the Leader how the flying squadron always cruised around this particular district at the end of Thirty-eighth Street and picked up any gangs of fellows who were gathered too long. The police were mentioned at the time Larry was telling how he could clean up the bank at Twenty-Third and Lexington. Steve said that would be easy because it was right across from the police station. He said, 'They never see what's right in under their noses.' Larry said, 'Police don't monkey with robbers because they don't want to get filled with lead.'"

The Leader comments on this:

"The discussion, although rather disconnected, was the first of that nature in the Leader's experience with the group. It started in the blustering type of talk in which one boasts of all the things he could pull. The Leader thinks Larry was just defending his point for fun but it would seem that he has respect for those that can get away with racketeering. The Leader can understand how some of these boys look at the question. Not taking into account the feeling of insecurity and unhappiness in the life of a robber, it would seem to be better to have a lot of money for a short time than to have nothing for a long time. But when it was called to their attention that gangsters are not happy even with their money, the rosiness disappeared. It is easy to see that the stories newspapers play up have quite an effect in idealizing crime. Even stories and pictures like 'The Last Parade,' which many think paint crime in its blackest, still have the effect of idealizing it. Undoubtedly the discussion was of some value because it made the fellows think somewhat.

"Steve's statement about its being better to be satisfied with your wages was certainly a social conclusion to the discussion. The comment by Joe about not wanting to get married on thirty-five or forty-five dollars a week shows something of the standard of living required by such fellows."

Note: This discussion reflects current attitudes no doubt common to the neighborhood and type of boy. (Larry's part in this discussion should be noted.) Could the Leader have handled the discussion better? Could he have led it to any more discussion of the effects of racketeering or of economic conditions, wages and vocational opportunity in which there is evidently some interest? How could this lead have been followed up by discussion of these subjects, by introducing vocational advising or outside speakers?

The party for the Jolly Jumpers was considered, committees appointed and plans made for decorations and program.

The club also agreed to put on a stunt at the inter-club party on May ninth.

April 6, 1931

The next meeting dealt chiefly with the selection of a pantomime for the stunt, with reports of committees on the coming party and with a discussion of a prize for the pinochle tournament now approaching its end.

April 11, 1931

This was the occasion of the party with the Jolly Jumpers. The Leader describes it as follows:

"When the girls came, Steve surrounded by the rest of the group was still making out slips for a game. The Leader suggested that someone receive them at the door but no one did until the girls had been in for a good part of a minute. Joe went in the front room then and volunteered to take the girls' coats. Larry evidently was the one who was going to be in charge of games; at least he introduced the first game when the Leader urged that they get started on the program. He explained the game to two or three at a time. When he was through, there was a question as to what the game was about so the Leader explained it further. When this was over no one made a move for another game so the Leader introduced another and finally took complete charge of the program for about an hour and a half. Tom and Steve were the only ones who did much dancing. The rest of the boys hung around together. The Leader pointed out to them that their responsibility was to see that their guests had a good time and that if they did not dance they might ask the girls who were standing around to play some games. They did mix better after that but there was a tendency on the part of the boys to observe rather than to participate.

"After the refreshments the Leader called time at twelve-twenty and for the next ten minutes the girls and boys in their separate groups sang popular songs. They ended by singing some together. Dave, who sings very well, was the outstanding singer for the boys. While they were standing around waiting to go home some of the girls showed the boys some stories. The Leader asked to read one and found that it was full of foul insinuations. The Leader made no comment but looked coldly at the girls and fellows. Inside of two minutes the girls had left. Tom said, 'I knew those girls were not what they should be. They're dirty.'

The Leader made no comment. He heard Jake and Dave talking about the stories. Jake said, 'That's nothing. They weren't nearly as hot tonight as I've seen them already.' "

The Leader comments:

"The conduct of the girls at this evening party was not much out of the way, possibly, for this group but the fact that Tom mentioned the subject of their conduct to the Leader shows that there is a conflict of standards in his mind. From the various remarks made by Tom from time to time, the Leader knows that this conflict is still in the budding stage. At least it does not control his conduct and talk when he is with such girls."

Note: Could this party be considered a great success? How could the Leader have planned with Steve and his committee so that they assumed more responsibility? Is it advisable for the Leader to step in and do it for them when they fail in their part? What would have happened if a leader refused to do this? How could the Leader have handled the situation in regard to the conduct of the boys toward the girls?

April 13, 1931

Two days later at the regular meeting the party was discussed:

"Steve asked if anyone had anything to say about the party. Joe said, 'What do you really think about it?' To which Steve replied, 'I think they had a good time; if they didn't it was their own fault.' Steve said he thought the committee did mighty fine work. Tom remarked that his committee on conduct thought everybody conducted himself excellently. The Leader added a few comments about the party, saying, 'I was sorry you fellows did not prepare the program the way you should have,' whereupon Steve blushed some, seemed at a loss and said, 'We owe Mr. S. a lot of credit for making the party a success.' "

The pinochle tournament petered out due to irregularity of attendance and was dropped at this meeting.

The agency at this time was putting on an operetta and several of the Hudsons had important parts in it.

April 20, 1931

A plan for an outing got under way at this meeting as follows:

"The big question of the evening was a plan for an outing. Most

of the fellows said they would like to select their own girls. After
this was settled the problem of food was considered. Steve said
he would appoint a refreshment committee later but in the meantime beer and sandwiches were hit upon for food. Joe volunteered
to make the beer (seventy some bottles) if they would give him
the money right then. Several of the fellows paid up their part of
the outing cost which was set by Steve at fifty cents apiece. The
Leader asked what they were going to do for entertainment. Steve
replied, 'Oh, we'll just dance around the fire for a while and play
some games.' 'Then we'll hunt for the bushes,' added Carl, much
to the wild amusement of the rest of the group. Steve had said
earlier that they could start from his house about eight o'clock in
the evening. The Leader asked what games they could plan. This
was greeted by chuckles from the group. May ninth was chosen
as the day for the outing. Before this discussion ended, Carl
asked if the Leader was to be invited. Steve blushed a little and
said, 'Sure I guess so.' He said the Leader would have to bring a
girl too, at which all roared with laughter."

The Leader comments on this:

"The party is somewhat of a problem. The Leader said nothing
much while plans for it were being made because he could see
that they were set on having the party and to cross them in their
plans would probably have meant that the subject would have been
dropped and finished outside the club meeting. Occasionally, side-
long glances were shot in the Leader's direction during these plans
but the Leader tried to appear neutral in his attitude.

"If the Leader can induce the boys to want him on the outing
and not just to tolerate him as their attitude seemed to be tonight
—the invitation tonight was in reality an afterthought—he will go.
He hopes to be able to bring them to the point where they will
want to plan a definite program for the outing. If the Leader cannot be of some help in this respect, he may as well not go because
he will be nothing but a wet blanket on their activities. His presence will not act as a balance wheel to any great extent because
the group does not consider this a Community House outing.

"While the Leader was getting the checkers out, later in the
evening, he met Steve alone and spoke to him about the party. The
Leader asked if such a party would not spoil the name of the club
if some of the fellows got drunk. Steve replied that he did not
think that would happen. 'Anyway,' Steve replied, 'the fellows
want that sort of a party.' Just before he went home, the Leader
asked Tom what such a party would do for the club's reputation.

Tom said, 'The fellows have been having these outings before and everything has been all right.' The Leader then asked whether Tom thought the girls should be out under such conditions, to which he replied 'Oh, they know what they are coming for.' 'But would you want a sister of yours to go to an outing like this?' he asked. Tom admitted that he would not. The subject of program for the outing was introduced next by the Leader. Tom said they would not need any program and laughed. The Leader explained then that generally what happens on outings when no program is planned is that people's emotions gradually get away with them. The Leader asked if it would not be better to plan some program so it would be easier to control these tendencies. Tom said he did not think the fellows would go too far, but if they did, they would not be broadcasting it to the others. 'What they do is a personal matter,' he said. In closing, the Leader said that he could hardly approve of such a party.

"Tom's attitude toward the question is interesting because he seems to be as well balanced as any of the group. His view that what each one does is his own affair is certainly modern but he has left out the social aspect of the problem, the effect on others.

"Possibly the talk about the party is much stronger than the party itself will be."

Note: Here again the Leader's standards and the agency's come into conflict with those of the group, this time on the point of sex practices as well as drinking. Since it is outside the agency they feel free to conform to their own rather than to agency standards. Can the Leader do anything about this? Is it wise for him to try to go to the party?

April 27, 1931

By the next club meeting plans for the outing had changed:

"Next came the matter of the outing. Larry suggested that it be dropped until later in May or in June. Carl objected to this but after the question was put to a vote at the suggestion of Tom, and the vote was five to three in favor of dropping the affair, he consented to dropping. Carl did not vote but when the result was known, he said, 'These guys are like the weather. They change all the time.' Larry asked the Leader previous to this vote what he thought about it. The Leader replied that he thought they could plan an out-door program and then plan to leave about eight when it begins to get cool in the evening. They could go to some fellow's house for an in-door party or have a theatre party. There was no direct response to this suggestion, however."

The Leader comments:

"The party plans were indeed a surprise. Evidently the Leader's talk with Tom last week was effective to some extent. Possibly his bringing up the subject may have been done because of a felt duty. It will be interesting to know if this idea of planning carries over into later parties. The change in the date of the party may be just to avoid having to invite the Leader but he feels that the choice was based on the reasons given at the club."

Note: What does this shift in plans probably mean? How much of it is merely a desire to get rid of the Leader and how much does it arise from a willingness to agree to the agency's standards without admitting it?

May 4, 1931

At this meeting a discussion arose:

"Carl said, 'Let's just talk.' On being asked what he wanted to discuss, he was at a loss. The Leader sat down and let the conversation take its course without suggesting anything. Steve looked questioningly at the Leader several times but the Leader took no notice of these looks. Gradually the conversation turned to the Naval Reserves which several boys had joined.

"To start a discussion, the Leader asked what the motive was for joining the Reserves. Larry replied, 'Why, to be prepared of course.' The Leader asked what there was to be prepared for. The answer was, 'War.' The Leader asked then if such preparations did not lead to war. All recognized the truth of the point but Tom asked, 'What are you going to do about it?' He added almost immediately, 'Boy, the U. S. has a kind of gas that will wipe out everyone almost instantly. The next war will be a lot different.'

"The Leader started a new line of thought by asking what he (Larry) was going to fight for. Of course, country, freedom and democracy were the answers. The Leader asked him to figure out who benefited by the last war. Joe and Steve came in here and said, 'Just a few fellows who have money.' Steve and Joe said they would never enlist and be shot down just because a couple of 'big shots' got them into the war. Tom said, 'Yeah, if there was a war and some of us signed up, all of us would.' Steve denied this and Carl said, 'You're a coward then; you're yellow.' The Leader said he was not so sure about that. The Leader admitted that a fellow who refused would be despised but asked if world peace was not a bigger principle to stand for than following the gang into anybody's war. The Leader closed this discussion by saying he very seriously doubted if he would go to war, not because of fear, but because war is futile and unnecessary.''

The Leader comments :

"In beginning the discussion, the Leader just let the conversation drift and entered with a new idea when opportunity offered. Whether the discussion was of much value is hard to tell. At least enthusiasm waxed hot most of the time—Larry's and Steve's voices getting so high the Leader cautioned them against disturbing other clubs. The Leader got a chance to air his pacifist views and was interested to find two supporters in the club. It will take time before Tom and Larry can be brought to a different point of view. It seems evident that most of these fellows are not socialists or communists in any sense of the word, for they did not respond to the idea of soldiers' fighting for moneyed interests and not for the country. The rest of the group failed to say much. Unfortunately the Leader became so much interested in the discussion that he forgot the others. Next time he will try to bring them in.''

Note: This is one of the few occasions when there is an interest in discussion. Could the Leader have secured better participation here or led it more effectively? Should he have been so passive when they turned to him for leadership? Now that this has happened can he plan on following it up in later meetings? What preparations can he make for this?

May 6, 1931

On this date a pantomime was put on by the club at an interclub party. At the next meeting the group discussed the results.

"All of the boys said they thought the play went over big and the Leader encouraged this attitude. Tom came to the Leader later in the evening and said, 'The next time we put on a play we want to do our own lines. This was a lot of fun but to talk would be more fun.' Steve and Carl expressed the same sentiment. Both Steve and Tom individually thanked the Leader for having helped make the play a success but Tom went further and said, 'You deserve a lot of credit for being so patient with us. We horse around an awful lot.' ''

May 25, 1931

In the interval the club had attended a party given to them by the Jolly Jumpers. At this meeting an invitation from another girls' club, the Gloom Chasers, was received and accepted.

Reference was also made to the postponed outing.

"Someone asked about an outing previously considered and Steve immediately tried to put the damper on the subject by saying that that could be discussed later. However, the group continued to talk about it but with a different tone from that appearing in the previous plans. Carl suggested a clam-bake. 'My old man can do that swell,' he said. Steve added that sometime the club ought to entertain the 'old-folks.' Nothing definite was decided about the kind of an outing it would be but a date was set for the middle of June.

"At the end of the meeting the Leader talked with Steve. He told Steve that he felt that he was a damper on the club discussions lately. At first Steve denied this but finally he admitted that he thought the Leader sort of old-fashioned. The Leader tried to show him, however, that he just had different standards that he felt were good and that the club might profit by some of them. Steve made little response to this latter point."

Note: The Leader is conscious of a lack of rapport evidently. Is he wise in discussing it with Steve? How can he interpret what appears to the group to be "old-fashioned standards" in any other light? How are shifts in values accomplished under such circumstances?

May 27, 1931

Two days later the club attended the Gloom Chasers' party.

During this period the Leader had some doubts as to his own relation to the group. Steve had commented that he was old-fashioned which made him consider his methods of approach to the conflict of standards. The Leader comments on this:

"The effect of the Leader's words in the discussion of the outing when mentioned several weeks ago has seemed only to estrange the group from him because the club now refrains from talking in his presence about its parties outside of the Community House. The fellows seem to think that the Leader is an old timer and doesn't know any better. The problem is not very serious but it is plain enough that the Leader should not pursue his original plan of making suggestions for the planning of these outside affairs. Possibly a solution for next year would be for the Leader to become a member of the club. He can then suggest entirely different activities from their old type of outing but make them when no other plans are being considered. Probably what was wrong this year was that the Leader interfered with the club's plans. At the time the Leader did not recognize it as interference but the group seemed to take it that way.

"What the club needs is to be directed into constructive channels. The Leader is hoping, more or less blindly that he may, by pointing out their deficiencies, change the members somewhat. This is not a good method, the Leader realizes, because it is hollow but when ordinary types of indirect group or personality control apparently fail, the point-blank type may bring results."

Note: How can the Leader deal with these attitudes toward himself and the standards he represents? Can he get a better rapport with the group by some more positive contribution to their activities? Can he bring them into contact with other groups that will be sufficiently beyond them to effect this? Is the point-blank attack likely to have any results except to estrange them further?

The Leader comments particularly on Larry:

"Larry is a problem. The Leader is sorry that it is the end of the year and that he will not be able to work further on this during the summer. In some ways the Leader sympathizes with Larry. He needs money and he cannot get a decent job. However, Larry is not satisfied to have a job that pays a small wage. Under the circumstances he should be glad to have the ten dollar a week job which he had at one time but 'that isn't good enough.' This attitude is natural because Larry is young and wants the sort of things the others can have. The Leader thinks Larry would probably settle down with a twenty dollar a week job but the Leader is in no position to offer him this sort of thing."

Note: Can the Leader do anything to help Larry in this period? Should he be urged to keep a ten dollar job? Should the Leader make any attempt to understand his family situation? To get him expert vocational advice? To try to arouse his interest in some avocation?

ANNUAL SUMMARY 1930-1931

The Leader in summing up the year's accomplishments comments upon the fact that the group seems to be dominated by a desire for fame. They want to see the Hudsons celebrated in the papers and to be the center of the stage at the Community House.

The sound foundation for such status in worth while accomplishments is often of less interest to them. The Leader feels that although they emphasize standards of conduct in their rules and constitution, they do not live up to them in practice. He attributes this discrepancy between the ideals they have been taught and their actual behavior largely to their environment. His chief hope lies in providing an environment within the agency which will create a better correlation of ideal and practice.

In so far as program is concerned the group shows some development in its interest in serious discussion but most of the time still is spent in the simpler forms of recreation. Some interest in other more educational projects has, he feels, been stimulated.

The group also shows development in its methods of control. The dictatorial policies of the president have been modified under pressure from the group and this is resulting not only in more participation from all but in a different type of leadership from Steve.

The reader may wish to ask in regard to this year's record:

1. How can the Leader better establish his relation with the group? How can he deal with the difference in backgrounds and standards between himself and the group? What definite contribution does he make to the group's activities? Does the Leader adequately and convincingly represent his own and the agency's values?

2. In relation to individuals does the Leader help Steve in his position as president to develop more democratic methods? Does he provide as much assistance in counseling as the group requires?

3. What progress is made in the methods of group control? How can greater participation be promoted? What type of leadership is being learned by Steve?

4. Is the program suited to the interest of the group? Is it giving them experience which will require the growth of new capacities? Is it vital to their interests and adequately presented?

5. What relation to the community can such a group have? Are its inter-group relations developing in constructive ways? What more could be done to prepare the group for active participation in the community in socially useful ways?

SECOND YEAR

The Hudsons open their second year with a membership of ten carried over from the previous year. Two new members were added during the year neither of whom were outstanding. Stanley is a friend of Steve's, of Polish parentage; he has a job in a wheelbarrow factory part of the time but is often unemployed.

Ed, the other new member, is a shy, backward fellow of Polish parentage; he belongs to the "Holton gang," a predatory gang of about the same age. He has a job in a butcher shop.

One member of the club, Frank, assumes a new importance this year. During the first year, he worked at night and was unable to attend regularly. This year he is unemployed and so devotes much of his time and energy to the club. He has marked leadership ability, although he is at times self-conscious. He begins to challenge Steve's place as undisputed leader of the group. He has developed interests which enrich the club program. He is energetic, responsible and is using his unemployed time constructively by taking music lessons, reading, looking for work and undertaking various volunteer jobs at the agency.

Larry during the summer of 1931 becomes associated with the "Holton gang." He claims to have broken off with the gang in September and after that time devotes most of his time to the Hudsons. He takes an enthusiastic and responsible part in many agency activities. Larry's family has been having a hard time because his father was partly unemployed. Larry has some difficulty with his mother over his connection with the gang and left home for a time, returning, however, in the fall.

Tom has, also, been having difficulties about his family. He is beginning to feel the burden of his family responsibilities since it means he cannot look forward at present to a home of his own. He is a skilled worker in a machine shop but his pay is very small. He feels the hopelessness of his situation and shows it in fits of depression in which the Leader can do little to help him.

September 21, 1931

The Hudsons started their year on September twenty-first with a meeting with the director of the agency, Mr. K. A question arose as to whether they should continue to have the same leader as last year. They said at this meeting that "he was a hell of a nice fellow but he just does not understand the Hudsons." The director of the agency withdrew therefore to let them make their own decision between their former leader and the other available leaders. At the conclusion of the meeting, they decided that they would take S. back. At the next meeting therefore he took up his responsibilities as leader for the second year.

September 28, 1931

The Leader reports the opening of the club meeting and his rapport with the group as follows:

"The Hudsons still have the same officers as they had last year: Steve, president; Tom, treasurer; and Larry, secretary. Larry read the minutes of the previous meeting omitting, however, all record of the discussion about a leader and not mentioning that Mr. K. was present. After the reading of the minutes there were some smiles around the room. In the treasurer's report Joe announced that there was over sixty dollars to the Hudsons' credit. The rest of the evening was spent in pinochle and carroms.

"It seemed to the Leader that the boys were overly cordial in greeting him at this first meeting. This may have been due to the memory of the previous meeting where they had discussed the Leader and his merits and this may have made them somewhat self-conscious. Naturally none of them said anything about the possibility of the Leader's not continuing with them. This attitude toward the Leader arose partly from his remarks about a suggested outing the previous spring. The type of party which they had intended to hold at this time was, however, held frequently during the summer according to the reports of some of the boys and on one occasion when there was a Community House representative there. The report is that the activities were as planned for the outing in May.

"A few members of the group had said that the Leader was somewhat superior in his actions and did not understand their type of people. The Leader has attempted to follow out the policy of maintaining the level of culture to which he is accustomed and not lowering his level to that of the boys with whom he is working, hoping that in this way after they have gained enough respect for him there will be something which they might imitate."

Note: Here we see the Leader consciously maintaining standards. What should he do under these circumstances?

October 1932

During the fall months, the Hudsons proceeded with their usual program of games and recreation. A dance was given in October which resulted in some controversy over an accusation made against the committee in charge of the beer, for drinking up the profits. The result of the dance was a profit of a hundred and three dollars. The use of this money created a serious conflict since the newer members, led by Frank, wished to spend it immediately. Some threats of withdrawal were made. The constitution provides that the club cannot break up without the consent of the five charter members who therefore would inherit the treasury in case the others withdrew. Charges and countercharges were made but eventually subsided without serious injury.

During the fall an increasing interest developed in volunteer work. Some of the boys assumed responsibilities as club leaders with groups of younger boys. The following is typical of that situation:

"Tom asked the Leader about his volunteer work with a club. The Leader went over several games with him so that he would be well stocked up in that line and then gave him some pointers as to ways in which he could get the respect and confidence of the group. He suggested Tom's showing the boys his printing press and possibly if they indicated an interest in it, their working up a monthly report of clubs. The Leader also suggested that he might be able to work out something in electricity if the group showed any interest since the club was quite small and could be handled in such projects. The Leader also talked to Tom somewhat about the purpose of boys' clubs."

The Leader comments as follows:

"The talk which the Leader had with Tom was very encouraging in that Tom seems to have picked up the idea of club work quite rapidly. It is evident that he has been thinking about the subject somewhat since it was first mentioned last week. The Leader hopes and believes that Tom's experience with the club will carry back to his own club work in that he will be seeing club work from a different angle and will probably think more about what the club experience in the Hudsons is doing for the various members of the club."

A month later the Leader reports in regard to Steve:

"This evening Steve had the Rangers at Community House.

This was the first meeting and Steve arrived about the same time as the club members. He began talking to the Leader right at the start and when the Leader suggested that he get in with the group and try to learn to know them as soon as possible he said, 'I will talk to them pretty soon.' The Leader urged him to get in with his group at once and finally Steve acted on the suggestion. At first he stayed very much in the background but later in the evening he was able to suggest some games which the boys played and seemed to enjoy.

"On that same evening Tom came to the house about seven-thirty and told the Leader that he planned to deliver some football tickets to prospective members of his club. He talked to the Leader for an hour and a half before he started out on this job and told the Leader quite a bit about himself during this time. He said, 'I was raised in a gang and now that I have a chance to associate with other people I'm going to take the chance. Last week I was at the Community House every night and boy, I'm not sorry for it.' He told the Leader about the pleasure he got out of greeting the boys at their homes. He said, 'Boy, that makes you feel good when little Pat Hogan says, "Hi there, Tom!"'"

Note: The significance of this experience seems to be very great for those participating. Could the Leader widen it any further by leading from it to a better understanding of community problems or the objectives of the Community House?

November 23, 1931

A new development in the program was discussed:

"Another item of old business which was overlooked by Steve but suggested by Tom was the idea of a discussion meeting once a month. Steve expressed himself very forcibly on this subject, saying that he did not think it would work out to choose one day and say this would be the discussion day because he said that such things had to come on the spur of the moment. Jim, Joe and Frank also expressed this same idea. The others were quite indifferent on this subject so no date for a discussion meeting was set but it was decided that when the fellows feel in the mood for it they will talk. The Leader left the subject with the suggestion that if they did have some subject which they wanted to discuss and could let the Leader know a few days in advance he would try to get someone in from outside the club who was an authority on the subject and could thus direct the discussion."

The Leader comments:

"The Leader feels that Steve and the rest of the club have a great psychological block against anything that might appear intellectual. The Leader imagines that there is some similarity also between their aversion to printed matter and a feeling of difference the boys have between themselves and the Leader, whom they speak about as having had a good bit of education. The difference which they feel the Leader would say is an imagined one. Probably the only way to get these boys over this stumbling block is through actual experience where they can find out their error. The fellows do enjoy the discussion meetings when they come about and show quite a bit of intelligence in their discussion. But the talking about such an activity seems to carry with it a certain amount of stigma. It will take quite a bit of time and patience to get over this."

Note: Could the Leader have followed up his suggestion for discussion more effectively? Would it have been more popular if he had had a subject of interest to the group to propose for a next meeting rather than making a general suggestion of having discussion? Or could he have introduced some outsider who could talk interestingly on some current topic?

However, informal discussion occasionally develops spontaneously.

The Leader reports the following:

"The fellows came over informally one evening. They said they had come to pay the girls a visit but in fact they retired to the cellar and down there indulged in a discussion. At first the fellows began telling stories and in a few minutes they were getting dirty. The Leader was forced to laugh at some of them because they were really funny. He made no comment as to the ethics of telling such stories. Soon Steve put a question to the Leader, 'Why is it that when a group of fellows get together about the first thing they do is to tell stories such as these?' The Leader tried to give him an explanation which would be satisfactory and scientific. He explained how the emotions are satisfied by release of tension and showed them that by telling these stories this satisfaction was attained. This was followed by quite an intelligent series of questions and answers in regard to sex and sex perversions. Following this the Leader told the fellows about the effect experience in childhood will have on the individual later in life. One of the boys brought out the question as to whether character is inherited. The Leader went into quite a bit of detail in explaining the genes theory of heredity and showed that there is no possibility of character being inherited. Tom was not quite sure but that if a child could have the physical characteristics of his parent, he could have the same kind of character as the parent he resembled. But when the group left most of the fellows expressed themselves as believing that the Leader's ideas about the conditioning of character were probably correct."

Note: This is an interesting illustration of the Leader's improved rapport with the group and also of his ability to use his greater knowledge to shift the level of the conversation. Does this discussion suggest leads which the Leader might follow up in further informal discussion or in more planned programs?

The following discussion is reported during this same meeting:

"Steve had mentioned earlier in the evening that he had gotten a letter from a communist worker just before he came to the Community House. The Leader asked him to read the letter to those sitting around. The letter stated that there was going to be another war run in the interest of the bosses and urged that workers refuse to fight. Steve said, 'Now isn't that just what I've been telling you fellows?' Jim expressed himself as thinking the letter was right. A discussion followed. Larry, although playing cards, took part in the discussion and upheld the idea of war.

"The discussion, while short, revealed the position of all the boys on the war question. Jim seemed especially interested in hearing the Leader's views which were essentially pacifist. Neither Stanley nor Ed participated in the discussion, although Stanley listened quite closely. Larry was pretty imperialistic in his views on war. No doubt his being a member of the Naval Reserves encouraged his views. Every now and then the fellows and the Leader, too, gave little digs to Larry and Dave because they belonged to the Naval Reserves. They kidded Dave about being a big, bold, bad man and said, 'You'd get homesick.'"

In December a new tendency made its appearance. The Leader reports:

"Steve went home from the Community House and the rest walked around by Tom's house. On the way Tom started talking about club programs for the junior clubs. Frank asked, 'What do the senior clubs do?' The Leader replied, 'Well, you see what they do. They all meet on Monday nights.' Frank's answer was, 'Nothing. We have a meeting, play pinochle and that's all.' The Leader said, 'Do you fellows want to do something else? I thought you knew pretty well what you wanted to do so I have not said much along this line.' Frank answered that the fellows did not know anything to do at club but would be glad to try something. Games were suggested by Frank but Jim said, 'Aw, we don't want that.' The Leader explained that there are a lot of things in the handcraft line which are pretty fascinating and then told of his own change in attitude toward handcraft. He asked them what they thought of a planned discussion. 'A debate?' Frank asked and then he talked about the possibilities of such a project. The Leader suggested that a program committee might be appointed to thrash out some of the possible projects. A list of programs for about two months of meetings could be made out. Both Frank and Jim thought this a good idea."

Note: Does this indicate some dissatisfaction with the present program which might lead to other activities? How could the Leader follow this up?

December 14, 1931

At this meeting the new attitude toward the program resulted in a discussion of plans for the next few months. A dancing class was suggested for those who wanted it. A Christmas party with small gifts was planned. An elaborate New Year's party of the typical Hudson variety was planned with plenty of drinks and a select list of forty girls "not too dead."

In addition to these rather usual activities the Leader reports the following change in attitude:

"The fellows who attend the volunteer leaders' meetings are bringing back suggestions to the club and in this respect the participation of some of the fellows as club leaders is beginning to have an effect on the club. The Hudsons certainly are feeling their responsibility more and more as a community influence. Ed has a brother in a younger boys' club and the Leader hears reports that this brother continually talks about the Hudsons as an ideal club. The Leader feels there are real signs of progress in the club and assigns a good bit of the credit to the work with volunteers.

"The club activities are taking up a good bit of the time of the fellows. This is especially fortunate since a good many of them are unemployed. It seems to the Leader that this club is fulfilling one of the objectives of club work in a time of depression such as this."

The Leader comments further:

"The picture one gets of this club from a consideration of the above interpretation is an ideal one in certain ways. One can hardly understand sometimes the two extremes of which these fellows are capable. At one time they are almost ideal in their conduct and in their attitude toward the other clubs and other fellows and at another time the whole bunch can be so drunk they can hardly handle themselves. The Leader understands that this latter is a habit with them but he cannot see much possibility of influencing them away from this even when it can be clearly seen that it is harmful. Not knowing what to do, the Leader, when plans were being made for the New Year's party, just had a good laugh with the rest of the fellows. He felt that to scorn such plans would only stir up ill feelings. At the same time he hoped that Dave was right in saying, 'This party won't be half as bad as it sounds.' It may be that these fellows will accept new attitudes in regard to such matters as they have begun to take a different point of view toward their responsibilities as a group. The Leader can see no chance for him to say anything until the opportunity presents itself in a discussion. It is difficult to tackle any problem such as this because drinking seems to be perfectly acceptable in the homes."

Note: By this time the Leader has changed his tactics and to some extent his point of view. Are his present methods likely to be more successful than those he used the first year in keeping rapport with the group or in affecting their behavior? How can the methods learned as volunteer leaders be used in other ways in strengthening the program of the Hudsons? What type of activities is the group now ready for?

The New Year's party was successfully carried through in typical Hudson fashion.

January 8, 1932

The Leader reports the following conversation with Steve at his home:

"Steve began talking about the club and asked the Leader what he thought about the club's situation at present. Steve said that some of the fellows refuse to cooperate and act as if they would like to break up the club. He said he thought the difficulty was that there was too much money in the club treasury and suggested that possibly it would be a good idea to spend the money on parties as rapidly as possible so that those who are in the club for the money only would drop out. The Leader agreed with him about the money. Steve then asked the Leader what he thought about the club. Steve said, 'You've got something to gain by having the club successful and I thought you might have analyzed the club.' The Leader told him that his analysis of the situation was based largely on the various degrees of development of the fellows in the club. He said, 'Some of the fellows are more socially developed than others and consequently, those who are not so well developed tend to hang with the gang because they feel more security in that kind of association.' The Leader was not able to give Steve any concrete suggestions as to what could be done immediately for the club except for the possibility of a discussion which would work around to the question of just what is the position of each one of the fellows in relation to the rest of society. Steve thought this would be a good idea, that possibly some of the fellows would begin to realize that the world does not owe them one big party after another. He pointed out the fact that what held the group together was the desire for good times and admitted then that probably this objective of good times was standing in the road of serious programs. The Leader acquainted Steve with the fact that some of the other fellows in the club were thinking seriously about the club program also and that if the subject were approached in the proper manner some progress could probably be made. The Leader said he would think out a way to present the discussion for Monday night and Steve said that he would cooperate as much as possible to make the discussion a success, adding that something had to be done to stop the conflict in the club."

Note: This is almost the only account of a home visit during the Leader's experience with the club. Could he have established his rapport sooner or helped the club to progress in its program if he had called more frequently on certain club members at strategic points in the club history? How could the club program be made more satisfying to Steve? Did the Leader seize his opportunity here as effectively as he might in helping Steve analyze the club's situation?

During January there was evidence of increasing friction between the group of charter members, headed by Steve, and a rival group, headed by Frank. The newer group was anxious to spend the money in the club treasury either on good times or on sweaters or jackets. The group of original members, which included the more developed boys in the club, felt themselves threatened by this group. This conflict came to an issue in the meeting of January eleventh.

January 11, 1932

The discussion of the treasury recurred again at this point:

"Steve suggested that the club, after all accounts were cleared up, arrange to have some sort of a 'good time' at least once a month. He said there was money in the treasury which could be used in this way. All of the fellows were in favor of this and Jim suggested having them oftener. Frank protested that that would be spending money too fast. He said that the club ought to spend more time on planning the programs for Monday nights.

"Larry came out quite bluntly with his opinion about spending the money. He said, 'There are some fellows in this club who don't care to do anything except attend the good times and I don't think we'll get any place until the money is spent because these fellows are just sticking as long as their money is in the club.' He pointed out that the attitude of those who joined late is that they do not seem to want to better the club. Frank interrupted for a moment to state that he wanted to better the club by working out a program other than pinochle.

"Steve went on, 'There's another thing about this club. A lot of you fellows spend your time hanging around on the corners. That corner gang stuff is kid stuff. When you fellows get to be nineteen and twenty-one you ought to be getting over that kiddishness and act like young men.' Larry disagreed with this point of view. 'What are we going to do in times like this? If times were better we'd have work and wouldn't need to hang around on the street corners.' This idea was seconded by Dave and Jake but it was not an answer to Steve's statement. He replied that they should find other things to occupy them and that if they did stick with the gang they did not have to act like 'kids.' He said, 'Another thing, you fellows don't want to change. When there is a chance to do something in a social way or to get out and meet people you won't try.' There was no response to this.

"'Speaking of behavior,' Joe remarked, 'a good friend of mine told me what he thought of the Hudsons. He said that they acted like kids when they are in a crowd.' Joe cited a party at the Community House where the Hudsons showed off somewhat. Steve asked who it was who made the charge. 'You can tell,' said Frank, 'this is a meeting.' But Joe refused to divulge the name of the person who made the remark. Dave and Jake tried to point out that just because somebody criticized they did not have to get excited about it. Joe replied that just the same other people judged the Hudsons by their conduct. Steve said that he thought there was a lot of truth in the criticism and admitted that he was as much to blame as anyone. He added that this was a case where the gang held together and acted as a gang when the fellows should really forget the gang and act as others in the crowd do. Larry agreed that if a person is to be liked by the people with whom he associates, he must conduct himself as they do but someone interpreted this statement to mean that when the Hudsons go some place they should act just like Hudsons, since it was by the Hudsons that each one of the group wanted to be liked. Steve disagreed at this point and said that while the group wanted to get publicity as a club, if the publicity was not good it would be better not to have it. The Leader suggested that even if the group did not take any stock in the criticism of Joe's friend it might be a good idea to try to improve their behavior anyway.

"Frank insisted that the group get back to the point and outline a program. Steve encouraged this with the result that various trips were suggested including an all day trip to Pittsburgh."

The Leader comments as follows:

"This meeting and all that has led up to it in the past week have been full of potentialities for future development. Certainly program has experienced a boost which will carry the club through the year. The possibilities for the club feeling are improved and an initial step has been made in showing the members in what ways they can develop individually. It seems that the cap has blown off and a club which was formerly quite self-satisfied is ready to move on to something better. But judging from past experience these are only possibilities and rejoicing should be reserved until some concrete results have been obtained.

"The suggestion that the program of the club be varied has been brewing over several weeks. It was first mentioned by Frank when he asked why the Hudsons could not have programs after he found out that younger clubs did. This resulted from having volunteer leaders in the club. Nothing was done at the time since there were other matters, mostly financial, which took their attention. The heated discussions which took place in club and out, threatened its continuance some of the members felt and as a result those who had the good of the club at heart began to think seriously about a plan whereby the energies of the fellows would be brought to some constructive work rather than being expended on useless and damaging criticism. The spending of the money in one way or another will be a good thing because it will test the members. Those really interested will probably stick and the others who are interested only in the money will no doubt drop out.

"The Leader was completely surprised at the way Steve tackled the problem of getting the fellows to see that they needed to improve their behavior but it was more of a surprise to find that the fellows took the criticism and discussed it. Then after pointing out weaknesses, Steve made a masterful stroke in showing the fellows how they could overcome their shortcomings by making more of an effort to get out and meet people. What followed was enthusiastically spontaneous and by the time the meeting was over it seemed that there was an almost sentimental 'one for all, all for one' feeling on the part of most of the club members."

Note: Is the Leader correct in his estimate of these developments? How can these leads be followed up individually and collectively? Is this program planning carried as far as it could be? How can these trips be made valuable? Did the Leader make effective use of this occasion? Could he have entered into it more fully or pushed it further toward a constructive solution?

January 16 and 17, 1932

"The week-end camping trip to the 'Y' cabin took place the next week. Immediately following supper, Frank and Dave got out the victrola and began dancing. This dancing evolved into an orgy in imitation of sex display. The dancing was followed by more of such activity. To this the Leader made no comment but indicated disapproval by acting as if the fellows should know better. Later on the Leader spoke to some of the fellows about their attitude toward women in this regard. The Leader told Tom, for instance, that he could not understand why it was that some fellows could think of women in no other capacity except that implied by Frank and Dave. Following this a general call was made for the dice and a crap game was started which lasted until

twelve o'clock. The boys played penny ante and no one lost very
much money. The Leader was not interested in the game although he watched for about an hour altogether at various intervals. As the fellows became broke they would come up to the
fireplace where the Leader was sitting and the Leader took this
opportunity to talk to them about the ethics of shooting crap.
Nothing definite was gotten from any of the fellows except from
Tom who said that he enjoyed gambling. He said, 'I know when
to quit and I don't lose any money particularly because of that.
But there's a lot of sport in it.' The Leader pointed out that there
were dangers involved in that the habit might grow. He also
indicated that as Leader he would be in a peculiar position if a
representative from the 'Y' should appear while the group was
indulging in this game. At the end of the game Charlie had won
one dollar and fifty cents altogether and threw up fifty pennies and
let the fellows scramble to get as many as they could. The boys
constantly spoke of the game as a 'sociable game' and at no time
did anyone become angry. Charlie remarked, 'Gee, I didn't know
Tom would enter into things like that. He's always so quiet.'

"At twelve o'clock a midnight lunch was served mostly by
Stanley and then everyone prepared to go to bed. The Leader put
his bed out on the porch so that he would not be bothered by the
talking which was bound to continue after everyone had gone
to bed. The Leader found out the next morning that no one
had gone to sleep before four o'clock and that during the night
Stanley, Frank and Tom came out on the porch to sleep also since
the fellows were continually running around and stealing blankets
inside.

"About seven o'clock in the morning Tom and Frank got up
and went to church at St. Paul's but the rest of the fellows did
not get up till about eight-thirty. Most of the fellows went to the
park to play football while Steve and Tom remained at the shack
with the Leader. Steve and Tom began talking about the club
situation and about the possibility of there being a break. Immediately after dinner the whole group left for home."

The Leader comments on this occasion as follows:

"The hike caused the Leader to do quite a bit of thinking in
that so many things not acceptable to his way of thinking were
done but at present the Leader feels that he should have quite
a passive attitude toward their crap playing and their sex displays.
The crap playing is an inexpensive way of getting the thrill of
chance which they cannot get in a more socially acceptable way.

Everyone gets enjoyment out of chance and this game is not bad in itself except as it is over-indulged in.

"The Leader analyzes the sex display on the part of some as an example of a latent homosexuality which is likely to be found in gangs which continue on through later adolescence. This is no doubt a factor blocking the social progress of some of the fellows. The attitude toward women in general probably can be explained in that the experience and knowledge of women, on the part of most of the fellows, consist in what they have seen of the intimate life of their parents. This is quite often true in cases where living quarters are very crowded. Few of the fellows can afford to have dates with girls so that their experiences can be broadened on a social level. Consequently they satisfy this aspect of their lives by talking about women and invariably the talk follows the trend of their experience at home and the pooled 'knowledge' gained from alley gossip. The Leader hopes that by introducing a study of Mary Ware Dennett's 'The Sex Side of Life,' the attitudes of some of the fellows will be changed. The Leader does not condemn them because of their present expression on such subjects because they are excellent examples of fellows who are starved so far as healthy social experiences are concerned."

Note: Is the Leader right in his technique at these points? How could he lead on from this to a constructive and adequate handling of the interest in sex? What else could he have done during the week-end?

January 18, 1932

On this date the club took a trip to the Food Show.

The Leader comments as follows:

"The thing which attracted the Leader's attention this evening was the conduct of the Hudsons as a group. Individually the fellows tend to be quite meek and docile but as a group they are quite boisterous. It seems that they feel that when they are together everybody has his eye on them. The Leader is trying to get the group to realize that when they are in public they should control their conduct so that they will not attract the attention of other people too much. At present they fail to realize that they have any responsibility in this respect. Of the individuals in the group who conducted themselves with the most propriety, the

Leader would say that Jim and Charlie probably measured up the best."

January 25, 1932

On January twenty-fifth a new project emerged at the end of the club meeting.

"The final item of business for the evening was the suggestion by Carl that the club have a monthly paper which would review its activities. The fellows discussed this idea and Steve said it would be all right to give it a trial but suggested that if it did not work out in a few months, it should be dropped. Steve suggested that if the report proved to be good enough it might be submitted to one of the newspapers and parts of it be printed for the public. The suggested name for the paper was 'The Rave Ons' or 'The Braggarts.' These names were treated somewhat jokingly by most of the fellows but Frank did not seem to be joking about his suggestion of 'The Rave Ons.' Carl was to be the editor and Larry and Frank the reporters and all three of them indicated that they were very anxious to start work on the report for January. Frank mentioned that he wanted to do it because it would fill up more of his time."

Note: What value could this activity have? How could it be carried out so that those participating could get the most out of it? Here is an opportunity for learning in various lines. Does the Leader take advantage of it?

The Leader comments on this new phase of the club's growth:
"The club is beginning to take on more work than it can handle. It is going to be necessary to cut down on the planned program so that some of the trips which are to be taken will not be taken without any thought. The club as a whole has the tendency to talk a lot about their plans and then fail to go through with them. This is not characteristic of the majority of the individuals in the club but is characteristic of their dominating leader, Steve. If the club is to come to have a saner attitude in its plans it will be necessary to change Steve's method of attacking the problem. The fellows are beginning to reply to Steve whenever he gets too dictatorial but they are still under his influence to a great degree. On the whole, however, Steve's influence is good for the club and he really has the interests of the fellows at heart."

February 1, 1932

On this date, a sample of the club paper was distributed. It was proudly displayed by Larry. After some discussion, it was agreed that the project be continued in the form of an enlarged issue to contain a summary of all the activities in the Community House.

February 4, 1932

At this point Larry got into serious difficulty. The Leader reports his handling of the situation:

"Frank called at the office along with some of the other club members and notified a staff member that Larry had been arrested in the morning and was being held at Central Police Station. The Leader interviewed Frank before going down to see Larry, and Frank said none of the club knew what Larry was charged with. The Leader assumed that the other club members knew but they would not admit it.

"The Leader went to the police station and was permitted to see Larry. He received the following story: (Larry's eyes lit up when he saw the Leader and he shook hands.) Larry said, 'It's true. It happened last July. A couple of us (no Hudsons) were up at Joe's place and we were drinking too much. One of the fellows knew the Poultry Market and said, "Let's rob it."' Larry said he tried to back out but they threatened to shoot him on the spot. 'And they would have,' he added. He said they got about a hundred dollars and that he got fifteen. 'How did they happen to get you at this late date?' the Leader asked. Larry replied that one of the fellows who was in on the job was being held for murder in another holdup and that this fellow had been arrested earlier in the week and had told about the holdup in July. Larry was arrested immediately and was identified by the victim. Larry said he had admitted being in the holdup but he said he would plead not guilty in the hope that having had a minor part in the robbery he would be put on probation. Some place in the story (the Leader is not clear at what point), Larry told about Nick Holton who came to a few of the club meetings last year and who was shot and killed last September in trying to get away from the scene of a holdup in Warren, Ohio. The Leader asked him if he had been associating with the Holton gang lately. He said he had not but had been spending most of his time with the Hudsons. Larry admitted that he was helping Nick Holton last spring in his bootleg work.

"The Leader told Larry how sorry he was that he was tied up in this thing but assured him that he had confidence that he had been traveling straight since summer. The Leader told him that he had good stuff in him and that he appreciated Larry's help as a volunteer worker at the Community House. He tried to encourage Larry and make him feel that he could still make good:

"The Leader called at the Community House to see a club and Tom. Shortly afterwards a group of five Hudsons appeared—Frank, Jim, Jake, Dick and Charlie.

"Frank asked, 'What's this going to mean to the club?' 'What do you mean?' asked the Leader. 'Well, you and everybody else will think we are tied up with this robbery or that we are just a common gang. People know we've got lots of money in our treasury and they'll think we got it crookedly. They know we wear pretty good clothes and that we stay out late at night.' The Leader said he never had thought that the rest of the club was tied up with this other group in any way. Frank replied, 'You think we're crooked. You acted this afternoon as though we knew and you acted the same way tonight. You don't trust us.' The Leader denied these charges by explaining that he did not distrust the group but he knew from his own experience that he had often shielded his friends when he thought giving information might be harmful. He explained that the group might be acting in the same way but that this was no charge against the fellows. Jim and Frank still insisted that others would look at the Hudsons as if they were a group of four-flushers.

"During this session the Leader appeared very much hurt that the fellows would take this attitude and in fact he was very much disappointed. He tried to explain again that he meant nothing by assuming that they knew about the robbery. He said, 'It just seems incredible that Larry could keep this thing a secret for six months. I believe you though and don't distrust you. I feel just as badly as you do about Larry's predicament and I'm going to do all I can to get justice done.' He added, 'I believe Larry has been shooting straight this fall. What I want for him is a chance to keep going that way.' Frank and the group still acted as if the Leader had injured their pride.

"The Leader suggested that it might be a good idea if he went to see Larry's mother so the group went with him to make the call. The Leader asked that one of the group go in with him and Jake finally did so since he lives just across the street.

"Larry's mother asked how long it would be and the Leader explained that court procedure is quite slow and that it may be a month before the trial. The Leader tried to console her by saying that Larry had been doing very well at the Community House and that this would no doubt help him a lot in his trial. She cried, saying, 'I tried to keep him straight but what chance did I have? Larry would like to work and there's nothing he can get and then he got mixed up with bad friends.' She continued, 'Last spring he said Nick Holton had given him a job. I was so glad because he hadn't had anything for a long time. I saw him come in with bundles under his arm and wearing overalls-like. I thought he was getting along until I found that he was going out too much and I began telling the fellows who called that he was not in when he really was in (referring to the bootleg business). What can a person do?' she cried.

"The Leader told her that he thought Larry had sterling qualities and that he had shown them. He said, 'I like Larry.' She broke in, 'And he did you too.'"

Note: Could the Leader have managed this situation any better in his relation to Larry or in his relation to the club? Does this reaction from the group indicate a fault in his approach or a super-sensitiveness on their part? The better relationship which he seemed to have established broke down in the stress of this situation. Is there any way in which this could have been avoided?

February 8, 1932

Larry's difficulty became a major issue in the club. He was out on bail during this period and he came to the club meeting on this evening.

"Larry told the group that he had something that he would like to bring up. He said, 'I guess you fellows know the scrape I'm in and know that I'm going to have a lawyer. Tomorrow morning I'm going to see the lawyer and I think that he's going to want me to pay some money down on my case and I wondered if you fellows could give me any help.' Larry went on to say, 'If I were the son of rich people it would not be necessary to pay money down but in this case the lawyer knows my parents have no money and that I do not have a job and he won't take the case unless some money is paid in advance.' Steve said then that it would be up to the fellows what they wanted to do and that not all were present. All of the fellows remained silent for a minute or so while they thought about whether money should be given and then Steve asked how much it would be necessary to have. Larry replied, 'About fifty dollars.' Steve pointed out that if Larry did get the money it would be just as good as lost to the club since Larry would not be able to pay it back at least for a long time and said, 'This money belongs to all of the fellows and I can't say you can have it.' Dick suggested that a special meeting be called some time during the week so that all the members could have a vote in this decision. Jake argued for Larry and presented Larry's predicament and indicated that he was in favor of Larry's getting a loan. Jim asked if his sister could not borrow money if she did not have it and Larry replied, 'If she'd do that she would have to mortgage her furniture and if payments would fall behind she would find herself without a home.' He said, 'I don't want anybody to be put out that way on my account.' No action was taken on the question. Steve later on said that he was not exactly opposed to letting Larry have the loan, although he said he would not have the money given to Larry directly but to the lawyer. He said in Larry's absence, 'I wouldn't distrust Larry but I don't want him to pull the wool over our eyes.'

"Steve, Tom and Dave stayed around until about eleven-thirty and talked with the Leader about Larry. Tom who had not been present during the discussion of the loan to Larry said that he thought if he were in Larry's place he would ask for a loan too and for that reason he would be in favor of helping him out. Steve, however, said, 'If Larry's unlucky and loses the case the Hudsons would lose fifty dollars and if he's lucky and wins, the Hudsons will be out fifty dollars the best part of the year.' He continued, 'I don't care but the fellows have put their money in the club and I hardly think it's right to just give it away.' Tom said to the Leader, 'What do you think of it?' and the Leader replied that he did not want to give any concrete advice in the case since it was not his money but all of the fellows said, 'That's all right. We respect your opinion and we'd like to hear what you've got to say.' The Leader told them that there were different ways of looking at the question but he said, 'Larry came to this club last spring and at that time he was running around with the Holton gang. Gradually he has fallen away from that outfit and is

spending practically all of his time with the Hudsons. Since his
mix-up last summer he's been with the Holton gang only once, so
he says. That's improvement. I've noticed Larry develop along
other lines too. He's taking more part in club program and in the
Community House work in general and I'm confident that he's
going absolutely straight.' The fellows admitted that what the
Leader said was true and the Leader went on, 'Now, we've done
some good for Larry just through having him in the club. He's
learned to like it and he's given more and more attention to it. It
has been the club which has helped him to develop himself and
to get away from the other gang. Now when we've brought him
this far and something from his old life is brought up, are we
going to desert him?'

"The Leader indicated that this point of view was only one
and that Steve's was another but that it did seem to him that the
Hudson group had been of great value to Larry and that to fail
to give him support now would not be in line with the ideals of
the club. The Leader added, however, that it was a good idea not
to vote the money to him tonight because in that way it would be
possible to find out if the lawyer is really interested in Larry's
case or only interested in the money."

The Leader comments:

"The group was greatly disturbed following Larry's arrest because, as they remarked, they were afraid people would assume
that the whole group was mixed up in such affairs. The Leader
thinks, however, that they were just feeling him out to see what
his attitude is toward them. On occasion the Leader has given
the fellows advice about their conduct and it may be that they
have had a lurking suspicion that the Leader thought they were
not what they should be. The Leader tried to show them the
reason for his questioning but he can only hope that it got across,
for they made little sign that it did.

"Steve's reaction to Larry's request for money was typical. He
was not thinking of the group nearly as much as he was of himself—the fact that he had about fifteen or twenty dollars in the
club bank account. He tried hard though to indicate that it was
the group that would lose by lending Larry the money. He was
right about the possibility of never getting it back. Steve's attitude
can be contrasted with that of Tom. Tom seems to be less selfish
and more able to put himself in another person's place. In this
discussion regarding the money, Jake said very little but he in-

dicated that Larry should be helped if he could get money from no one else."

Note: What does this issue of Larry's request for money indicate about the real objective of the group in comparison with its stated purpose and the strength of the "friendship" which they have talked about earlier? Could the Leader have done anything more than he did? Again the size of the treasury and its importance in the life of the group seem to hinder the growth of other attitudes. Would an earlier handling of this question in terms of the purpose of having a treasury have helped at this point? There seems to be a lack here of any real friendship for, or loyalty to, Larry. Is this typical of groups of boys of this age? Does Larry's experience seem to have affected the group's attitude toward racketeering? Could the Leader do anything more about Larry himself?

There is no record of any further discussion of this loan but the club did not grant it.

February 14, 1932

On February fourteenth the club embarked on its long planned trip to Pittsburgh. The group visited a settlement, met another club of boys, was taken about town and given supper in the apartment of the settlement headworker whom they had previously known. The following excerpts give glimpses of that occasion:

"The group met at Jim's and Frank's home at eight in the morning. All were neatly dressed. One of them had a 'uke' which was later 'thumbed' by Larry and Dave and this was taken along although no one knew how to play it and it was miserably out of tune. All talked much about the trip and such expressions as 'paint the town red,' 'find the speakeasies,' 'got your liquor' and 'they'll have the band out for us,' were heard. On the way to the station the group fell into double file and was very orderly.

"By the time the group could get on the train it was well loaded and the fellows were forced to occupy a pullman smoker much to their pleasure. Immediately they made themselves at home in spite of the fact that one person was already in the car quietly reading a paper. Prior to this, in hunting for seats, they shouted from one end of the car to the other about the poor service. Dick, Dave and Jake were most prominent in this. Their songs ranged from 'Sweet Jenny Lee' to 'St. James Infirmary' and lasted the better part of one hour and a half. The Leader read a paper during this time and after he thought there was enough of it he told Dave that perhaps the people in the car would not like so much noise since it was Sunday. At this the Leader left the smoking car and took a seat in the main car. Later Steve organized a snake dance to go through the whole train. He asked the Leader to go but he refused the invitation, saying he did not care for that sort of thing.

"The trip consisted of a ride around the University of Pittsburgh and Carnegie Tech Buildings, Forbes Field, Conservatory of Flowers, Carnegie Museum of Natural History and the Art Museum, giving them a view of the city from Mt. Washington, a trip through the tunnels and some free time in the downtown section. Some of the comments were: 'Conservatory? What's this place for?' 'Cleveland doesn't have anything like this.' At the Museum—Larry said, 'I'm coming back here sometime and take a day to go through. Let's go upstairs and see the rest. Isn't that good work!—taxidermy.' It had been planned to be in the Museum for only about twenty minutes but it was an hour before they could be gotten away from the place.

"The trip and 'bumming' lasted from one to five o'clock. At five the group was directed to the home of Mr. T., the headworker of the settlement. Most of the group, after being introduced to Mrs. T., visited a men's group in the settlement. The whole group got together later and was served a lunch of sandwiches and coffee. After this Mr. T. told the group about his work and what settlement work can do. He used some of the Hudsons—Steve and Tom—as examples and pointed out the changes they have made since five years ago. He commended them on their work as volunteers. The Leader added to this point and explained that the club leadership was only a stepping stone to more prominent service to their community. Steve and Tom participated in the conversation while all the rest listened. Mr. T. asked the group about their education, remarking that Steve once thought of college. He went on to say that if one had little trouble going through high school he could do college work. Tom asked about requirements for social work and Mr. T. gave a review of present day requirements, saying that if Tom wanted to go into social work he could get the education if he was patient.

"The fellows ate heartily and commented on the food as being so good. Steve and the Leader helped wash the dishes while the rest of the group talked to Mr. and Mrs. T. From about eight-fifteen to eight-forty-five the group sat around listening to the radio and talking among themselves while the Leader talked with Mr. T. All left at eight-forty-five. On leaving the fellows thanked the T.'s again. The major speakers there were Tom, Steve, Larry and Jim."

The Leader comments:

"The group acted as if they had never been away from home before and this was true. The Leader supposes that their behavior was not any worse on the train than that of a group of college fellows of similar age. The motive for their 'show off,' however, was different. It was all a big drive to make people think they are 'big shots.' Some of their ideas have been gleaned from college humor, no doubt, as was indicated by the 'uke.' Their behavior lacked wit except for a few occasions and for the most part was just loud. This was particularly true of Steve, Dick and Jake. Tom, Jim, Stanley and Ed were more calm. It is obvious that Stanley and Ed are followers in the group and do not pretend to lead in anything. The trip around the city was educational without a doubt and has stimulated some interest in the fellows in similar things about Cleveland. Most valuable of all, though, was the visit to Mr. T.'s home. The discussion was stimulating and although only a few took part, the others listened and at least they saw that a man they respected thought seriously at times."

Note: Was this trip planned in such a way as to make the most of the experience? What learning could be expected from such an occasion? Was this as profitable a way to spend the club treasury as could be found?

February 15, 1932

At the next meeting of the club one of the results from the trip to Pittsburgh appeared:

"Steve asked, 'Where do they get the money for that settlement?' The Leader replied, 'They get their money through some such set-up as our Community Fund. If you would like to find out about how such organizations are financed and run, I can show you where you can find the material.' Frank replied that he would rather know about the Community House. 'Why was the Community House put in this neighborhood anyway?' The Leader gave him a few reasons: (1) 'There are many nationality organizations and churches to work through.' (2) 'The neighborhood has never been worked before,' etc. Frank intimated that the work was rather like missionary activities but the Leader indicated that group work could be of service to any community no matter what the economic standing. The Leader explained that he expected group work to be a public service some day as education is today. Frank's face was blank and Dick and Ed looked as if they were ready to sleep so the Leader did not push the subject. Steve asked the Leader to come prepared to explain the why's and what's of the Community House at the next full meeting and also asked the Leader to tell them about the Community Fund. On the latter point the Leader said he would show them material and if they were interested enough someone could make a report. 'But if you don't want to do any hunting for yourselves my report won't mean much,' he added."

Note: This questioning of the reasons for settlements and their support opens the way for further learning which the experience in volunteer training has provided for some. How could this best be followed up?

February 29, 1932

"The first item of business brought up by Steve was concerning the yearly summary which the Hudsons planned to put out for the whole Community House. Steve suggested that the regular newspaper staff have charge of this issue and that Frank use any of the other fellows he needed. The Leader suggested that he might announce to the staff what the Hudsons were doing so that the leaders could help in getting each club's summary written up in good form.

"Tom had one final point of business to bring up and this was in regard to the forty cents which the House Council is asking that all senior clubs pay for the cards that disappeared at the January House Council party. Steve said, 'What do you think about it, Tom?' and Tom replied that he did not care. Jim and some of the other fellows stated that if the other clubs were paying forty cents the Hudsons should pay also. He went further and said, 'Give 'em fifty cents.' This suggestion was greeted with the approval of all the other members and the club agreed that fifty cents should be given to the House Council, instead of forty."

Note: These items indicate a growing consciousness of relation to the whole agency and a willing participation in its activities.

The Leader comments on this meeting:

"It seemed that this whole meeting was constructive. All of the points of discussion had value from the social point of view. All the members except Stanley and Ed put a word in on all of the points. Both of these fellows are comparatively new to the club and naturally do not have as much interest in the House as the rest and consequently they have less to say. The club is dominated by Steve, Tom, Frank; Jim and Dave have a pretty strong voice. While these fellows apparently do most of the thinking and talking the others share in making the decisions and are good followers. Fortunately the leaders are coming to have quite social attitudes and all the members are absorbing these. The fact that Steve initiates most of the business only means that he is a good planner and comes with his docket pretty well prepared. The items on the docket, however, are selected during the course of the week from the suggestions of the group. At this meeting honors were pretty evenly divided between Steve and Frank."

Note: What does this meeting show about the development in their methods of group control and their inter-group relations? How is the type of leadership changing?

March 3, 1932

At this meeting the discussion on the purpose of the agency was continued. The Leader had given some material about the agency to several of the club members. Several members of the Red Jackets, a younger boys' club, were present.

"The first point in the minutes from last meeting was the report on the agency. Steve asked the Leader for that but the Leader referred it to Jake and he read the report. This report emphasized the fact that the Community House hopes in time to turn over its work to organizations already in the neighborhood. The fellows took this point up and asked how this was being done. Reference was made to work done by the agency at the Polish Church and at the schools. The Leader pointed out the rôle of the Advisory Committee from the neighborhood in respect to the policy formulation of certain work of the House. The House Council was referred to as an example of neighborhood control. Frank said, 'If the House Council has some control, why does it pay two hundred dollars to the House for light and fuel? Why doesn't

it use that money from dues for improvement of equipment?'
'Yes,' added Steve, 'two hundred dollars wouldn't mean much
to the House if the Community Fund pays for it.' The Leader
replied that every little bit counts and that if the House Council
would use the money for equipment the budget on light and fuel
would be increased. The House has to count on the house dues
to help pay expenses, the Leader explained and added that in
most organizations the members pay for privileges and that some
of the money generally goes for upkeep of the buildings. Steve
and Frank maintained that the House Council should not make
that donation, intimating that the suggestion in the first place had
come from a staff member. The Leader professed ignorance of
this but suggested that the group might investigate the matter in a
House Council meeting.

"The discussion then turned to the purpose of having clubs.
Steve pointed out that most clubs do not know what they are
organized for. 'What are you organized for?' asked Steve, referring to the Red Jackets. Andy, the president, said something
about, 'for fun, trips and recreation.' He was not definite and
Steve told him, 'How do you fellows expect to accomplish anything if you don't know any better than that what you want?'
The Hudsons laughed at this. The Leader asked what they wanted
from their leader if they did not seem to get what they want now.
Tom interrupted and said that the leaders did not help the clubs
enough. 'They should give games, new ones and not the old ones,
and the House should provide better equipment,' he said. The
Leader asked, 'You wouldn't want the leaders to provide entertainment for you, would you?' They intimated that they did and
Frank said, 'The House aims to satisfy the recreational needs
of the people but they do not have enough equipment. The Community House just provides a meeting room.' 'What do you mean
by recreation?' asked the Leader and Frank mentioned basket ball
or pool. To this the Leader replied that a lot depended on the
definition of recreation and stated that in many ways club activities are recreational. The basket ball need is met outside the House
in the High School and the Church gymnasiums which are co-
operating with the agency. The Leader said, 'One of the aims of
a good club should be to become self-sufficient and to be able
to furnish its own recreation and program without very much
help from the leader.' 'But the leader ought to give lots of suggestions at first,' said Frank. 'Quite right,' replied the Leader, 'but
most clubs expect the leader to be an entertainer all the time and

many clubs which don't seem to do anything, definitely resist advice and suggestion.' Steve remarked that such clubs should be thrown out.

"At this point, some of the Red Jackets told about their leader and complained that he was always talking—either 'beefin' (bossing) or else talking about politics or the like. They said that if they talked about politics they could stay at the house longer but they indicated that they did not like such talking. After this speech Jim particularly looked at the Leader and grinned and let out a hollow laugh as if to say, 'That's what we think of you.' Steve asked the Red Jackets if they did any 'crabbing' and they admitted that they did sometimes. Steve pointed out that they were probably partly at fault. The Leader asked them if they ever went to their leader about their dissatisfaction with the club and offered to work the problems out together. They said 'No,' so the Leader advised them to do this. Later he talked to them further on the subject, with emphasis on the idea of cooperation with their leader. The Leader told the group that he was glad to get all of these points of view because unfortunately the group did not express itself on these things very often. He said, 'I hope I'm not carrying this too far (Jim and Frank squirmed in their chairs as they had been doing) because I don't want to bore you, but I'm learning a few things.' The Leader indicated that the points which were suggested in the evening's discussion should be written up and presented to Mr. K. and perhaps later to the House Council. The Leader said, however, that they should not be disappointed if some of their suggestions bore no fruit because in the matters of finance no one could very well dictate what should be done with money but the persons financially responsible."

The Leader comments on this:

"The discussion, the Leader feels, was valuable in that the fellows did think about the policies of the House. Some of their criticisms of clubs' not doing anything worth while were true even though their interpretation of worth while activities does not correspond with the Leader's. On the other hand, such statements as 'The House doesn't do anything for clubs which aren't active and for members who fail to take part,' indicated that the fellows in their hyper-critical state are mentally lazy. Of course it can be understood that they would not be aware of the fact that through a group work process some of the inactive people would eventually be 'brought out.' The Hudsons certainly show that they attribute their club growth almost entirely to their own work. The

Leader is willing that this should be because it gives them the feeling that they are independent.

"In the discussion the Leader decided that discussions as such must never be forced nor carried too long. Often a leader goes home feeling that he had a wonderful discussion meeting when, as a matter of fact, the group goes home feeling that they never heard such a 'windy' leader before. This meeting certainly made the Leader more awake to the fact that all work with groups must consider the immediate effect on the group, as well as the ultimate effect.

"The best part about the whole discussion was the fact that the fellows made up a list of suggestions which will be handed to Mr. K. and from that there will probably be some results in the form of a report on the House that can be passed out to groups. The club pointed out one very important thing—that too many clubs are meeting for no good reason at all that the clubs themselves can state."

> Note: This discussion again indicates some lack of rapport with the Leader since they enjoy putting him on the defensive. On the whole, however, it would seem to indicate an increasing maturity in their demand to understand the basis of the agency and their feeling that clubs ought to do something worth while. The number of them who have been volunteers probably has helped to bring this about. Should the training in volunteer leadership have made them more understanding of the values to be sought? What can be done with this attitude of demanding more equipment and more entertainment as their right? And their spirit of criticism without appreciation? How could this be met by the Leader?

March 10, 1931

The next meeting was significant chiefly at two points—the follow-up of the discussion on the agency and the further plans for the paper. The Leader indicates that no feeling of conflict was present in the following discussion:

"Frank asked if the report of the suggestions made at the last meeting had been given to Mr. K. The Leader replied that they had not been given formally because Steve had not written the points up but that Mr. K. had been informed verbally about the discussion. The Leader told the group that the proposals they

made were well received and that Mr. K. had given their suggestions very careful consideration. The Leader warned the group,
however, that they should not expect action on their suggestions
at once because some of them involved the spending of money,
and that budgets were set up for the year. Steve replied, 'Don't get
us wrong. We're not trying to tell you what to do. Those were
only suggestions.' The Leader said that he understood that they
were only that but that they would be used if at all possible."

Discussion of the paper followed:

"Following this, Frank made a report of the meeting which was
held Thursday evening in regard to the House Annual. He outlined the plans and told the group that each fellow would have
a job, although he made no assignments at this time. He has already assigned committees to collect information from the various
clubs and told the fellows to be sure to get their material in by
the middle of the next week.

The Leader comments:

"In the working out of the Annual, Frank should be given
all the administrative work he can handle because he needs the
experience. In general the club's problem is to lose its self-con-
sciousness. Gradually this is being accomplished. A place for a
stroke will be in advising the group not to include a dispropor-
tionate amount of Hudson news in the paper."

Note: How could this project be made to contribute to a cooperative attitude toward House affairs? What can the participants learn from it?

March 19, 1932

The club participated in a banquet of the men volunteers and
staff at which a speech was given by Mr. S. from the University.

"Following this, Frank, Steve, Dave and Tom presented a playlet which they had worked out themselves with some slight help
from one of the staff. The playlet was in three acts. The first
act showed the group as of 1926 playing craps on the corner of
Seventy-first and Indiana. They were met by a House leader and
invited to come to one of the houses for meetings. This the group
accepted. The second act showed this same group of boys meeting
about nine-thirty in the evening after their own clubs which they
were leading had adjourned. They talked of some of their club
problems which they are actually meeting today. The third act
showed the same group, after ten years, as leaders in the com-

munity with Tom as the Executive Secretary of the district planning commission, making preparations for a new community center building, Frank as director of the Community House, Dave as coach at High School and Steve as councilman of this district. This group holds a meeting and Steve reports that he has secured a five hundred thousand dollar appropriation for the community center building at the corner of Ohio and Twenty-third Street."

This was followed by a speech on the subject of the agency and its leaders by the director of the agency. The Leader comments later on the effect of this experience:

"The banquet was an inspiring experience for the Leader and the reaction of the fellows shows it had the same effect on them. The vision which was shown in the skit, the Leader feels, was not entirely a part of them although they do have a rather superficial understanding of it. They will, however, need much more true educating before they will come to the point where they will see community service from the point of view of the community and not themselves. Mr. S.'s talk was helpful in that it stimulated the fellows to think but perhaps the stimulation was not as strong as the Leader at first thought for the group failed to say a single word about it at the Monday night meeting. The speech did help the Leader's standing in the group since it made some of the fellows realize that they were receiving the type of leadership that Mr. S. described and that the Leader who entertains is not doing the job properly. It was of interest to the Leader to know that Steve and Frank gave him some credit and this bit of recognition, though it came in a roundabout way, will certainly stimulate the Leader's interest in the group."

Note: This experience probably helped in creating a more responsible attitude toward the agency. How could this be followed up?

The Leader continued to follow Larry's case, having contact with his lawyer and his mother, going to see him in jail and testifying in his behalf at the trial. On March twenty-ninth the Leader reports that Larry will not get probation but will be sent to the reformatory.

April 1, 1932

Meanwhile work continued on the paper. The Leader comments: "The paper is taking quite a bit of time but the Leader feels that it is well spent in that Steve and Frank, while unemployed, have something constructive to do. In addition to this the fellows are getting some idea of the amount of work in preparing a publication. Then, too, they, as well as the club, are engaged in a piece of work which is of considerable good to other people. They are really doing it for the recognition they will get out of it. The sad thing about it all is that what recognition they do get goes to their heads. They get the idea that there is no one or no club as good, with the result that they are subjects for a good bit of criticism and razzing.

"The Leader is actually proud of the work the fellows are doing on the paper and feels that through the work he has gained their confidence. He admits that the fellows are quite conceited and at times he gets discouraged because of this characteristic of theirs. But looking back over the change the group has shown in the past year he sees that whereas they used to be conceited without any grounds, they now have something to found their pride on.

"In a way the Hudsons' attitude is a defense for an inferiority feeling. In the mores of this country is the attitude that a young man of twenty or twenty-two should make his own way and even though the opportunity for this is denied the fellows, they are still measured by the mores. Either a fellow in this situation is going to lose what pride he has and openly admit his inability to 'measure up' or else he is going to put on a false front and carry on such boasting as will tend to cover up this feeling of inadequacy. The Leader believes that some of the group are reacting in the latter way. At the same time, they are trying to do things which give them reasonable grounds for pride."

Note: Is the Leader correct in feeling that the group has accomplished a commendable amount this year?

April 7, 1932

"Frank and Dave arrived at the office at nine o'clock in the morning to mimeograph the Annual. Dave did the mimeographing while Frank and the Leader punched holes and took care of the stencils. Frank beamed all over as each sheet of paper came out. The Leader said, 'Boy, doesn't this give you a kick to see this coming out so well? It does me.' 'You bet,' Frank replied, 'it took a lot of work too.' 'We can be proud of this,' said the Leader. In answer Frank said, 'We are.'

"Later in the day Steve and the Leader talked for quite a while about the club and Steve asked, 'Do you think the Hudson Club should be given credit for putting out the Annual?' The Leader replied that they probably should have credit in that they were footing the bill in case there would be a financial loss. 'But,' replied Steve, 'only a few fellows in the club helped to do it so the whole club should not have credit.' The Leader admitted that that was another way of looking at the question and intimated that some of the other fellows might have been asked to help and that others could not help very much because they were working."

April 11, 1932

At the next meeting:
"Steve said the first item of business would be a report of the paper. He asked the Leader what the bill at the office would be and he estimated it around six dollars. Frank reported on the sale of the Annual and indicated that there would be about seventy some copies sold by the end of the evening. In addition to those sold he enumerated those which were to be given away. The Leader had spoken to Frank previously about giving some papers to certain friends of the House and Frank brought these names up for the approval of the club. For a moment Steve looked as if he were being imposed upon and the Leader intimated that, if they felt the club should be paid for these copies, funds would be found some place. But in a moment Steve said, 'I think it would be a good idea to give copies to these men if they have been helping the House because the purpose of the paper was to be of some good to the House.' Tom had given a few papers away previously to several of his friends who had been at the House. The whole club wished to send some copies to the Pittsburgh people who were visited earlier in the year and it was debated whether two copies or five would be sent. It was decided to send five. Frank reported that he had sent one of the Annuals to Larry with Larry's sister."

The idea of reorganizing the club appeared in this club meeting:
"The Leader was absent from the meeting for a few minutes but returned to hear Steve laying down the law to the group about a reorganization of the club in which the constitution would be gone over, new laws made and provision made for strict application of these laws. He said, 'Our meetings aren't being carried on right and we've got to have more order.'

"Under new business Frank suggested that a lot of the group's troubles were due to having too much money in the bank. 'Anyway,' he said, 'if we're going to get more members in the club we should get rid of our money so there wouldn't be any difficulty about their laying claim to it.' He said the club members ought to have something that they could wear which would indicate that they were members of the Hudson Club. Steve attacked this point by saying that a Hudson should be known by his work, not by what he wears. He then turned his attack toward Jim and Jake and the fellows who had not participated in preparing the Annual, mentioning that if those fellows had helped to do that work they would have been known as Hudsons. But the rest of the group to a man decided that they would like to spend some of the money for sweaters, rings or pins. Frank followed with a motion that fifty dollars be spent for some club remembrances. Everyone voted for the motion. Steve asked the Leader what his vote was but the Leader reminded him that he had no money in the treasury and therefore was not qualified to vote. The discussion raged for about half an hour as to what should be bought with fifty dollars but no decision was reached. All of the fellows except Dave preferred to buy sweaters but Dave, since he has plenty of sweaters, would rather have something else—what he did not say."

Note: There are signs here of a serious rift in the club. Could the Leader have seen to the distribution of work on the paper so that more could have participated? Should the Leader have taken a more active part in discussing the use of this money? Are there not some other uses that would have been more valuable than that proposed?

Steve also presents some problems to the Leader by his attitude toward the House. The Leader reports that at a banquet which Steve attended as one of the volunteers, "He mentioned the fact that the volunteers were senior club members leading groups without a particular education for the job. Miss M., the girls' worker, told the Leader that she thought Steve had poise and spoke very well. Later on in the evening the Leader mentioned to Steve what Miss M. had said and told him that he might work on his job, developing himself more along that line since he did have some native ability. This time Steve said that he would like to improve himself and get more education. He said, 'I'm sick and tired of working in a greasy old steel mill and I don't want to live my life that way. What I want is to educate myself.' During the program after the banquet the volunteer leaders put on the skit which they presented at the banquet. In this skit Steve brought out the fact that the regular leaders of the staff were supposed to be educated and made some sarcastic remarks about people of education."

The Leader comments later:

"The Leader's conversation with Steve at the banquet is rather significant in that Steve admitted to the Leader that one of the sources of his feeling of inferiority was his lack of education. It will be noticed that Steve continually makes sarcastic remarks about people who have had quite a bit of schooling but at the same time admits that this is the very thing which he would like to have. It would seem that most of his slams against the so-called 'big shots' are merely defenses which he sets up to prevent himself from recognizing his own inferiority."

Note: Steve is evidently struggling here between the sense of his own inferiority because of lack of education, his desire to excel in the opinion of the staff and his desire to compensate for his own inferiority by belittling the staff. Could the Leader have handled this attitude more successfully?

About this time the Leader brought to the club a letter from Larry written after reaching the Reformatory:

"The fellows read it and Frank repeated this line: 'This is a place to find out who your friends are.' Frank said, 'That's a good idea all right,' and noted Larry's reference to the club and the Leader. Larry advised the fellows to stay out of trouble and said he was going to learn a trade at Northfield. The Leader said he hoped Larry would not tie up with the fellows he meets in prison. Frank remarked then that the problem would come when Larry gets out of the reformatory. 'He'll probably never come back around here.' The Leader added that the club should try to keep in touch with him and Frank said he would take a copy of the Annual to Larry when the fellows went to see him on Friday."

As a result of this a further discussion occurs:

"Jake brought up the question of whether or not the club could send a present to Larry. Steve replied with a question, 'Who asked you to bring that business up? Larry?' Jake was somewhat upset at this and said, 'No. Frank is the one who asked me to bring this up,' and Frank said that Larry's father had suggested that Larry would appreciate a present. Steve objected to sending a present since it would cost the club about five dollars which was more than any active member of the club was getting at the present time. Steve maintained that Larry would be benefiting more from the club than any of the active members. Then the discussion shifted to a consideration of what presents could be gotten for Larry and it was found that the boys would be limited pretty much to a sweater and inasmuch as the prisoners wear uniforms most of the time, the group felt that a sweater would not be very practical. The Leader suggested that probably Larry would appreciate just hearing from the club members as much as he would getting a present. Steve volunteered then that every club member should write to Larry at least once a month. This seemed agreeable to the group and no decision was made as to a present for him. The Leader asked the group at this point whether they felt any responsibility whatever for Larry now that he was not active with the group. Steve replied that he did not think the club was bound to give Larry money or presents. The Leader clarified his point then by asking them if they were thinking at all about the time when Larry would be out of prison and the course he was to follow at that time. There was no response except silence to this question and the Leader went on to point out that Larry held the club in very high esteem and counted them as friends and that probably the way the club could do the most good for him would be to capitalize on this friendship and keep in touch with him all the time that he was down at Northfield."

April 18, 1932

On April eighteenth 1932, a final report was made on the paper. "A meeting was held at the Community House. Steve first called for a report on the Annual. There had been one hundred and ninety copies made and one hundred and fifty-five sold, twenty-seven complimentary copies given away and about twenty-five copies were not accounted for. Expenses were five dollars and sixty-two cents plus a few other incidental expenses and the club received one dollar and eleven cents clear money. Charlie had been requested to buy some presents for the secretaries at the office for their help and purchased a handkerchief for each for a total of one dollar and fifty cents. Thus the project actually cost the group the grand total of thirty-nine cents. Frank was charged with giving copies away but this issue was not forced."

Note: This project of producing the Annual was evidently a great success from the viewpoint of the producers. What value did they get from it?

The successful conclusion of the paper and the continued large treasury produced another crisis in the club. The Leader reports it first in a conversation with Steve:

"Steve said, 'That's right. Frank puzzles me. Sometimes he is all for himself and then just the other evening he said, "Our club ought to form two clubs; those that are interested in good times could be in the other."' Steve intimated that this idea was pretty good and that it would be satisfactory if worked out but the Leader reminded him that possibly the members who already had an interest in the House might assume some responsibility for those who were not interested at the present so that later on their interest would be developed also. Steve saw the point but indicated that nothing could be done with some of the fellows in the club."

The next few weeks were uneventful. Nothing further was done about the drastic revision of the constitution proposed by Steve and the conflict between the two groups seemed to have died down. A dance was planned and put on on April twenty-eighth. A wiener roast similar to the outing proposed a year before was discussed. The Leader comments on this on the basis of his previous experience:

"The Leader made no comment about the wiener roast although the plans this spring are almost identical with those made last year. Probably it would be best for the Leader to attend this one and perhaps have some control through mere presence but it is not likely that he can attend. The Leader does not believe the plans should be criticized in such a way that the fellows would think he is 'old-fashioned' because it is probably this more than anything else that the fellows dislike. If the fellows give the least hint that they would accept help in working out the program for this event though, he will offer his services and make constructive suggestion with no hint of don'ts."

Note: Is this decision on the Leader's part a wise one under the circumstances? Has he any function in regard to standards which he can successfully perform?

May 2, 1932

After one of the meetings the Leader reports the following conversation:

"The business meeting was adjourned about ten o'clock and a

discussion about the good and bad points of liquor was started. After a while Ed and Frank left but the other six remained and participated somewhat in the discussion. Dave maintained that any one who would drink too much liquor was 'losing his head.' Jake expressed himself as being in favor of liquor and plenty of it because it was good and gave you a good feeling. Steve advocated a certain amount of wine or liquor if a person wanted to feel good but to take enough to make you drunk was bad for you and the people around. Tom was against drunkenness and Dave, although he does get drunk sometimes, declared that he was opposed to too much drinking. Jim thinks drinking is all right. The Leader commented about the psychological significance of alcoholism indicating that sometimes a person gets drunk when he has something else the matter with him besides a mere liking for liquor; that drinking offers an escape from situations that are hard to face. The Leader admitted that he liked some wines and had tasted some whiskey which was pretty good but he could not see any advantage in drinking until he could not stand up straight.

"As soon as a lull came in this discussion, Dave burst forth with the idea that there is no such thing as true love. Jake sided with him and Jim was quiet on the subject, although he seemed to lean towards Dave's side. Dick continually made wise cracks during the discussion but Steve and Tom attempted to uphold the side of true love. Steve told Dave that he believed everything he was told, otherwise he would not think that there was no such thing as love. Steve cited all the married couples who continued to live with each other year after year and asked if they would live together if they did not love each other. Dave had no answers for the questions which Steve put to him except as he cited cases of married people who lost interest in each other. All through the discussion it seemed that the fellows looked at life merely from the sexual point of view. The Leader asked if there was not something probably greater which played a part in real love and asked if true friendship was not quite similar. Steve thought there was some similarity, that it was probably friendship brought about by common purposes that would hold a man and wife together through many years. The Leader asked what part respect for the other partner had to play in true love and asked whether a man should expect his wife to love him if he gave her no reason to love him. He added, 'Do you think that love is something which comes naturally without the putting forth of some effort?' There was no answer to this question. The Leader pointed out that sometimes men expect to have everything done for them. He explained that where both a man and woman are of this type lack of harmony is bound to grow out of their living as intimate a life as marriage imposes. Jim nodded his head as if he understood this argument. The Leader pointed out that while there are a great number of cases of divorce, after all down through the centuries monogamous marriage has been the common, normal thing and probably there must be some sort of feeling that holds a man and woman together throughout life. It does not matter what this feeling is called; some people call it true love."

The Leader comments: "In spite of Steve's braggadocio character, it will be found that he is probably the most conservative among the members of the club. It will be noticed that in the discussion about liquor he was the most moderate and in the question of love was the idealist and the most conservative. The fellows for the most part are opposed to drinking excessively but Jake, the Leader believes, gets considerable satisfaction out of this pastime. This may be traced to the fact that he does not have so many other interests and that it does offer him some sort of escape. In regard to the interest in love, it may be that Dave's point of view is colored somewhat by his own experience in that what they were talking about was unattainable for most of the fellows. This point was brought out during the discussion when one of the fellows said that he was not getting married for quite a number of years yet because he did not have the money. It is probably all right that the fellows have this attitude because in this way love is something which will not be so desirable to them since they cannot get married anyway. Most of the fellows are looking forward to the day when they will be able to support a family. No doubt one reason for the discussion is to be found in the questions which the fellows have in their minds about married life. In this discussion very few of these questions were cleared up, inasmuch as the boys were quite facetious most of the time and were not very serious."

Note: Here we see the Leader functioning again as the bearer of different standards and a different experience. His contribution in this case is accepted with better feeling than on some previous occasions. What part can a leader play in such discussions? Could the subject have been treated more adequately?

May 9, 1932

The club this evening reported a gang battle at a recent dance which had involved Jim.

"Steve told the Leader about a fight which Jim had had at the Polish Hall the night before in which he hit a young fellow over the head with a chair and possibly fractured his skull.

"Toward the end of the club meeting, Tom went to the door and came back with the report that there was a gang out on the corner. The others took a look and it was ascertained that it was the gang which was after Jim. Jim became rather flushed in the face and smiled in a sickly way. The group became very quiet and although the Leader tried to start a conversation the fellows remained silent. It was debated as to what to do since they knew if they went outside they would be mobbed by the gang which numbered twenty-five.

"About nine-thirty three of the gang came into the house asking how to spell Jim's name and what his address was. No one would tell and Jim stood up saying that if anyone was to find that out it would be the police. The fellows got rough and said, We came in here like gentlemen and if you won't do what we ask, you're going home on a stretcher tonight.' With that they left. There was less talking than ever after this. Finally Steve and Frank said, 'Call the paddy wagon to take us home.' The Leader did this and the police came to find no gang in evidence. They took the group away from the house but told them they should not be involved in that sort of thing."

The Leader comments:

"The Leader does not blame the group for wanting to be delivered to their homes because the other gang was in a rage and would certainly have given Jim a beating. Jim insists he used the chair in self-defense. The group took the incident as a joke at the beginning but when they saw the gang on the outside they immediately became serious. The silence indicated fear and it was written all over Jim's face. Frank and Steve took the initiative in asking for the police. The wagon was called by the Leader because he was afraid Frank might pull a knife which he carries as a matter of course with the result that the situation would become more serious than ever."

The Leader reports the next day:

"Called to see Frank to advise him and Jim not to carry weapons of any sort. He said they would take care of that and informed the Leader that Jim had left town for a time until the trouble blew over.

"The Leader went to the police station to see what they had on Jim. He discovered that there was a warrant out for him. The Leader explained to the sergeant that Jim had left town because he was afraid of what the gang might do and not because he wanted to escape justice. The sergeant said it did not make any difference since the warrant was good until it was served. When asked if Jim would be given protection from the gang, the police said, 'There's no use in crossing a bridge until you come to it.' They said Jim could not have been much of a gentleman to have used a chair."

A week later:

"The Leader dropped in at Jim's and Frank's home to find Dave, Charlie, Ed and Jake there. The Leader asked Jim how things in his case stood. Jim replied that he was not sure whether he would have a lawyer or not since one would cost him not less than fifty dollars and the fine if he should lose would be only twenty-five dollars and costs. The trial is set for May twenty-sixth."

After Jim's trial on May twenty-sixth:

"The Leader met Jim at the House Council party and found out that he had gotten off with a five dollar fine. There was an article in the paper which indicated that Jim had learned that he was in the wrong. The Leader laughed with Jim about it and said that some reporter just wanted to make a story."

Note: This incident indicates chiefly the mores of the neighborhood and the dangers inherent in them for boys like Jim. The Hudsons, while not a predatory gang in any sense, are embedded in a community where they could not escape this sort of situation occasionally. Could the Leader have played a more effective part in this incident?

During the three weeks following Jim's fight, the group did not make its appearance at the agency. The club still owed the agency a small sum for the use of its property for a previous dance. The Leader did not know whether this lapse was due to fear of the other gang or to the hope that the Leader would forget about the bill. The former seemed more likely, however. The fight also had its effect on the club's reputation and so on its morale.

"Steve said, 'I thought I was doing something by belonging to a club but it seems it doesn't mean anything if these fellows get away with this thing on Jim. The cops even said we were just as bad as the other gang.'

"The Leader finally called on Steve to ask him why the club did not meet. Steve said he thought it best not to hold meetings for a while so there would not be any fights. He said there would be a meeting on Thursday evening at his house and invited the Leader to come."

Steve further reported to the Leader that the fellows were no longer interested in the club. But he and Tom came around to pay the bill for the spring dance.

The Leader met Tom in June and was told that the Hudsons had definitely broken up. The money in the treasury was divided up so each individual received approximately ten dollars. He stated that the group might start again in the fall but for the time being, the fellows felt that they might as well divide the money.

ANNUAL SUMMARY 1931-1932

The Leader summarizes the year as follows:

During the year the club has had a fair attendance and has shown an ability to run business-like meetings and to plan its major activities effectively. It participated in activities at the Community House with more sense of responsibility than previously. More interest is evident among certain of the boys in volunteer work and this has proved to be a constructive factor in their individual adjustments.

On the other hand, he points out that there are conflicts between the members and difficulty over the club treasury. Interest in community affairs is very slight. The most serious problem in the club arises out of the unemployment of its members. Vocational guidance is needed but most of all the stabilizing effect of work. Most of the difficulties arise, he believes, out of their lack of opportunity. How much such activities as the club can provide can compensate for these serious deficiencies, the Leader questions.

The Leader evidently feels considerably discouraged at the end of this year. In reviewing the year, however, progress can be noted at the point of a more responsible interest in the agency, a better planned program, some actual achievements and a gain in the relation with the Leader. Against this must be set the conflict in the group and the final split up at least temporarily. The conflict in standards is still unresolved but there is evidence that several of the members are maturing into more responsible attitudes.

The reader may wish to ask about the year's record:

1. Has the Leader worked out his relation to the group in as constructive a way as he could? Does he cease to function in the situation as a bearer of values or does he simply do it less obviously? Does he make as definite and positive a contribution as he might?

2. Does the Leader carry through his relationship to individuals, Steve or Larry, for example, as effectively as he should?

3. Are the conflicts, evident in this year, handled constructively? What more could have been done in the basic conflict between the two subgroups? Does the hostility occasionally evident toward the House and the Leader work itself out constructively?

4. Does the group progress in handling its own affairs effectively? Is active participation confined to a few?

5. Does the interest in a more developed program advance as far as it could have? Could the Leader have been of more assistance in a better planning of program? In the provision of more adequate handling of interests?

6. Does the group progress in its community relations? Does it show an increasing sense of social responsibility? Does it develop better inter-group relations? What significant social attitudes toward the community are developed during this period?

IV

THE MERRY MAKERS: THE STORY OF A STRUGGLE
FOR POWER

THE Merry Makers is a club of twelve and thirteen year old girls. At the time this record opens it has thirteen members, four of whom are old members and nine are new.

All the children have grown up in the Polish community. Some are of the second generation in this country, some of the third but they are all members of the Polish church and most of them attend the parochial school. They live in a closely knit neighborhood within a few blocks of each other and are together frequently on the street and in school.

The parents of these children are, when employed, either manual laborers or the owners of small businesses. Several of the families during this year are on relief. Six of the children have mothers working occasionally outside the home.

This club has been in existence nearly three years before this record opens. It had been organized originally by the Dubinski twins and remains a constellation centered about them. The Dubinski sisters control the admission of new members and manage to hold office most of the time. No girl whom they do not like or who threatens their power can long keep her place in the group. The club has concerned itself chiefly with the simple forms of handcrafts, with cooking and with numerous parties. A play, "Cinderella," had been given the previous spring with a great deal of enthusiasm.

To the group worker this record is of interest chiefly at two points: the problems of discipline presented and the related problem of the development of democratic control. Problems of self-government and discipline are common with children of this age. This group in its exuberance, its changeable moods, its spontaneity, its petty squabbles, is quite typical of its kind. In the interest of the development of all the group the Leader struggles to maintain some degree of order and to develop the capacity for group discipline for its own ends.

The dominance of the Dubinski twins presents certain difficulties both in any exercise of the Leader's authority and in the development of self-government. Here the Leader has to consider both the undoubted capacities for leadership which the twins possess and the resulting submission of the club. The problem of how to convert this miniature dictatorship into a democracy runs through much of this record. The need for education in democratic leadership and followership presents here a recurrent and often baffling problem to the Leader.

This record is also significant in the indications it reveals of the developing interest in boys typical of the early stages of adolescence. It is interesting to compare the form this takes with the similar interest in girls in a group of adolescent boys displayed in the following account of the Pirates.

DRAMATIS PERSONAE

Gertie Dubinski—one of the twins and identical in appearance with Stella, described as having straight red hair, a pinched face and drooping mouth; possessed of marked leadership ability, intelligent, original, dominating, distinguished from Stella as being the "cheerful one" and more popular.

Stella Dubinski—twin to Gertie, distinguished as being the "solemn one," shares her twin's traits in regard to leadership capacity; the family during this year was in destitute circumstances and part of the time on relief.

Maud—a child of Polish parents in a home which is dingy and unattractive but apparently happy; adaptable, intelligent, willing, rather dependent.

Margaret—a friend of Maud's, in a family on relief with the father unemployed; intelligent, capable, happy, clever, adaptable.

Annie—a child of a working mother, father deserted, intermittently on relief; restless, energetic, clever, intelligent, superstitious, carries partial responsibility for the housework.

Connie—a child from a family on relief; nervous, unstable, comparatively well dressed and tidy, humorous and entertaining.

Madge—a substantial appearing child, rather naive, intensely interested and active in the club, articulate and outspoken in her opposition to the twins.

Jean—a follower of the twins and so admitted to the inner circle, somewhat passive and lacking in initiative.

Emma—a quiet, unassuming child without outstanding abilities but responsive, a former member who returns in the middle of the year at the suggestion of the twins.

Fannie—a plump, cheerful child, enthusiastic, rather slow and not wholly accepted by the group.

Julia—a thin, wiry child, who does acrobatic dancing, and "loves" parties, somewhat younger than the others and with a tendency to complain that the girls are "mean" to her.

Mabel—a friend of Julia's, also somewhat younger than the rest, quiet and good-natured.

Hazel—one of the younger members who remained only a short time, a center of conflict with a habit of yelling in order to get her own way.

Edith is proposed for membership and discussed but not admitted.

FIRST YEAR

The Merry Makers opened this year, the fourth of their history with a new student leader. On her first contact with them she comments:

"The group is very active and full of pep as evidenced by the fact that they jumped around and ran continually from room to room. Their interests seem to be wide and varied. Everything that was suggested usually received an enthusiastic, 'Oh, let's!' This interest, however, is short-lived; they jump quickly from one thing to another. No one activity was participated in for more than five or ten minutes at a time. The group seems to be dominated by Gertie and Stella, for the club does what they wish although they themselves seem to do little in the way of actual bossing."

October 12, 1932

The first weeks of the year were occupied with cooking and the planning and carrying out of a Hallowe'en party. At the second meeting on this date, an election was held.

"Jean nominated Stella for president. Margaret was also nominated. For vice-president Julia and Jean were nominated. For secretary Gertie was nominated but made a face and said she did not want to be, so the Leader said it was not necessary for her to run. Connie and Margaret were nominated. Mabel and Gertie were nominated for treasurer. Gertie smiled in a pleased way at this. Jean then said that the nominees for each office should go out while the others voted. The results of the elections were as follows:

President	Stella
Vice-president	Jean
Secretary	Margaret
Treasurer	Gertie

The Leader comments as follows:

"Stella and Gertie are very evidently the leaders of the group since both were unanimously elected to office. The Leader cannot understand why Gertie declined to be secretary and yet was quite willing to be treasurer. It may be that collecting the money gives her more social prestige than being secretary.

"The group is very enthusiastic about planning activities of their own as shown by their absorption in the Hallowe'en party. However, they have no definite ideas of organization and need quite a bit of assistance when they are planning a regular program. The group is very prone to yell their ideas all at once and the Leader found that the only way to silence them was to refuse to listen or to talk to any one until the group quieted down."

November 2, 1932

On November second an incident occurred which shows the control of the twins.

"In the midst of their meeting which was devoted to painting, Connie came to the Leader and said that Julia and Mabel were upstairs and wanted to see her immediately. The Leader found these two outside the door and Julia said in a soft voice, 'Shut the door, please,' before she started to talk. 'Are we still belonging to the club?' she asked. The Leader said, 'Of course,' and asked why they thought they did not. Julia then told a long tale about Stella's and Gertie's having slighted them at school and therefore they thought they should not come. The Leader asked if they always did everything Stella said and they immediately nodded their head 'yes.' The Leader explained that the club was as much theirs as Stella's and that they should come in. This they refused to do until the Leader had gone and asked Stella. The Leader returned to the basement and said to Stella, 'You girls want Julia and Mabel downstairs, don't you?' Stella hung her head and said, 'Whatever the kids say.' No one else said anything so the Leader told Mabel and Julia to come down. They both sat very quietly, working on their paper and demanding nothing. Julia always came to the Leader and said, 'I'm ready for the brush,' instead of asking any of the girls for one."

The Leader comments:

"The Leader feels that Gertie and Stella rule the group by ridicule and exclusion of those who will not do as they say. They were very rude and silent with Mabel and Julia and yet before the Leader they were unwilling to admit that their personal feelings were the cause of Julia's and Mabel's staying away, saying it was 'whatever the kids say.'

"These two evidently are the chief recruiting forces of the club, bringing someone different each week. The Leader wonders if these new people are the 'favorites of the week.' "

Note: Can the Leader influence at all this method of determining the personnel of the group? Is it desirable to have it made up only of those of whom the twins approve? How could the Leader affect this situation?

The Leader further comments on the behavior of the girls in the meetings:

"The group seemingly has no idea of cooperation, each one yelling and screaming and demanding what she wants for herself. This selfishness may tie up with their quick change of interest. Each one wants to keep ahead of the others by suggesting new things to do."

Note: Can the Leader do anything to affect or control their type of behavior? What could be done? Should the Leader exert authority in order to control or is there some other method of handling the situation?

The Leader discovered that pressure from the twins and from Connie who also enjoys "bossing" was being brought to bear upon Julia and Mabel to get them to leave the club.

"Margaret said that Connie had told Julia and Mabel that they could not come to club any more because they did not pay their two cents. Gertie further explained that Connie was the one who always said, 'We don't want her,' to any new member they suggested. Upon inquiry the Leader found out that Connie tried to boss the others in school but did not play with them outside of school. Margaret promised to tell Julia to come to club and not to heed Connie's bossiness."

November 11, 1932

The next meeting was devoted to a cooking lesson. The hubbub and confusion at the table following the lesson were so great that the Leader attempted to control it.

"Then followed so much noise and talking that the Leader could not even hear her own voice so finally she said she had a story to tell if they would listen.

"She told them the story of a girl who was in a strange place where people made much more noise and talked more loudly than she had been used to and ended with, 'What would you do if you were in her place?' Connie piped up, 'Slap them.' Annie said, 'Yes, and kick them out.' Ida said, 'I'd yell just as loud as they did.' The Leader pointed out that this would only disturb others. Then the hubbub set in again until above the clamor Gertie's voice said, 'Tell us another story, Miss L.' The Leader explained that the story she had told was about herself and explained that it was impossible for anybody to get anything done when everybody talked at once. Maud said, 'We're used to it. That's the way it is at home.' 'Yah,' Margaret said, 'at home it's "Get the h——"' and then stopped, grabbing her mouth. Then everybody laughed and all began admitting how their parents talked."

The Leader's comment on her own technique is as follows:

"As to the noise and yelling which predominated in the club this time, the Leader thinks that the home situation described explains their rowdiness. The fact also that they come directly to club after school, which in the majority of cases is a strict one, means that they are ready to 'let off steam' after the suppression of the day. The Leader finds it very hard to remain calm and collected and not show too much displeasure at their conduct.

"The idea of telling a story to bring them to a realization of how impossible it was to accomplish anything under such conditions probably accomplished little except that they were quiet for a few moments and seemed to understand the Leader's viewpoint."

Note: Was this method of the Leader's appropriate to the situation? Is the story method a good device here? What relation has this type of disorder to the program of the group?

The Leader gets further light on the case of Julia and Mabel. She reports:

"The fact that Julia and Mabel did not appear at all this time is indicative of the fact that pressure is being brought to bear on them to stay out. The Leader feels that this pressure is exerted by Connie but at the wish of Gertie and Stella."

Note: What action does this call for from the Leader? What can she do about Julia and Mabel if the twins have decided to oust them from the club?

November 16, 1932

On this occasion the Merry Makers embarked upon a project of self control by means of regulation. The suggestion of a previous leader some months before that they might have some rules for the club bore fruit as follows:

"When the group went inside Stella said, 'We're going to have a business meeting today. We haven't had any for such a long, long time.' Margaret said, 'And are we going to make rules?' Gertie began collecting the money and asked the Leader how much was in the treasury. The Leader said about twenty-five cents and Gertie replied, 'Aw, it must be more than that.' The Leader promised to find out by next time. Jean then arrived and Annie suggested that the group bring their chairs 'close for a meeting.' Stella asked, 'What shall I say first?' The Leader suggested that she call the meeting to order. This she did, then said, 'Is there any old business?' There was no answer. 'Is there any new business?' she then asked and everyone sat on the edge of her chair as Gertie answered, 'Rules.'

"The following rules were then drawn up:

"1. Anyone who comes late pays one cent (this was given by Margaret who stood up and asked the president if she might speak.)

"2. No cursing during club meetings or parties. The Leader said, 'Does that mean Polish or English?' They laughed and then shook their heads 'Yes.'

"3. If a member is absent three times without an excuse she is to be dropped from the club.

"4. No talking during meeting.

"5. No chewing gum or eating candy during the meeting.

"6. Nobody leaves the meeting without permission of the president."

The Leader comments:

"The Leader feels that this business meeting and the rules that were drawn up may be a very good means of control of the noise and boisterousness that had hampered the club during previous meetings. The group were very much quieter this time which might also be attributed to the fact that they were very much interested in what they were doing.

"As to the rules, the Leader felt that the ones concerning the lateness and absence were directly aimed at Mabel and Julia who were often late to club. The other rules were probably patterned after those of other clubs that the girls knew of, especially those in which the older Dubinski girls were members."

Note: This tendency to formulate rules seems to occur spontaneously in such groups. How can this be used for the development of more actual self-government?

The rest of the meeting was spent in making decorations for a Thanksgiving party and planning for a craft program in which they were to make leather purses.

November 23, 1932

The account of the next meeting gives a vivid picture of the struggle for law and order:

"In the meantime Margaret began fixing the chairs behind the table to have places for the president, secretary and treasurer. When she had finished, Connie shouted, 'Let's get going.' Stella reminded her that the others had not yet arrived and that the 'meeting shouldn't start till they're all here.' At three forty-five Margaret said, 'Come on, kids, it's time to get this business meeting started.' At this everyone brought her chair as close to the table as possible and Margaret said, 'Aw, not so close!' The Leader then suggested that a circle around the table would be better so that everyone could see. Whereupon they all moved back and made a circle.

"At this point Mabel arrived to be greeted with loud shouts of 'You're late, you owe a penny!' The Leader intervened to remind the group that they had decided that Julia and Mabel could be fifteen minutes late because they have to come a longer distance from school.

"As Mabel took her place in the circle, Stella looked expectantly at the Leader and Margaret poked her, saying, 'Go on, start!' Stella looked at the Leader again and said with a giggle, 'Shall I say, "Meeting in order"?' The Leader said, 'Yes,' and it began. When Stella asked for new business, Mabel said, 'We'll have a Christmas party, won't we?' and Stella said, 'Sure.' She then asked for the reading of the minutes and the secretary, Margaret, began, 'The meeting was adjourned' and then went on to read what happened. When she had finished, the Leader explained that 'adjourned' meant the meeting was over, when she had meant the meeting began. Stella then asked Gertie to collect the dues and she got out a little notebook and marked each one's name as she paid.

"She asked the Leader how much was in the treasury and on finding it was sixty cents, Margaret piped up, 'See, I told you! Miss L. said it was only twenty-five cents!' in a condemning tone.

"Stella asked if there was anything else and the Leader said she would like to bring up the matter of dues. She explained that, since some people did not have money to spare and the House dues had been lowered, maybe it would be a good idea to lower the weekly dues. There was a loud cry of 'No!' at this and Connie said, 'Aw, we want lots of dough.' The Leader explained that it was hard for some nevertheless and Margaret said, 'It is hard for Annie. Sometimes she doesn't have it.' All were silent on this and then Margaret said, 'Why not let those who can't pay, pay only one cent and the rest of us pay two cents? We could try it that way and see how it works.' The group protested at this suggestion saying it was not fair. Maud said, 'Well, we could each bring a penny a week and collect extra money for parties and things, if we needed it.' 'Sure, that would work,' Gertie said. 'Well, then, we only need to bring a penny every week from now on?' Connie asked and the whole group nodded assent.

"Julia just then arrived and Stella pointed a finger at her, rising to her feet, 'You owe three cents today, a fine for being late.' Julia put her money down and said apologetically, 'I'll bring the rest next time,' and then quietly brought a chair into the circle.

"Gertie interrupted the meeting at this point to say, 'Connie's chewing gum and so is Maud.' Whereupon Stella ordered them to throw it away and Maud smiled mischievously and started to get up. Connie blurted out, 'Aw, I won't throw mine out. What's the use of buying it if you can't chew it?' and then she began to pout. Margaret spoke up and said, 'If it's a rule, why then you must get rid of it. What's the use of rules, if you don't keep them?' Whereupon someone discovered Stella was chewing gum too and the subject was dropped after Stella grinned sheepishly and asked the Leader what they were going to do that day."

As the Leader says of this meeting:

"The group likes rules and wishes to enforce them until they concern themselves and then they are reluctant to give up their 'rights.' The chewing gum episode illustrates this excellently.

"No one in the group exactly trusts anyone else and therefore in any situation which calls for the whole group's participating and getting a fair deal, they ask for authority from above. This is probably due to the fact that their parents settle their disputes and also their teachers. They are used to this kind of discipline."

Note: Could the Leader have done anything to uphold the impartial administration of the law in this case? What, if anything, can the Leader do about this? Should she respond to their demand for authority from above?

November 30, 1932

The next meeting was devoted to the making of simple leather purses and was quite uneventful.

December 7, 1932

At this meeting there are some evidences of conflict between the group and the Leader. The Leader had been asked to bring the money to the club treasurer at a previous meeting and had forgotten it which had made a bad impression on the group. The conflict centered about two factors—the money and the continuance of Julia and Mabel which the Leader had been promoting by home visits to them.

"As soon as the Leader came up and took her place in the circle in which each one was seated, Stella called the meeting to order. Margaret read the minutes of the last meeting and said to the Leader, 'Did you bring the money, Miss L. ?' The Leader explained that it had taken all the money in their treasury for the leather purses they had been making and that there was none left, whereupon there were loud 'Oh's' from everybody concerned. Ida said, 'Well, we'll just give them back if they're going to cost ten cents apiece.' Margaret said, 'But we got them last year for nothing.' The Leader explained then that it was impossible to give them to them for nothing because the leather, the thongs and the buttons all cost something and there was no other money with which to buy it. Jean said, 'Well, we could have bought them at the ten cent store,' and the Leader said, 'But you wouldn't have had the fun of making them,' at which the whole group laughed."

Note: What does this indicate about the Leader's relation to the group? about the group's planning of its activities? Should they have embarked on making these purses without understanding about the expense?

"When Stella asked if there was any new business, Margaret suggested that names be drawn again for gifts for the Christmas party, since two of the girls had not been there, whereupon Stella wrote out new slips of paper and passed them around. While they were discussing when names should be drawn, Connie said

she did not want Julia and Mabel to come back any more and
the Leader asked why. 'Aw, they're too little and they're always
hanging around.' The Leader suggested to Stella then that the
rule on such matters be consulted and Stella informed the group
that the rule stated that an absence of three meetings dropped a
member from the club. Connie asked Gertie how many times they
had been absent and found it was only twice. Jean said, 'Well,
you wait till next time and when they don't come, then they just
won't be members.' 'We'll do that,' said Stella, and Gertie added,
'And they won't come either.' Jean spoke up saying she had talked
to Julia and Mabel, and Julia said she did not want to come to
the club because she lived so far that she could not get there on
time and did not want to pay a penny. The Leader asked Jean
what she thought and she said she did not care whether they came
back. This time Connie spoke up saying, 'Aw, Miss L., we don't
know where we're at. You ruined our whole club by going and
calling on those kids who didn't come back.' The Leader explained that she had not asked them to come back but merely
inquired their reason for not coming. 'Well,' said Connie, 'they
think they're supposed to come back now and they came and
asked us why we had not asked them.'"

Note: Was the Leader wise in urging Julia and Mabel to return against the wishes of the controlling group? What indications are there in this meeting of favorable and unfavora-
ble attitudes to the Leader? How should she react to them?

The Leader's plan to meet this situation is to let the matter of
Julia's and Mabel's membership take its course since they have
been outsiders for so long that there is little chance of their being
accepted. She plans also to work with Stella hoping to get her to
run the club with more cooperation from the others and less
domination.

December 14 and 21, 1932

The group planned its Christmas party and carried it out successfully. The program included games and a present for the
Leader as well as ten-cent presents for each of the members. On
this occasion the Leader comments that the group was very polite
and orderly at table and were cooperative about clearing up afterwards.

January 4, 1933

"At the first meeting after Christmas plans for future meetings were discussed. The immediate demand was for cooking. The group decided to make popcorn balls next time. The Leader discovered that the kitchen would not be available because another club was using it. Upon reporting this to the club the whole group sent up a howl and said, 'We want to cook.' The Leader went into great detail explaining that since the party had been planned by the other club, nothing could be done about it but the group still kept insisting 'We want to cook.' The Leader said that they had cooked four times this fall and Gertie said, 'When?' So the Leader had to name the times. Still everyone insisted on cooking. The Leader said that she was sorry that nothing could be done and that it was time to go home. Whereupon Stella said, 'We won't go home till we know we can cook.' The Leader laughed and said, 'Well, then you'll have to stay all night,' and everybody sat down in a chair and Fannie said, 'All right, we'll stay all night.' The Leader turned out the lights, went to get her hat and coat and from the next room she could hear various comments as, 'What a club!' 'What a House!' 'We won't come next time if we can't cook.' The Leader then went to the kitchen to see if a part-time arrangement could be made with the other club but again found it impossible and returned to the Merry Makers to say that nothing could be done about it. However, no amount of explanation had any effect and still they sat. Finally the Leader went to the door and opened it and said it was time to go. Whereupon Fannie got up first, followed by the others who slowly came to the door. They all went out saying they would bring stuff for popcorn balls anyway next time and they could be done on the register! The Leader laughed and said it would not do them any good and that she would see them next week."

Note: Again the Leader has to exercise her authority with this group. This time she is confronted with evident hostility. Was this an adequate way to handle this situation? Is such hostility to be expected at times? How should a leader react to it in order to establish an effective relation to the group?

The following incident on the street throws further light on the twins' hold over the group:

"While on the way to make a family call, the Leader met Annie

on the corner with another girl and on learning the Leader's desti-
nation, Annie asked to accompany her. Annie explained to the
Leader that the rest of the members of the club, especially Stella,
made her feel bad when she did not bring money to the club. The
Leader replied that Annie was to come every time regardless of
whether she brought money or not. The Leader then asked if the
other members always did as Stella and Gertie asked them to.
Annie said, 'No,' they did as they pleased because they paid."

January 11, 1933

Annie's difficulty was thus dealt with at the next meeting:
"As the Leader was taking off her coat in the other room, Stella
came in and said, 'We want Annie to come to club all the time
and we know she can't afford to pay dues so from now on she's
not to pay any dues. Only when we do have something that we
can bring materials for, such as cooking, she can bring it.' The
Leader said she thought this a good idea and told Stella that she
could tell Annie. Stella refused to take this suggestion and asked
the Leader to do it, saying she did not want to. (The Leader gave
Annie the news during the process of the meeting when an opportunity offered itself to speak to her alone.)"

The problem of not being able to tell the twins apart had been
a serious one to the Leader all the year and at this time she tried
to deal with it.

"As soon as the Leader opened the piano, Gertie sat down to
play but when the Leader called her by name she discovered that
it was Stella, whereupon the Leader asked Gertie to come and
stand by Stella and asked that the rest of the group tell her just
how Stella and Gertie were different. At the time Gertie was
wearing a pink scarf and Stella a brown one but the group said
they could tell them apart by their faces and yet no one could
say what part was different. Fannie then asked to do the Virginia
Reel. As the Virginia Reel began Gertie played the piano and
Stella refused to dance. Fannie said, 'Aw, Stella's mad but let her
go. It's just because Miss L. asked about her and Gertie.'"

The Leader realized afterward that this may have been a false
step.

"The situation of the identification of Gertie and Stella was
badly handled and the Leader realized that the ground she had
gained so far in their identification may have been lost since Stella
seemed to be offended by the Leader's action. The Leader will

now try to identify them on the basis of the fact that Gertie's face is supposed to be broader and a little fatter than Stella's."

Note: How is this incident likely to react on the Leader's relation to the twins?

January 18, 1933

The group had decided that it wished to have half an hour of tap dancing every week, after which it would work on a play. A good deal of wrangling arose over the selection of a play. "Robin Hood" was decided upon and then after the meeting the Leader heard that the decision was reversed.

January 25, 1933

At the next meeting the Leader felt a firm stand was necessary in order to get some decision made on the play. The following account gives the setting of that decision:

"The question of the play was discussed again and after some difference of opinion, 'Snowdrop and the Seven Dwarfs' was suggested. They were very scornful of fairy plays at first but as the Leader told the story with some help from the group enthusiasm rose. The Leader said she could get the story in a play and everybody began saying, 'Oh, let's give that, let's give that!' Stella asked to write the parts on a slip of paper and let each one draw. The Leader agreed and the following parts were finally decided upon: Snowdrop, Madge; Prince, Stella; Hunter, Jean; Queen, Annie; Dwarfs, Margaret, Maud, Gertie, Fannie. When they first drew, however, Annie had been Snowdrop, Stella the Queen and Madge the Prince but by trading around they were more satisfied with the above arrangement."

The Leader states her interpretation of this occasion:

"The group's decision on a play came, the Leader feels, as a result of the fact that she took a firm stand and let them know that they could not change their minds every week and make any progress. There are times like this when it is necessary for the Leader to take more of an authoritative rôle in order that the group may come to some sort of cooperation which will later lead to achievement for the group. This is the pattern which they have been following in school and at home and therefore it is the Leader's only means of control at times.

"It is interesting to note that the play finally selected was a fairy story which from the very beginning the whole group definitely said they did not want and refused even to consider. The Leader feels that this proves her contention that this sort of play was much more suitable to their age and type than any other."

Note: Is the Leader right in feeling here the necessity for an element of control from her? Does the group actually desire such control for their security?

February 1 and 8, 1933

The next two meetings were devoted to tap dancing and the rehearsing of the play. At the second meeting, however, Gertie and Stella did not appear and the girls reported that "they think tap dancing is silly" and that "their mother doesn't want them to come any more." In the drawing for parts in the play one of the twins had received a minor rôle. The Leader wondered whether they were repeating their tactics reported in previous years, of withdrawing whenever they were not given the most prominent positions.

February 15, 1933

At the next meeting the twins were back again and Stella, as president, insisted upon a business meeting. This is the occasion for an interest in boys to appear for the first time.

"Stella said, 'We want to have an Easter party and invite another club,' and then with a giggle added, 'Shall it be boys?' The whole group then began tittering and giggling but Fannie in a loud voice said, 'Oh, no. They're too dumb and I know 'cause I've never seen any but dumb boys.' Stella then asked for a show of hands from those who wanted boys and only Connie put up her hand, whereupon everybody went into a loud burst of laughter. Margaret stopped the confusion by announcing, 'No. We'll not have boys,' and Stella added, 'Oh, we'll let them go.' The group then asked the Leader to get the file of girls' clubs that they might ask to the party. Every single one which she suggested they voted down with a 'No, not them!' No decision on this was reached, although they asked the Leader to find out what boys' clubs might be invited."

The Leader comments that there are indications of an increasing interest in boys evidenced by giggles and silliness. These plans for a party, however, were never carried out.

Note: Most of the group at this period are twelve years old. This first sign of the interest in boys is natural, of course, at their age. How should the Leader treat it?

Rehearsals were continued and the interest in the play was maintained. The Leader planned to have it given as soon as possible so as not to lose the impetus.

February 22, 1933

The following meeting again indicated the stage of self-government attained:

"The Leader asked the group if they would like to stay and rehearse the play upstairs since no one was working in the office that day and was greeted with an enthusiastic, 'Yes!' Everyone made a mad rush for the office chairs and those who were not lucky began inspecting everything on the desk until the Leader reminded them that things were to be left just as they were found. The Leader began setting the stage in the other room when Gertie said, 'Oh, we have to have a business meeting first,' and the Leader said, 'Do you want one?' Everyone clamored, 'Yes.' This decision, however, caused a dissension since the officers insisted that they sit in the 'nice' chairs and those who already had those chairs resented having to give them up. After much unsuccessful hounding the officers finally took other straight chairs with the exception of Gertie who merely stood up in the middle of the floor for the rest of the meeting. Just as the meeting was starting, Gertie discovered that Connie had chewing gum and told her to throw it away but this she refused to do, saying, 'I guess youse guys never throw yours away. What's a rule anyway?' The others merely looked at her disgustedly but said nothing.

"A discussion of possible new members arose. Margaret stood up and announced in a loud voice, 'We don't have Edith in this club.' The Leader then inquired if they had asked her to be a member or how her name had been brought up. 'Oh, she asked us and we thought we wanted her but now we don't.' Stella then called for the collection of dues which was followed by a few

minutes' silence until Stella suddenly announced, 'Meeting's over.'
There was a general rush into the other room.

"The rest of the time was spent in rehearsing 'Snowdrop and
the Seven Dwarfs' which was very difficult, due to the mischievous capers of most of the cast. They continually walked all
over the stage and raced back and forth into the other office.
Lines were merely said mechanically.

"During this period, while Margaret and Maud and Connie were
offstage, they did so much running around, darting in and out
and pulling up the curtains that it was difficult for those on the
stage to continue. The Leader called the group out and asked if
they would please cooperate and be quiet while other people were
doing their parts. In about fifteen minutes or less the noise was
worse than ever. The Leader called the group on the stage and
asked what they wanted to do about the play, whether they were
willing to work hard and be quiet in order that the play might be
put on in a couple of weeks. Gertie said, 'What's the use of it?
Let's don't have it,' but she was immediately quieted by the others
who said they very much wanted to have it. Once again rehearsal
was started and in five minutes there was as much noise as ever.
This time the Leader told the group that since they were getting
nowhere they could stop and go home. There were many groans
and exclamations of 'Oh, let's finish.' The Leader, however, stuck
by her decision and the group departed at five-thirty."

The Leader comments on this occasion:

"The general lack of attention on the part of the characters in
the play and the noise and confusion during the rehearsal was
probably due to the fact that this was a holiday and most of the
children had been at home all day, cooped up in the house and
that this was their first opportunity to 'let go.' The fact that Stella
and Madge and Annie were not entering so much into this noise
was due to the fact that they were kept busier than the others
during the play and became very much more a part of it, thus
taking it more seriously. The Leader's being quite firm in dismiss-
ing the group without finishing the play may be the cause of their
being more settled and quiet the next time."

Note: How does the fact that Gertie has only a minor rôle
enter into this? The discipline problem here assumes a major
importance. Is there evidence of continued hostility against
the Leader here? How can she handle the situation wisely? Is
the authoritative approach the best one here?

March 1, 1933

The next time the Leader attempts to control the situation further:

"Rehearsal for 'Snowdrop and the Seven Dwarfs' then began with the Leader's asking all those who were not in the first scene to get chairs and sit in front to make an audience. There was much running around the curtains and dodging behind furniture but finally everyone was out in front except Annie and Jean.

"During the rest of the time the play was rehearsed with very little attention given to it by the group. Connie especially did much jumping around and talking until the Leader finally took her out of the play and asked her to sit beside her until she was quiet enough to go back. Connie pouted for a second or so and then began watching the others. After ten or twelve lines the Leader told her she might go back to the play.

"During the most of this rehearsal the Leader had interrupted frequently to tell them of some mistake they were making or to suggest some different way of interpretation. From this point on, however, she told them that she would not interrupt them but would tell them at the end what was the matter. They all gathered in an interested circle around the Leader after the play was finished and the Leader went around the circle making suggestions and praising various ones."

The Leader comments on the results as follows:

"The Leader's solution of the problem of so much noise and confusion by having those not in the play sit as an audience worked very well this time and there was much less confusion than during the last rehearsal. Some of this may also be due to the fact that the Leader told them the play was to be given a week from Saturday and for this reason they were very anxious to do it right. The idea of not interrupting the play at all until the end of that particular part on which they were working proved to be much better than the constant interrupting which tended to make the group restless and dissatisfied. Furthermore, they were very much interested in the criticism at the end and discussed it quite freely."

This meeting was noteworthy, too, for an attempted revolt against Stella's domination. She and Gertie were absent on this occasion. During the business meeting this incident occurred:

"The question of new members was then brought up and Annie began complaining of how Stella dominated the rest of the club and consequently they had just whomever Stella might approve of. Connie backed her up in this, saying that Stella always decided whether they would have a new member or not. 'Well, I'll tell you what let's do about Edith (the member discussed at a previous meeting). Let's vote and see if Stella is going to tell us what to do.' The Leader suggested they close their eyes to vote and she would count the hands. Margaret, Jean, Maud and Hazel voted to have Edith. The others were quite jubilant that they had gone against the 'powers that be' and were having something the way they wanted it."

The Leader's reaction to this is as follows:

"The Leader was very much amused at the stand that was taken against Stella's domination in her absence. However, the Leader thinks that just such things as this may be the beginning of a feeling that will make the whole group rebel against the domination of these girls which has continued over a period of years. Such revolt will be encouraged by the Leader."

Note: Is the Leader's technique in dealing with this problem of autocratic leadership a sound one? Earlier in the winter she had decided to work through Stella. There is no evidence that this plan has been tried. Now she decides to encourage revolt from the established authorities. What should she do?

There is no evidence in the record that Edith ever entered the group. Evidently the revolt here pictured did not succeed.

March 8, 1933

"This meeting was also occupied with the rehearsal at which there was some squabbling about costumes and some confusion. The dwarfs made a lot of noise back stage when they were not doing their parts until the Leader finally said, 'You'll have to be quieter or we'll have to quit.' The group was quiet for a while after this but in a few minutes the noise was as great as ever and the Leader exclaimed, 'All right, you can go home now.' She further explained that she had given the group a chance and they had failed to take it and therefore could not finish. Three of them said they had not even heard the Leader give them 'one more chance.' The Leader consented to another trial and the play was finished with less interruption."

Note: The problem of control remains largely unsolved throughout these rehearsals. How should the Leader have handled it?

March 11, 1933

The play was put on at the Playshop along with several other plays by groups of about the same age. The Leader reports:

"The production itself went very well and several people remarked about how well done the play was. The whole group was very much excited, arriving half an hour before they were supposed to and dashing from one room to another, saying lines to each other with such remarks as, 'Oh, I'm so scared,'—'I know I'll forget,'—'I'll bet everyone laughs.' In the midst of this uproar Annie began to cry hysterically because someone grabbed her beret off quickly and her braids came tumbling down (she had not wanted the group to know she had braids). During the dressing process there were constant shoutings for 'Miss L.' for lost articles, pins, fasteners, and so on.

"Just before the other plays began the group went downstairs and sat in the back with their coats on (covering costumes). They were very quiet and orderly but remarked that these plays were not as good as theirs. They were third on the program and after their play they again went to the back of the auditorium to watch the last play.

"After the program was finished they dragged the Leader out into the hall and Fannie said, 'Say, our play was best, wasn't it? Those others laughed and giggled—they didn't think it was serious.' Gertie then chimed in with, 'And dos kids said our play was stiff. But I think dey were terrible.' At no time during the play did they mix with the others except for a few remarks about the merits of their respective activities."

Note: What were the attendant learnings here in regard to other groups? Is this competitive attitude necessary and desirable on such occasions? What could the Leader have done to produce a more magnanimous attitude toward the achievements of others? Is the temporary cohesion and order within the group related to this expression of hostility to other groups?

March 15, 1933

At the next business meeting two significant incidents occurred:

"Stella then said, 'Say, we want a new name for dis club. Merry Makers is too old and everyone laughs at it. Why, whenever anyone asks what de name of de club is and you say "Merry Makers" dey just laugh. And den dey say, "What a dumb name!" ' When anyone said she thought it was a good name she was 'booed' down. Everyone then began talking and jabbering about names until no one could be heard. The Leader suggested to Stella that she go around the circle and get a suggested name from everyone after they had done some thinking for about three minutes. Everyone was silent for that period and when the Leader said 'Timeup!' they all sat up to listen attentively. Some of the names suggested were the Junior Aid Society, the Red Cardinals, D. O. B. (Dat's Our Business), Rinkeydinks and Sky Blue Maidens.

"The slip of paper on which these names had been written was then passed around and each one checked the one she wanted. 'Merry Makers' had also been added to the list at the Leader's suggestion that perhaps some would like to keep the old name. The vote stood six to six for 'Merry Makers' and 'Sky Blue Maidens,' with a few scattering votes on the others. Madge objected to Stella's saying *we want.* 'It's always "we want" and we just always have to do what you and Gertie want.' Stella became indignant and told Madge to 'shut up her trap' saying that if she objected why was not she president. The Leader asked if they thought the president told everyone else what to do. They all nodded assent and the Leader explained that the president was supposed to carry out their wishes and that what they wanted to do was what the president should want. 'Well, the President of the United States doesn't do that,' Gertie hastened to say. 'I guess the people didn't want the banks closed but I guess that's what he did.' The Leader said that they may have not wanted them closed but they did want something done about the depression and that was the only way he could do it. Gertie made no answer and Madge came back with, 'Well, I'm tired of youse always having your way. Oh, I know that tomorrow in school I'll get the dickens from youse but I don't care. Why should your saying "we want" be the rule always?' to which Gertie replied, 'Aw, you're just mad and stubborn, that's all. Why don't youse make Madge president 'cause I don't want to belong to dis dumb club anyway.' This last remark was lost in the general buzz of talking that followed and the club divided into the two sides. They decided finally the matter would be held over until the next time when everyone should bring more suggestions. During all of this latter time Stella was sitting back in the corner, leaving the president's chair vacant but reluctantly when urged by her followers said, 'Meeting's over.' "

The Leader comments:

"The old struggle of leadership has arisen again as can be seen by the incident of the names. Never before, however, had anyone dared to say the things in meeting which Madge said. This was very interesting to the Leader, especially the remark about getting 'bawled out' the next day in school. That was probably just what had happened before. Every time anyone had dared to defy or stand out against the 'powers that be' the next day the wrath of the governing power descended upon them. The Leader had been of the opinion that more and more each one was standing up for her own rights and today's evidence pointed in that direction. At any rate the protest was becoming more articulate and the Leader encouraged this whenever it occurred feeling that in this way Gertie and Stella would eventually be forced to assume less and less authority."

Note: This is the first open challenge to the authority of the twins in a club meeting. What part should the Leader take in this situation? Should she attempt any assistance to the twins themselves in using their capacities? Should she encourage the revolt? How should she handle the feeling evident in this conflict?

This conflict was forgotten in the intervening week and no action was taken on a change in name.

March 22, 1933

Since clubs close for the summer in April the Leader announced to them at this meeting the plans for a Play Day for all intermediate clubs.

"The Leader said, 'I have something to tell you. You know clubs are closing in two weeks and so on the last Saturday we're going to have a Play Day. That means that all the clubs your age will go. There will be games and folk dancing.' At this Margaret immediately inquired where it would be held and the Leader said probably at the Park, at which there were loud groans from the group. The Leader suggested that they went there often for a hike but Emma said, 'Aw, tell 'em we can't go, that we have a date.' At this there were suppressed giggles all around the circle and Emma looked at the Leader and burst out laughing. Stella wanted to know what kind of dances there would be and the Leader said they would be easy to learn, the Red Handkerchief being one. 'Aw, we know that,' said Stella and began demonstrating the dance in an exaggerated manner and singing the song in a squeaky, high pitched voice; all the others joined in this activity. When it was over the Leader said, 'Then you want me to say that my club doesn't want to come to the festival.' There were nods all around the circle and the Leader again inquired, 'Do the Merry Makers want to be known as the "high hat" club, one that doesn't do anything with any other club and thinks they are too good?' 'Of course,' 'Sure,' greeted her. Annie said, 'Aw, we don't want to do those babyish things,' and the Leader explained that the games and relays to be played involved teams, score keeping, etc., just like days in college. Stella piped up, 'Oh, we've gone to college,' and everybody began chattering in a way somewhat resembling a New York accent. This was evidently to convey to the Leader what the group thought of college. The subject of Play Day was dropped after this. The group stuck to its determination not to attend."

Note: It is hard to tell how much of this reaction is directed against the Leader and how much is a dislike for contacts with other groups. What does it suggest of the Leader's relation to the group at this time? How could she deal with these attitudes?

March 29, 1933

The Easter party was the subject of discussion at this time.
"Plans for the party were taken up and the group asked the Leader to get the list of clubs so that they might see whom they could invite to the party. They disagreed about all the clubs that were suggested and were not able to come to a decision about any of them. Emma interrupted to say, 'What about the boys' club of Comrades that Stella's sister suggested?' The Leader told them the Comrades were too old for them but she would ask Mr. F., the boys' worker, for groups nearer their own age. When she returned she told them that there were only the Flying Seven and the Hot Spurs who were near enough their age. Everyone said the Flying Seven were too young although Stella said the Flying Seven wanted to be invited. They kept asking the Leader who the boys were in the Hot Spurs and although she said she did not know except that they were the same age as the Flying Seven, they kept insisting on knowing their names and 'could not understand' why the Leader had not looked up the names. They kept arguing that they could not do anything until they knew the names

and the Leader kept saying that the group was too young anyway. Finally the Leader said she had not had time to look at the names and that seemed to end the argument.

"The group next discussed inviting Miss O., the girls' worker in the House, and Miss B., their former leader, to the party and otherwise having it only for themselves.

"Having agreed on this they spent the rest of the meeting planning the games, decorations and refreshments."

Note: What does this argument over the boys to invite mean about their real desire to have them? Compare this with the similar period in the Pirates' record. What does it indicate in the relation to the Leader?

April 6, 1933

The closing Easter party was the high point of the year. The crêpe paper tablecloth with its Easter chickens, the rabbit's nest centerpiece, the white candles, the jelly bean favors—all were their own creation. The guests were treated with unusual politeness. And then the twins, hurrying up to the Leader, said, "Oh, we have something special we don't want the rest to see, you know, a surprise!" They gained permission to add a final touch in the way of candy eggs with the Leaders' names done in chocolate. The other Merry Makers looked on enviously, muttering, "They always get to do everything!"

ANNUAL SUMMARY 1932-1933

In summarizing the year's work the Leader points out certain achievements and certain obvious defects. She feels that the group has planned most of its activities and has shown a developing initiative in doing so. The Leader has herself made suggestions at points in order to vary the program but on the whole it has been self-determined. The last two projects, the play and the Easter party, have provided opportunity for this. She also feels that the club has made some progress toward greater participation by all in the control of the life of the group. Resistance has appeared to the domination of the twins and there is evidence that this may in time affect their methods of leadership.

On the other hand, the Leader indicates that there has been continual conflict running through the group over the domination of the twins and frequent disorder and confusion as they have attempted to carry out their projects.

The reader may wish to raise questions such as:

1. Does the Leader establish a satisfactory relation to the group? How can she deal with their occasional hostility to her? Does she create a control which provides them with enough security and also a chance for experimentation and adventure? What is her contribution to the life of the group?

2. Should the Leader have more contact with individuals than is evident here? Could she make contacts with the twins which might be helpful to them as leaders? Should she try to discover what lies back of their drive for domination?

3. How can she more effectively deal with the interactions within the group? What is the best way of handling the almost continuous squabbling? How can she provide harmless or useful outlets for such mutual hostilities? How can she create cooperative attitudes? How can she help to provide recognition for their various needs within the group process?

4. How can self-government be promoted? How can greater participation be secured from all? How can the type of leadership methods used by the twins be modified in the direction of democratic control?

5. Is the program of activities here described adapted to the group? Does it grow out of their interests? What are they learning from it directly and indirectly?

6. What relation to the community is this group developing? In their inter-group relations what feeling are they expressing? What are they learning from their inter-group experiences?

V

THE PIRATES: A GANG WITHIN SETTLEMENT WALLS

THE Pirates were organized in October 1930, a year before this record opens. They are a rollicking, boisterous lot with the ethics common to boys in this neighborhood and that curious mixture of good intentions and depravity found in adolescents. Some of the members had been in younger clubs in previous years. The group, at the time the record opens, consists of thirteen regular members. Of these three are fourteen years old, four are fifteen, three sixteen and three seventeen.

A certain amount of subgrouping on the basis of age is evident in the club, the older boys sticking together and the younger ones sometimes making themselves a nuisance to their elders. This division is not sufficiently marked to split the club but it becomes increasingly obvious and constantly affects the unity of the group and the program it can undertake.

All the boys were born in this country and most are of Polish parentage. There are three pairs of brothers in the club and several cousins. Only one boy in the group is Protestant. He is the child of an American father and a Polish mother.

The street on which most of these boys live is an arm jutting out from the Slovenian neighborhood into the Polish section. The fact, therefore, that this is a mixed group is indicative probably of the diminishing influence of the nationality factor.

Of the thirteen boys only three are out of school at this time and only one of them is employed. Five of the others attend trade schools, three the parochial school and the others the public high school. This separation in school is compensated for by the proximity of their homes. Several live on the same street and all are within five blocks of each other.

All the families represented here are on a low income level with the exception of one or two boys whose fathers are saloon keepers. Several of the families are on relief. In other cases also there is unemployment and a very low standard of living.

This group is a gang, typical of boys of this age and kind. They are constantly together outside of club meetings, have played together all their lives, and have many of the usual loyalties of such groups. Although it adds new members and drops old ones, the thirteen who form its central core are regular attendants. The desire for organization and for admission to the Community House seems to have been motivated largely by the material advantages which the house provides. During the first year the club had joined for basket ball only but had become interested in camping trips, games and other activities which they found available. The club was mischievous but not seriously destructive. It was suspected of stealing electric light bulbs and food on various occasions, and these incidents gave rise to various discipline problems.

Unlike many gangs there is no strong leader. Their elected leadership changed several times during the first year, and no one of their presidents proved wholly adequate to the problems of control in the group.

The record is interesting to the group worker in the problems it presents to the Leader who attempts to "civilize" such gangs, control them sufficiently to make life possible for other groups and help them to develop to a more mature social level. This record is valuable also in the light it throws on the emerging interest in girls and the relation of such group experience to it.

It is interesting to compare the discipline problems presented to the Leader here with those of the Merry Makers and with the conflict in standards evident in the Hudsons. The Leader is confronted not only with the natural exuberance of adolescence but with certain problems which may develop into serious anti-social behavior. How can such a group become the means for the building of constructive social attitudes and the creating of responsible citizens?

The developing interest in girls also presents an opportunity and a problem. Here in the first stages we see the attitudes forming which will have great significance for the future relations of these boys. How can the group contribute to this situation?

The group leader assumes that by bringing the gang off the street and into the Community House the "natural process" can be thereby turned to constructive ends. The attempt to "civilize" the Pirates gives us a picture of what is involved in that process.

DRAMATIS PERSONAE

Henry—president of the club, a fifteen year old of Polish parentage, the son of a saloon keeper; alert, evasive, deceitful, indifferent in school, unsupervised at home, with a family history of unemployment, bootlegging and dependency.

Fred—a former president, a seventeen year old of Polish parentage, out of school and unemployed; dependable, capable and unafraid, likes to pose as a "hard guy" with a highly colored vocabulary.

Charles—Sometimes known as Speed; a sixteen year old of Jugo-Slav parentage and a counteracting influence to Henry; grave, tall, strong and responsible.

Art—better known as Blackie; a fifteen year old of Polish parentage, attending a trade school; small, swift, silent, and gracious, also wishes to be thought a "hard guy" but is good-natured, honest and responsible.

Paul—known as Goosie; a seventeen year old of Polish parentage, good-humored, athletic, honest, also wants to be known as a "hard guy," attends the trade school.

Stanley—a follower of Henry; a sixteen year old of Polish descent, out of school and unemployed, occasionally involved in a theft, under Henry's leadership, lacking in initiative and ability.

John—a mature boy of seventeen of mixed English and Polish parentage; employed as a stock boy, the only Protestant in the group, honest, dependable, intelligent, good-humored, outstanding in athletics.

Carl—known as Smiles or Bubbles; a sixteen year old of Slovenian parentage, quiet, resourceful, dependable, interested in reading and wood work, lacking in athletic ability.

Leonard—the fourteen year old brother of Henry; quiet, reserved, frank, a mischief maker, known as a "guy wid brains."

Bert—a fourteen year old of Polish parentage, son of a saloon keeper, also supposed to be a "guy wid brains" and to have a "lotta jack," an easy talker and a constructive influence in the club.

Albert—a slow, awkward boy of fourteen, the butt of many jokes.

Walter—occasionally known as Puvak; fifteen year old brother of Fred, bright, likeable, intelligent, mischievous, the club clown.

Joe—a fifteen year old of Polish parentage, agreeable, mischievous, with a reputation for being light-fingered.

In addition to these boys there are several others who are inactive or irregular and so do not require characterization.

FIRST YEAR

The club year of the Pirates opened on October sixth, 1931, with the Leader Mr. T., who had been with them the previous winter.

October 6, 1931

The Leader reports the meeting as follows:

"Henry accosted the Leader on his way to the Community House: 'Club tonight?' he asked. 'In five minutes,' replied the Leader. At seven fifteen, the appointed time, the crowd burst into the House.

"'What do you say, Mr. T.?' said Henry and Bert. 'Can we meet with girls, huh? You fix us up. Boy, we'll have the fun.' The Leader said that he could arrange to have a girls' club come down once in a while and have joint meetings with dancing following the meeting. The question did not go any further. Later, however, a senior girl came in for a House Council meeting. Her entrance made all but Charles and Paul jump up and escort her to the committee room. Bert was the first to return. 'Boy,' he said, 'I got a date already. Boy, ain't she dressed up. You ought to see all the powder and paint on her face.'

"As soon as the meeting was called to order the Leader addressed the club somewhat as follows: He told them that last year the club had had many good times. On certain occasions the group had displayed a spirit of unity which had resulted in a very happy time for everybody, including the Leader. At other times some of the younger members of the club had been entirely too careless in what they considered propriety. There were times when the older fellows really wanted to talk or play and the younger ones like Joe, Walter and Leonard ran around the house poking into every drawer and in general showing disrespect for other people's property. Charles spoke up, 'Them kids,' he said, 'they always monkey around. If they do it this year, I'll kick them out.' Then the Leader said, 'Who else will be in the club?' and they replied, 'Carl (whom they call Bubbles), Art and Albert.' They would all be at the meeting the following week since Charles had told them to come that time.

"Then the Leader said, 'Let's put down here what we did last year and what we want to do this year as a club.' During this talk

Charles asked the Leader to 'git that camp.' The tension which had been over the club while the Leader spoke to them of their having to assume responsibilities in the house relaxed. Talk of camp loosened everybody and stories of how they had cooked and spoiled the pancake batter, broken an electric light and skied, came thick and fast and put all into a jovial mood again. When the talk had finally made the group very jovial, the Leader suggested that some games be played."

The Leader comments on this:

"It is unusual for a leader to devote the first meeting of a club to delivering a sermon on the propriety of its actions. In this instance the Leader took this course because the last few meetings of the Pirates last year showed an attitude of lessened responsibility towards the House. The youngsters got more and more free in their behavior; the older boys were less unified as a result of conflicts on their own street. Last year they were accused by the Leader of having stolen a large quantity of ice cream from a senior club meeting at the House. They denied the accusation to the Leader and insisted that they had been elsewhere at the time. The incident, however, served to scare them away from the House porch where they had been making nuisances of themselves during the night the girls' clubs met. This year the Leader determined to impress them with a sense of responsibility the very first meeting so that they would govern themselves accordingly. Charles and Blackie, as the older fellows, are very tractable. They talk readily and to the point."

Note: Was this good technique on the Leader's part? It indicates a rather authoritative approach. Is this necessary in groups of this kind? The interest in girls is evident from the opening episode. How can the Leader best help the group to meet this interest?

The Leader also records here the following incident which illustrates Henry's behavior:

"At this moment a member of the Leader's group at another house called him out saying that the club had come around to say 'hello' to him. As the Leader stood talking to them outside for a minute or two he noted Henry coming out to see who the visitors were. Some of these boys started to roll their own cigarettes and in the process dropped one of the papers. Henry scooped it up and then made his way to the rear of their group. The Leader saw him digging into the pockets of one of them for tobacco and said,

'Henry!' Henry looked up and said, 'What's the matter?' 'Better go inside,' said the Leader. Not a bit abashed Henry turned to the group and said, 'Hey, give us a feeney.' They gave him the cigarette wanted and he went back.

"Henry's lying and stealing tonight are in accord with his whole attitude. These traits which seem to be habitual to him—for he lies even when he does not need to—are like his numerous wise cracks and exclamations, designed simply to get a laugh, especially from Joe. The Leader hesitated to call the attention of the visitors to the fact that Henry was searching their pockets, but he is going to talk to Henry. It will take more than words, however, to break that particular habit of Henry's."

Note: The Leader is obviously disturbed at Henry's behavior and seems to consider attempting to deal with it individually. Should he try to do so? What could he do? Should he attempt to get below these symptoms of psychological difficulty? Should he get more expert help?

October 13, 1931

The next meeting was concerned with elections, plans for football and a camp week-end. Henry was elected president and Bert treasurer.

October 20, 1931

Law and order entered the group at this point as Henry assumed his new rôle as president.

"Henry, the president, arose, 'We got new rules,' he announced. 'There's five of 'em and if you don't obey them three times you get kicked out of the club for three weeks.' 'Well, do you have to pay dues even if you ain't there?' said Fred. 'Sure ting,' said Henry, 'that's the worst of it.' While Bert, sitting next to Henry, leaned over to help him decipher the rules, Henry announced each one in turn:

1. No one can speak when a member is speaking.
2. Don't wear caps in club.
3. Good manners.
4. Anyone who doesn't pay dues for three weeks, he's out of the club if he don't pay.
5. Nobody must break things in the House or hang around the porch.

"Henry read these and was about to put them away when Bert said, 'Read them again. Then these guys can't say, "Well, we didn't know what was going to happen to us."' So Henry read the rules and the penalties again, eliciting from Charles the comment, 'That's the only way. Them kids mustn't monkey.' Hearing no further comments from the group, the Leader said, 'Henry, wouldn't it be a good idea to have the fellows vote on each rule separately so they can know them all and feel that they are not having anything put over on them?' 'That's a good idea,' said Henry and forthwith took up each rule individually. To each rule all present assented, except the rule of loitering on the porch. To this all but Henry and Bert dissented, laughing as they did so. 'Hey, I'm going to get kicked out of the club,' said Fred with a laugh, 'I got to come here and meet my bim (girl).'

"Henry then said, 'Now we got to plan the party.' The party is to take place next week and will be participated in only by the Pirates. Aided by Bert who looked over the list continually to make sure nothing and nobody were omitted, Henry compiled the list of food for the party. He would say, 'We got to have spuds. Who's gonna bring spuds?' About six promised to bring them. Then he would say, 'Who's gonna bring bread?' If nobody answered, Bert would run his eye down the list and say, 'Here's Joe. He ain't bringin' nothin'. Henry would say, 'All right, Joe, a loaf of bread.' Henry then appointed committees to prepare the food, set the tables, and wash the dishes. In appointing these committees, Henry seemed a bit hazy about what he was doing, for he kept re-appointing the same boys to different committees. All who were appointed accepted the jobs, although the dish-washing committee laughed as if to imply that their appointment would not necessarily mean their fulfilling their obligations."

The Leader comments:

"The first thing to catch the Leader's attention was Henry's behavior as president. Last year he had been considered by outside boys as the leader of the club. Whenever they had spoken of the gang from Seventy-seventh Street they said, 'Henry and them guys,' but in the club he had had to resort to sly sayings and eye-rolling to gain attention. Tonight, however, he evidently meant to take full advantage of his presidency, for he maintained order at the meeting, had a prepared docket and in general brought life to the business meeting of the Pirates.

"The thoroughness of the business meeting was unusual. The discussion lasted a whole hour and Henry did everything logically.

Henry's assumption of the dictator's rôle may be a good thing for the club.

"For the first time in many meetings neither Walter nor Joe left the meeting early to roam around the house and pry into things. Bert, as treasurer, took his duties seriously and kept strict account of what money he took in.

"The Leader wonders how much of tonight's live meeting can be traced to the influence of his stern talk at the first meeting. In many instances the Leader's taking on of a sterner demeanor brings vitality into the club; how long it will last depends largely on the result of the Leader's talks to them and on Henry's ambition as leader."

Note: The effect of responsibility on Henry is very significant here. If it can be maintained, it may be the first step toward a change in attitude. What could the Leader do to use this opportunity? It is significant that the group is considered Henry's gang although the Leader was unaware of any strong gang leader in the club. Should Henry be encouraged in assuming a position of dictatorship?

October 27, 1931

The party previously planned was put on on this night.

"The party took place this evening, but the afternoon found the entire membership of the club arriving at the House with baskets of food. With no hesitation they began to peel potatoes and set them in pots on the fire to boil.

"When the Leader arrived at seven o'clock, the whole club awaited him. Charles, Bert and Carl good naturedly drove everybody out of the kitchen and set to work on the food in earnest. Albert, Henry, Fred and Walter helped them at times. With those not preparing food the Leader played Hallowe'en games. He tried a new game involving disguising the voice; this the boys liked. The next game did not fare as well until a feminine member of a senior club meeting in the next room entered. Finding Henry blindfolded and ready to guess the identity of those who walked around him, she stole up behind him and stroked his face. 'It's Fred,' said the unsuspecting Henry. All laughed in great glee. The lady kept on thus with Henry, once even giving him a none too gentle dig in the ribs, while he kept calling names. When he finally removed the blindfold, his eyes opened wide and he exclaimed,

'Was it the bim?' He was assured it was indeed the 'bim.' 'Did she give me that dig in my ribs?' pursued Henry. And when he learned she had done just that, he smiled knowingly and offered to teach her how to play football.

"There were 'hot dogs' in rolls, meat sandwiches, French fried and boiled potatoes, relish, jelly and a large cake baked by the sisters of Charles and Bert. There was too much food; most of the potatoes were hard and were left uneaten; so was some of the jelly, relish and coffee. Joe salted the jelly and took it down, together with potatoes and bread, to the Hudson gang meeting in the basement. Fortunately, the Hudsons were too hungry to detect the salt. But even after they finished eating there was a heaping plate of potatoes to throw out.

"Nobody was eager to wash the dishes. Charles volunteered and did the job, assisted by Albert, Art and Carl. At that, it took the Leader over an hour to clean the pots and kitchen well even after Charles had finished his work."

The Leader comments on it:

"The party was very uneventfully run but since the Leader wanted it to be entirely of the boys' making, he interfered in no respect. The food committee filled up on food while preparing the repast and lacked appetites when it was served. The games were difficult to manage because the players kept sneaking back to the kitchen to see whether they could steal a bite or two."

Note: Could this party have been more successfully planned? The growing interest in "bims" is evident at nearly every meeting. Should the Leader provide for some activities with girls?

November 3, 1931

At the next meeting the Leader reports:

"Everybody waited for the Leader to do something. The Leader looked at Henry, the president, and Henry looked right back at the Leader. 'Well now,' said the Leader, 'haven't you brought a list of things to talk about, Henry, the way you did last time? That's a good way to get things done. Remember, we had our best meeting last time.' Henry said he had not.

"Then Leonard spoke up, 'Hasn't the secretary got the minutes?' but the secretary, like his minutes, was nowhere to be seen. The Leader discovered him a few minutes later sampling the food in the kitchen.

"Finally Henry thought of something. 'How about them club emblems, Mr. T.?' he asked. 'We want to get some quick.' Bert announced that the club had a surplus of two dollars and forty-seven cents with which to buy emblems. All understood, of course, that each was to pay an extra amount in addition to the surplus. Henry's eyes began to reflect his usual sly look when a cunning idea came into his head. 'You going to get an emblem too, Mr. T.?' he asked. Everybody turned and looked at the Leader. The moment was critical. 'Why, yes, I want one, too,' said the Leader. 'Where you gonna wear it?' asked Walter. 'Oh, he's got a sweater,' replied Albert.

"But Henry had a point to make and he made it. He spoke again to the Leader, 'Well, if you're gonna get one, you're gonna pay for it, ain't you? Got to soak up forty cents.' 'Oh, I'll pay for it,' said the Leader. 'Just wait till we get the things ready to buy.' Henry's intentions in this matter hurt Charles. 'Listen fellows,' he began, 'after what Mr. T. has done for us he ought to get an emblem for nothin'.' They all agreed with that and everybody's face relaxed. Indeed, even Henry was so won over to the cause of giving the Leader an emblem as a token of the club's esteem that he offered the Leader, who had been standing, a chair."

Note: This incident shows something of the Leader's standing with the group. What does Henry's attitude indicate?

Later in the evening the following incident took place:

"About this time sounds of life from the other rooms created an element of unrest in the Pirates Club. 'Thar was food in them there rooms' and these boys knew it. There were girls, too, and the Pirates of late had been particularly conscious of their existence. It was not surprising then that at this instant seven or eight Pirates were smitten with terrible thirst and could slack it only by walking through all the party rooms into the kitchen. The Leader had asked them not to interfere with the revelers but he was determined to make sure they did not do so. Leaving the few who had remained in the room, he made his way to the kitchen. There he found Henry rushing off with a slice of bread, clutching it as would a refugee who had been given food after several days of hunger. He placed his cap over the bread before he thought the Leader could see him. One or two of the other boys were also cramming bread into their pockets. Not so Bert. Bert was a man of influence. He was receiving a gift offering of a sandwich from one of the party sponsors himself. Finally by tactics comprising persuasion and herding, the Leader got the Pirates back into their room. There he found Henry munching happily on an apple. The Leader looked at the club and said, 'I understand that you fellows would like to be invited to a bite or two of food and I know you gave these same fellows some of your own food last week but you're disturbing them by going into their rooms and they were really nice enough to let you have the whole house.' 'We didn't take nothin', Mr. T.,' said Henry. 'Them guys gave me this.' That ended the incident for a while."

The Leader comments on it:

"The incident of stealing food is of no great account this time, although last year the Leader was concerned when these same boys were twice accused of stealing other clubs' food through the open windows of the House. This time it was just as dishonest but it was so openly done as to seem the normal behavior of growing boys. The Leader did chide the club for it, however."

Note: What should the Leader do under such circumstances?

November 7, 1931

The Leader had arranged for a football game with the Cubs, another club at the agency. He reports the results:

"The Leader refereed, kept time and distance and acted as general peacemaker. Before starting the game, he introduced the clubs to each other and reminded them that this was to be a friendly game.

"The Cubs scored in the first quarter when one of them intercepted a pass and ran nearly seventy yards for a touchdown; a pretty bit of dodging. They scored again in the second quarter on a pass over the goal line.

"The Pirates scored in the third quarter when Charles went around the end for the touchdown. The game was close and well played. It was marred, however, by the 'dirty playing' of Henry, Joe, Stanley and Albert for the Pirates. Paul also 'played dirty' in the first quarter. When the Cubs complained to the Leader of this he took Paul aside and asked him to play fairly which he did play during the rest of the game."

The Leader comments:

"Henry's dirty playing is to be expected; he is sly in everything else. Joe, Albert and Stanley who were rotten players, saw a way of getting attention by following Henry.

"The final score was Cubs, thirteen, Pirates six. After the game Dave, the captain of the Cubs, asked the Leader to walk home with the Cubs, saying that the Pirates meant to 'get' him. This the Leader did. On the way home the Cubs expressed happiness at their victory and all agreed that Charles, captain of the Pirates, had played a clean, heady game. 'Tell him that the president of the Cubs tells him that as captain of the Pirates, he played a clean game,' this from Dave."

Note: Has the agency any responsibility for the kind of game played by such teams? What could the Leader or the agency do to improve this type of situation?

November 10, 1931

The time for the week-end camping trip was approaching so the club gave their attention this evening largely to planning it.

"The Leader suggested that since the group was going to camp on November twentieth they get all their planning done now. Henry persisted in conducting this business in his own way. 'We got to get committees,' said Charles. Henry arose to 'git' the committees. At first he tried to give the same duties to the same fellows for the whole trip. Finally, Charles persuaded him that he ought to divide the duties up. Whereupon, with further explanation from the Leader, Henry began, 'Who volunteers to wash dishes the first meal? That's the easiest meal. I'm on that committee. Who else volunteers?' Several hands went up and Henry chose Joe and Bert. In like manner he appointed the other committees. This took a long time.

"Henry then set to work to plan the menu. His procedure brought criticism from Fred and from the Leader but he paid no attention. 'Who's going to bring what?' he asked. 'Potatoes?—everybody,'—this with a sweep of his hand. 'Coffee?' 'I'll bring some,' said Speed. 'Who else?' said Henry. No reply. 'Al, you bring coffee.' 'Eggs? We're needing a lot of eggs. Who's going to bring eggs?' No one answered. 'Oh, we'll let Cap (Art). Oh, he ain't here. He ain't bringing anything.' 'Sugar? How much will we need?' 'Oh, two pounds ought to do,' said the Leader. 'I'll bring that,' said Henry, 'that don't cost so much.' 'Why don't you find out what we want to eat and then get the food?' said Fred, 'then we'd know.' 'Oh, we can do it this way, too,' said Henry. 'Hamburgers?' Henry consulted Bert, his right hand man. 'Can you bring that, Mr. T. ?' The Leader replied that he would. 'Bring five pounds,' said Fred. 'I can eat it all. Well, bring as much as you want to—three pounds or so.'

"It developed in the meeting that thirteen Pirates, the whole club in fact, intended to go out for this week-end. The Leader explained that the cabin was small, there would not be enough mattresses or blankets and that everybody would have to cooperate to his fullest extent if the week-end were going to be beneficial. Speed promised the club's cooperation."

The Leader comments on this:

"The Leader permitted this camp planning to take up the entire evening because he wanted very definitely to let the boys plan every bit of it; he knew that if Henry assigned them to committees there would be more chance of their enjoying the committee work than if the Leader did and he knew, too, that even though the boys failed to see the efficiency and saving in planning each meal and then pooling their money and buying food together, they would still have as good a time through their own efforts."

The competitor for the boys' interest in camp was again the 'bims.'

"Once during the evening two of the club girls came through the room. Immediately all talk of camp was forgotten and once the boys fixed their eyes on the girls they kept them there. When finally the girls had left the room, Fred said, 'The bims!' and Bert took a picture of a girl out of his pocket and announced that she was his 'bim.' He did this several times."

The Leader reports that he is trying to find out the possibilities of inviting the Pirates to a party with girls. He is also arranging for a swimming party.

November 17, 1931

At the next meeting:

"The Leader spoke to them about various matters of conduct. The first of these transgressions was that someone had scribbled the club name with a pencil on the white wall of the Community House and on the door of the Playshop. After describing how ugly this looked and how it gave the children the idea of doing the same, he asked who had written that. 'We didn't do it,' Joe said. 'Naw, nobody here would do it,' said Blackie. 'Well, that may be so but no one else would write your club name. And, whether you've done it or not, I'd like to see that erased from the walls before we go to camp.' This announcement did not create a great stir but Blackie arose and, asking the Leader for a rag, erased the name from the wall of the House.

"'What's the other thing, Mr. T.?' said Henry. The Leader answered by relating how the 'teachers' of the girls' club had been telling him for the past few weeks that the Pirates plus a few others had been hanging around the porch, interfering with the meetings and constantly calling to the girls as they came and went. The Leader told them that they were hurting the fun of the girls, the work of the 'teachers,' the reputation of the House and their own neighborhood. Not only that but the policeman on the beat was investigating every suspicious character he saw. That very night the Leader had met him as he was mounting the steps of the House to learn who all the boys were on the porch. 'It might be,' continued the Leader, 'that they had no other motive than to sit there and watch the girls but if they were arrested as suspicious characters it would be just as much a black mark against their names as if they had really meant to do damage. The policeman would be doing nothing more than his duty.' The boys all listened quietly and seemed by their expressions to be impressed with the Leader's arguments.

"A little later the Leader noticed that Henry and Joe were missing and had been missing for the last ten minutes, now that he thought of it. Earlier in the meeting the Leader had suddenly descended into the cellar and had found Henry and Fred there both gnawing on slices of bread taken from a basket of supplies in the kitchen. They had told him then that they were planning the camp program. This time as he started downstairs Albert was with him and he found the door locked. 'Mr. T.'s coming,' shouted Albert, 'Mr. T.'s coming.' 'Open the door, Henry,' said the Leader. Activity followed the Leader's voice. There seemed to be a good deal of running and chuckling and the door remained locked but the Leader caught a glimpse through the open stairs of several boys hastily leaving through the cellar window. He rushed up and out through the side door but they had all run away before he could learn their identity. Mr. Maxton, landlord and neighbor, came hastily over. 'Those boys,' he said, 'they break the windows; they break the porch. Can't have it this way.' The Leader assured him that he himself did not want such things to happen and would try to curb such practices. Then he returned to Henry and Joe and bade them come into the meeting room again, saying to them, 'I'd like to see you fellows after the meeting.' When all were together again, the Leader said, 'Listen, fellows, this has got to stop. If you are coming here to meet you've got to meet together and in one room. If some of you are going to play down in the cellar and some of you smoke on the porch and the rest of you play around here, you're not going to have much of a club meeting.' None answered the Leader.

"It was nine-thirty now and Joe said, 'I'm going, Mr. T. You want to see me now?' Leaving the club to continue playing games, the Leader walked through the kitchen with Joe and Henry. He pointed out to the boys that while they knew he was their friend in many ways, he was not a sucker—they could not make merry at his expense. If they chose to meet they were welcome but if they chose to disturb things in the house they were not welcome.

"Speed and Albert came in at this point and joined the conversation. Speed sat on the edge of the seat with his feet on the rungs of a chair, Albert was perched on the edge of the gas range and Henry, Joe and the Leader sat in chairs. The Leader continued, 'Who were those fellows down there tonight, Henry?' 'I don't know,' said Henry, 'I didn't see them.' 'If you didn't know,' pursued the Leader, 'why did you keep the door locked until they could go through the window?' 'I didn't keep it locked,' said Henry, and Joe here protested his innocence too. 'We were down there talking to Speed and them big guys came in. We said, "How did you get in?" They said, "The door was open." They sat here and when they heard you coming they all beat it through the window.' 'Didn't they take anything?' said the Leader. 'Naw,' said Henry solemnly, 'they didn't take anything,' and Joe supported him."

The Leader comments on this:

"There are several elements in the club which do not harmonize. Paul, Charles, Fred, Carl and John will play any game. Leonard tires of new games before the rest do and drags down enthusiasm by refusing to play and having to be drawn into these games by being 'It' or some other device. Joe has the wanderlust. Henry keeps making for the cellar, where the Leader suspects he smokes although he denies it. Stanley does not know his own mind and circulates between the groups. Bert renders all frivolous with his Polish chatter. Consequently, it is difficult to lead the club into an attitude of unity and the spirit of organized play."

Note: These are typical discipline problems with adolescent boys of this kind. How should such problems be treated? Could the program be managed so as to provide more engrossing activities? Are such incidents to be expected and ignored with boys of this age? Are the Leader's methods likely to get the results he desires?

At the beginning of the basket ball season the Pirates entered a league of teams of their age playing in the gymnasium of St. John's Church.

November 19, 1931

This was the date for the camping trip.

"A truck hired by the boys took all to camp. A game of touch football was first on the program. After a dinner of soup, baked beans, salmon patties, bread and coffee, dishes were washed and at the Leader's suggestion all took a long walk. Stirred by the gentle wind, the boys frolicked—now they sang, now they marched in fours, again they set themselves for a football play and then raced down the road. Bedtime was marked by the toasting of marshmallows. Bert carried on playfully for two hours; until midnight he played Indian, heartily amusing everybody. Breakfast consisted of bacon and eggs, bread, butter and coffee. Rain prevented sports; some of the boys climbed hills, others went 'grsszibi' (mushroom) hunting and still others read two Flight Story magazines brought by Carl, or played 'Hearts.'"

The Leader comments on the success of the trip:

"The Pirates clicked in harmony on this camp trip. Everyone worked willingly and sometimes without first having been asked.

"The Leader complimented the Pirates, both after the first meal and after the hike, saying that when they showed such a spirit of cooperation as they had this week-end he would surely secure camp again for them."

November 24, 1931

The tactics of Henry as leader appear in the following:

"All but Charles arrived on time. Quickly Bert began collecting dues, while the boys crowded around him to pay. This done, Henry arose and began, 'Charles ain't in the club any more. He don't want to pay the dues. How many vote to have him out?' When no objections came forth, the Leader raised some. He explained that since Charles had been one of the founders of the club and was vitally interested in it he deserved a chance to give his side of the case. 'Sure,' Blackie approved. Henry said, 'Yes,' too, but added, 'how many want to vote him out?' Whereupon the Leader repeated his objections. 'I'll go get Speed,' said Henry and disappeared.

"While he was gone, the club described the jackets it wanted the Leader to secure for it, black buckskin with white collar, cuffs, waist band and Pirate emblem. By this time Henry and Charles arrived. Henry greeted him with, 'We were voting you out because you don't want to pay dues. You get rent from six houses; you can afford to pay like the other kids.' 'From six houses,' echoed Speed mockingly, 'only three! I can pay but Bert there says to me on the street, "You gotta pay for the truck ride to camp like we all did; if you don't you'll get boosted out of the club." He ain't supposed to talk to me that way. I don't care if I'm not in the club. We ought to have a new treasurer anyway.' The Leader took charge; he explained to the group that Bert had been within his rights to ask Speed to pay what he had used with the rest but had overstepped his authority in his zeal. He then explained to Charles first, that he should have paid or promised payment of what he justly owed; and second, that he should avoid confusing a personal quarrel with another member of the club with his interest in the club itself. Neither Charles nor Bert said more and a bit later were playing games together as if nothing had ever come between them."

The Leader comments:

"Henry's haste to 'vote Charles out of the club' strikes the Leader as a move on his part to gain a stronger hold on his leadership by eliminating the influence of the older boys like Charles and Blackie. The Leader does not want these older boys to leave the club; they are its stabilizing element."

Note: What does this small conflict indicate about the attitudes between members of the group? Is the Leader's solution of the conflict the best one?

The interest in "bims" now reached the point of an active demand for joint activities.

"Henry now suggested a party 'with bims.' The Leader said he thought the idea a good one. All but Carl promised to bring 'bims' and many were the comments centered on these girls."

The Leader comments:

"The party with 'bims' may steady the Pirates. They go crazy about girls, talk about them all the time in a frivolous fashion and hang around the House to meet them. The party may give them an idea of socially accepted ways of meeting with these girls."

December 1, 1931

A next step was now taken in this direction.

"Henry brought up the party again. 'How about the party, Mr. T.?' he asked. 'You see we ought to appoint committees.' The Leader said that they probably would get the work done more easily and so Henry appointed the following committees: Food— Fred, Joe and himself; program—John, Carl, Bert, to meet with the Leader; decorations—Carl, Paul, Charles; dishes—Albert, Stanley, Art. Later when Carl suggested that coat checking ought to be taken care of Joe, Walter and Stanley volunteered to do the job. Several boys thereupon accused Walter of wanting the job so he could go through the pockets of the clothes but he disclaimed such intentions.

"The approaching party with girls led to a demand for dancing and the rest of the evening was devoted to a dancing lesson.

" 'How do you hold the girl?' asked Henry. The Leader described the proper way to ask a girl to dance and how to hold her. 'How does she know what steps you're going to take?' The Leader took several of the boys and led them in simple movements explaining how the slightest pressure of the hand or foot could indicate to a partner what the next step was to be.

"John alone knows how to dance. The rest could not even beat time properly. The Leader tried several ways of making them grasp the three beat rhythm of the waltz. Time and again he would say, 'Well, now, do you understand this?' and everybody would say, 'Sure.' Then the Leader would say, 'Now you're not fooling me. It's you who have to learn how to dance. If you don't understand, tell me frankly so I can try another way of teaching you.' At which Henry and one or two others would smile and say, 'No, we don't understand.' While everybody indulged in the dancing and took particular pains to shout at the Leader so that he might watch them try the steps, Fred alone caught the rhythm that evening. The rest learned the simple waltz step and the box step. To teach the simple waltz step the Leader tried for example to say, 'Now put your left foot out and bring your right to it, then left out and pause, then right out, left out, right out, and pause. Now come on, say to yourself as you're dancing, "Left, right, left, stop; right, left, right, stop." ' None of the boys would say that out loud. They all started the left right, left right movement and got their feet tangled up. Finally the Leader found that they did remember when he formed them in a straight line all facing the same way and made each grasp the arm of the other and then very slowly do the steps with him. He did the same thing for the box step and these repetitive movements were caught on to more easily than any of the others.

"Walter and Joe danced violently about the room, whistling to themselves in an ear-splitting manner. Everyone else chuckled as he thought he had grasped the step, bumped into everyone else, shouted to get the Leader's attention to himself and never gave up dancing. The noise was terrific but the enthusiasm was clear from the actions of the boys."

The Leader comments on his attempts to teach the Pirates to dance:

"The Pirates talk a great deal about their 'bims' but unfortunately lack the social virtues to make an impression on them. Under the cover of their loud talk and swagger there is evident the desire to acquire a little more polish. Even at their own parties where no girls are invited the boys arrive with neckties and washed faces."

Note: This is a typical picture of the adolescent. The new and demanding interest in girls is at last afforded some outlet here. What more could the Leader do to help the group in its new adjustment?

At this point the Leader heard that the boys have adopted as a hang-out a new speakeasy just opposite the club house. The store had recently been opened by a bootlegger and boys went there because they could smoke and watch the two "bims" who were daughters of the saloon keeper.

Note: The gang is rapidly growing up from a gang of little boys to a group of young adults. As it does so its tendencies to social or anti-social behavior become more defined. The presence of their new hang-out offers serious competition to the agency. Can anything be done about it by the agency? by the Leader?

December 8, 1931

The adolescent attitude toward the girls was again revealed in the uncertainty over the party. As the meeting began:

"Henry spoke up. 'I don't think we're going to have the party, Mr. T.' 'Why not?' said Charles. 'Oh, the kids don't want a party now. They want to save their money for jackets.' 'Why, I invited a bim,' said Fred. 'Oh, you didn't invite no bim,' came from several. 'Who is she?' Fred named some girl, but the rest laughed it off. Remarks came from both sides until Henry leaned forward and said, 'Should we have a party, Mr. T.?' 'Well,' said the Leader as everybody turned to look at him, 'you're the ones to decide. If you want to have one, why I'll be glad to be in on it and help you with it. But if you don't want one, why perhaps it would be better not to have one and thus keep the money for the jackets.' 'Well, let's have a vote,' said Henry. 'All who want a party, put up their hands.' Four put up hands, one putting up two hands. 'One, two, three, four,' said Henry. 'Now, who don't want a party?' Five put up their hands. 'All right, we don't have a party,' said Henry. Albert, Joe and Stanley had not engaged in this conversation at all but they voted against the party. The decision aroused the ire of Charles and Bert. 'The kids,' said Charles, 'they go ahead and plan a party then they back out because they ain't got the nerve to invite girls. What's the good of planning it?' Bert pointed to Fred, 'That's the guy that told us he had three bims on the string and now he don't want the party.' No more was said after this about the party and the Leader immediately introduced a new game."

The Leader comments on this:

"Why the Pirates have decided not to have a party is not clear except that in spite of all their loud talk of the 'bims' they are afraid to invite them.

"One of the major interests of the group at this point was saving enough money in the club treasury to buy jackets. At this time the club had seven dollars in surplus money and was considering charging members half a dollar for dues the first meeting after Christmas because they would be flush with gifts then."

The Leader further comments on Henry's behavior:

"Henry is more and more of a puzzle. His shifting eyes belie his smooth talk and his actions are always suspicious. Tonight for example, he was found rummaging through the bathroom. Last year a shaving brush and a razor disappeared. The Leader checked up tonight and could find nothing missing. Henry is also a disrupting factor in the club program. He leaves the thing he is participating in to go off to smoke. More than that, he seems to be planning all the time how best to satisfy himself. He makes sure to be in everything that's good, but unpleasant jobs he wishes onto others.

The Leader received a letter from Henry's teacher recently in response to one he had sent the teacher, saying that Henry was continually absenting himself from school and now his parents were being compelled to see to it that he went to school."

Note: Henry's reform during his presidency was short-lived. Should anything be done by the Leader to deal with these problems or should he attempt to get more expert service through some other agency? Should the Leader be responsible for attempting to handle such individual problems as they appear in his group? Should he cooperate with the school or see Henry's parents about situations in the club?

The Leader met several boys on the street and fell into conversation with them:
"Fred asked how one could become a leader of a club. He and Carl said they would be old enough next year and wanted to become leaders. The Leader outlined the requisites of a good club leader and steered the boys into thinking that the best way to start was in their own club. That club needed unity of spirit and action which they could supply. The Leader learned later that Fred had announced that next year he was to be a leader.
"They spoke of putting Henry out of the club because, though he was president, he created the most disturbance. On the way back the Leader met John and chatted with him also about club leadership. He, too, is interested."

Note: The opportunity to become junior club leaders is an honor in the agency and one which is desired by the more ambitious boys. It often proves one of the best methods for developing a sense of responsibility and capacities for leadership. It is significant that the older and more responsible Pirates are now seeking this opportunity.

December 17, 1931

Though the more responsible boys were developing in this direction, several continued their customary raids on the food supply of other groups.
"While some of the Pirates were presumably busy with metal craft in the basement a bag of cookies brought by the Gay Girls for a party that evening disappeared. Together with their Leader they descended to the cellar and accused the Pirates, naming Bert

in particular as having acted suspiciously at the moment. Bert had left in the meantime. The Leader assured the girls he was sorry and would see that the thieves paid for the cookies. The girls left after evaluating their loss at fifty cents. Events seemed to point to Henry and Stanley as the thieves."

December 18, 1931

For the first time the older boys assumed some responsibility for this situation:

"Early the next morning Carl came to the House, soon to be followed by Charles, Fred and Bert. They completely absolved Joe who had previously been suspected. The money to pay for the cookies, they said, the Leader was to take from the club money which he held for them; Henry and Stanley would pay it back. Not only that but if Henry and Stanley were caught hanging around the House at other times than club meeting, they would both be dropped from the club. Fred told how he had elicited a confession of theft from Henry. 'I came around,' he recounted, 'and I said, "Did he have the cookies!" and Henry said, "Yeah, we got two whole pounds of them."' "

December 20, 1931

The following day:

"The Pirates dressed in their Sunday clothes, were standing on the street when the Leader passed. They hailed him and he stopped to talk to them. He asked the group whether they had given Henry the word of warning they had intended to give. Blackie and Fred said they had. The Leader added another word to Henry but Henry paid little outward attention and kept changing the subject. The cookie money was returned by the Leader to the Leader of the Gay Girls."

The Leader comments on this:

"A leadership movement is growing up around Fred, Carl, Charles and John. In the near future, the Leader suspects, they are going to oust discordant elements like Henry and Stanley and unify the club. Until that time, however, the Leader will deal through them in treating Henry, for he is sure Henry will continue getting into trouble around the House. If necessary, however, the Leader will personally and swiftly bar Henry from the House or visit his parents. These are two good weapons."

Note: The Leader's attitude toward Henry is obviously that of punishment or of protection of the House property. What else if anything could he do about him and his relation to the group? Is this method of attempting to control his behavior through the other members a wise one?

December 22, 1931

After a business meeting devoted to plans for another camp week-end and more swimming, the urgent matter of the jackets was discussed but the cost was still far above the resources of the club.

Following this discussion, the Leader seized the occasion to discuss the club's accomplishments:

"The Leader began by a public evaluation of the Pirates Club right then and there. All paid heed to his words, but Bert's Polish remarks and funny movements kept them giggling continuously. Between bursts of laughter and Bert's Polish jests, the Leader pursued his theme. Had the boys noticed any change in the club this year? Yes, they had. Leonard said they had had more fun this year. 'More swimming and camping,' added Joe. 'Were there any other changes?' continued the Leader. 'Yeh, we're taller and weigh more,' Bert snapped back, chuckling aloud with the others. 'Well, we like to do different things,' said Joe seriously.

"The Leader explained that he felt enough friendship between the club members and himself to talk freely with them; that if he did not like them he would not be so concerned about their welfare; that he knew they could work together more harmoniously at meetings; witness the week-end camp when everything went off so smoothly. He told them that the reason he had sought to find out whether they had noted changes in themselves and the club was that he had noted such changes. The boys were bigger, had new interests, such as girls and four of them, Fred, Carl, John and Charles were hoping to be club leaders in the near future. They were having fun at the meetings but they could have more fun if all took part in the same activity instead of going off into groups. Not only that, but several in the club acted very suspiciously at times. Henry, to be specific was not only putting himself in danger of constant suspicion but was implicating everyone who was with him at the time. The Leader had been very lenient last year when food had been stolen from the house; he felt that

the thefts were more in youthful frivolity than in earnest; but
that this year, while the club had promised to punish those who
loitered around the House and stole things, from now on the
Leader, too, would keep offenders from meetings or even discuss
their acts with their folks, drastic as this latter action was. He
affirmed stoutly that he knew everybody here was no crook—he
knew Henry was no crook, at which Henry smiled slyly and rolled
his eyes in the manner of one who knows better—but the boys
would have to be more careful of their behavior. The Leader
wanted to help them have the best possible time."

The Leader comments:

"The Leader's words had not been prepared for this meeting.
He had intended to keep the last meeting before Christmas cheerful. It was cheerful up to the sudden point in the business meeting
when the spirit of expectancy that had lain on the group all through
the afternoon suddenly resolved itself into a perfectly passive attitude of listening. Even then the boys lost little of their cheerful-
ness but they did pay strict attention and they left with friendly
farewells."

Note: This is a modification of the same authoritative technique used by the Leader on other occasions. Is this a valuable
method with this group? Is this the best method of dealing
with Henry?

January 5, 1932

"The jackets became of increasing importance. Some of the
boys were very anxious to get them but several, including Charles,
Blackie and Carl, could not afford them. The Leader explained
that while getting the jackets was a good step as a club project, no
member should or could be compelled to get one against his will.
The Leader also made it clear that if jackets were bought with the
present club money, that money would first have to be apportioned
among the members so that those who were not getting jackets
should still have their share."

The persistent interest in girls reappeared.

"Bert then brought up a new subject, 'Hey, how about that
party. You promised us that the girls would invite us.' 'Well, you
got to learn to dance,' said Blackie to him. The Leader assured
him that the invitation would come in the near future and added
that the ability to dance would bring more invitations."

Note: In spite of the rising interest in girls and social demands of this kind no party with girls is included in this year's program. Should the Leader have pushed this through?

January 12, 1932

"The club treasury and the jackets now became a serious cause for controversy. As soon as the meeting opened the discussion began on the jackets and went from them to the state of the treasury. 'Bert,' said the Leader, 'how is your treasury coming?' Someone beat Bert to the answer. 'He gave Blackie and Bubbles and Speed (the boys who could not afford jackets) their money so now everybody's going to pay only two cents for dues and the other money goes for jackets.' 'Bert,' said the Leader raising his voice a little, 'did you really give these fellows their money?' 'Sure,' said Bert. 'You told me I should. You said it was their money.' Whereupon the Leader explained his position again. The money, he pointed out, did belong entirely to the Pirates and they could do with it whatever they wished. The thing that they had to remember was that if the treasurer had the right to give back money to anybody without the consent of the club they were going to get into difficulty. Bert took issue with those who had advised him not to pay out money without the club's consent. He burst out with, 'Well, Henry told me I could give the money out to Speed and Blackie and Bubbles. He's the president, ain't he?' 'Of course Henry's the president,' answered the Leader, 'but remember this,' and here everybody leaned forward to listen, 'the president is not the club. The president's powers are only these, that he directs the club meeting. Don't you see that you have chosen him. You're the ones to decide what goes on in the club. He is the one whom you have chosen to carry out your decisions. Remember then that the club, not the president, has to decide what it wants to do.' There was no answer."

The Leader comments on this:

"Bert's move in giving out money from the treasury despite the Leader's continued injunctions not to do so illustrates the fact that the Pirates still have the strong gang attitude towards their leader. If Henry said he could give back the money, then he could do it regardless of anything the Leader might say."

Note: This assumption of the rights and duties of the president appears in several groups. This is one place where training in leadership is essential. Is the Leader handling this wisely?

For several weeks the meetings were uneventful, the program consisting of games and story telling. On January twenty-sixth, a jacket salesman, introduced by Henry, came to the club and measured them for the jackets. On February ninth the jackets arrived and were proudly worn on a swimming party at the nearby "Y" pool.

February 16, 1932

This meeting too was uneventful. The Leader records the following conversation:

"Some boys outside suddenly shouted, 'Brown elected, extra, extra!' Hearing them, Fred leaped to his feet, poked his head out the door and bellowed, 'Hey, shut up,' then came back laughing. 'What's the matter, Fred?' said the Leader. 'Are you a Bogart man?' 'I sure am,' said Fred. 'Brown ain't gonna be a good mayor.' 'How many of the rest of you are for Brown?' asked the Leader. Every hand went up. 'Well, why are you all for Brown?' asked the Leader, counting votes with a prominent forefinger. That started a discussion on the relative merits of the two candidates and what they stood for. Finally Fred spoke up, 'Brown sent an innocent guy to jail. I mean Morton.' The Leader caught up his words and asked him what he would do if he were prosecutor for the city. Fred was a bit hazy but said he would see that the police arrested those that should be arrested. One or two others took part in this discussion but the rest listened. It was broken up all too soon by Walter and Joe who rose abruptly and left the room."

Note: It is significant that it is the same younger members who interrupted the discussion. How could the Leader follow up this interest in local politics? Could the Leader have gone further with this type of discussion?

February 19, 1932

Henry had been trying to curry special favor with the Leader. The Leader at this point explains what his plan is for handling him.

"Henry is very evidently trying to use the Leader for all he is worth. There are several ways of course of treating a boy like him. One is to take an intensive interest in him, cultivate him and deal with him as an intimate adviser; for such a course the Leader unfortunately has not the time. Another way would be for the Leader to treat Henry exactly like everybody else; he merits more attention than the rest, however. What the Leader is doing now is to treat Henry like the rest but dealing very firmly with him where special interests come up."

Note: Are these the only alternatives in dealing with Henry? Has the Leader any further responsibility for him? The Leader has apparently made no direct contacts with his home, his school or any other social workers that may be dealing with the family. Should this have been done before the Leader decided upon the plan he would adopt?

February 23, 1932

The following gives a glimpse of the street life of the neighborhood:

"The talk turned to movies. 'I'm lucky,' said Walter, 'I always get in for fifteen cents; I always pay children's prices when one guy at the box office ain't there. He knows me.' Fred burst out laughing, 'I ain't going to take my hat along any more when I go to the Grand (movie house). They pipe the lid and they says, "thirty-five cents." When I leave it home I get in for fifteen.' Walter and Fred went on in this manner telling how they used to sneak in at times; how at one time Fred had paid his way but the usher insisted on putting him and his friend out, claiming that they had not paid. 'We says to him,' said Fred, ' "We paid," but he doesn't believe us and he grabs us by the arms and wants to throw us out. Boy, did we rip his suit! I rips one pocket, my friend rips the other. We paid. The manager comes up. "Put them in the cellar," he says, so they put us in the cellar and we had to stay in the dark till the movie closed. Then they wanted us to sweep the place or they'd call the cops. But we wouldn't do it. We got out without doing nothin'.' 'That's a joint,' said Walter, 'there's always a mob of kids standing. You go in and you stand for an hour and then when there's two seats the usher comes back and says, "Hey, let them girls come through. They been waiting for a long time." Then they meets them after the show.'

" 'If you got a t'in wrist you can get candy at the Grand,' said

Walter. 'They got a slot machine in the lobby and when a crowd of kids gets there some kids bring a school bag under their coats. Then the kid with the t'in wrist sticks his hand in the machine and pulls out all the candy. Then they fill the school bag up. Nobody can see them. There's a crowd around.' 'That's all right if you got a t'in wrist,' said Fred, 'but boy, if you ain't!' and here he waved his drooping hand at the Leader. 'I stuck my hand in the machine once and it got stuck and I couldn't get it out. Somebody hollered, "Here comes the manager," so I pulled my hand out but did it get cut up!' "

Note: There is no evidence of the Leader's response to such conversation. How should he react to these remarks?

March 15, 1932

At a later meeting:
"Bert started the discussion by announcing that the club team now held first place in their class in the St. John's Basket Ball League and needed but three more games to win the championship. Victory would bring them a cup and individual medals. From basket ball the talk went to uniforms for a moment and from there to jackets. Henry entered in time to hear, 'We got gypped on these jackets, Mr. T. Is that there Mr. C. a Jew!' Henry laughed, 'I told you, Mr. T. Didn't I tell them kids not to buy them if they didn't think they were worth it?' The Leader said, 'I think you got your money's worth. That's exactly the kind of jacket you wanted, more for looks than for warmth.' Henry spoke again, 'Just because a couple of kids on the block say them jackets ain't worth the money these guys don't like their jackets.' "
So the experience of the much longed for jackets ended in disappointment. The Leader suspected that Henry got a rake-off on the jackets but he had no positive proof of this.

Note: Had the Leader any responsibility in this buying of the jackets? Was this perhaps a good experience for the group?

Again the casual discussion among some of the older boys illuminates the accepted values of the neighborhood:
"Then crime came up. The immediate cause of the discussion was the announcement that George, who lived on the block, had just returned from a ten months' visit to the state authorities at Columbus. One remarked, 'If he's like he was, nothin' ain't safe

any more.' At first the story of George led into general talk of crime. George's older brother was perfectly honest. 'Why,' asked the Leader, 'did George turn out to be a thief?' The Pirates made answer that George had never played around the block much with them but had always preferred to hobnob with 'the gully rats,' a group of shabby but harmless looking boys who loaf around the Playshop and who at one time or another had been in Community House clubs, notably in metal craft. Art explained that what may have led George to play with a group away from his own block was perhaps a chance acquaintance in that distant group or a school chum who was a member of it. That gang of 'gully rats' has a very great reputation for petty thievery among the boys. George, so the Pirates felt, had probably been misled through his companionship with them. 'Well,' put in the Leader after some talk, 'why do these fellows steal? Why don't the rest of you steal?' Charles answered immediately, 'Boy, there's nothing doing on our block like that.' And Art said, 'I'll tell you how it is. It's the parents around here that are most to blame. A kid goes out and brings something home and instead of asking him where he got it and making him take it back if he's stolen it, they just pay no attention to him. Sometimes they even tell him that it's a good way to get things for himself."

The Leader comments :

"The discussion tonight was interesting because the boys spoke quite frankly and trustfully. The neighborhood is so much their ówn world that they know the habits and the reputation of all its better known juvenile delinquents. The Leader wonders just why the Pirates were so receptive to having a discussion tonight. The reason probably is this : that these boys present tonight are the leaders of the club and are interested in things like discussion when the rest of the club is not present. They feel, the Leader knows, that when the whole club is assembled, games or some form of amusement are in order."

Note: Was the Leader right in his method of handling this discussion? What attitude toward George on the part of the Pirates will have the best results for themselves and for him?

March 29, 1932

This was the day for a basket ball game with a club of colored boys at Talbot House, another settlement, to be followed by a trip to a radio station.

"Along Broad Avenue the Pirates were merry but reservedly so. Blackie pointed to lighted windows and said, 'Those are the places, boys,' making everybody laugh.

"The settlement was reached at seven-thirty. At eight o'clock they were on the floor. The game was close and fast all the way through. Charles made some very pretty shots and together with Art easily led the playing. The Pirates lost, however, thirty-two to eighteen. Down in the locker room again, as they were making ready for a swim they said not a word about the roughness of the other team, while the other team whom the Leader could hear in the very next compartment, kept on complaining about the roughness of the Pirates. Yet to the Leader, the Pirates played a very clean game. A shower, a swim and the boys were ready to visit a radio station."

The Leader comments on this occasion:

"The Pirates enjoyed their trip to Talbot House. Their behavior throughout the trip was faultless and their enjoyment loudly proclaimed. It is very curious that several other members of the staff who have had more or less contact with the Pirates consider them a hard group to handle. Yet the Leader has always found them amenable to proper program activities, and on hikes, camp trips and outings they have worked together harmoniously. Although this harmony has been obtained on club outings, it has not always been achieved at club meetings. Here several cliques exist, each seeking its own interest and it is not always possible for the Leader to strike upon an activity appealing at once to all.

"Blackie's comments on Broad Avenue were harmless but evinced the desire to show to the other Pirates his knowledge of the city and to impress them with his being a man about town. His remarks are typical of the feeling around here that colored sections of the city are characterized by frills and vice. On several different occasions the Leader has tried to interpret the colored people to the Pirates but their prejudice is one of too long standing to be easily swayed. Incidentally the Pirates have a new name for Negroes. They used to call them 'shines'; now they call them 'boons.'

"Basket ball games can very easily become causes of combat. The Pirates this evening prepared for battle just as their colored opponents did. 'See how big them guys are,' this from Henry in the dressing room. Just before the game the Leader suggested to the team to be friendly and fair and to count on their team work to carry them through."

Note: The behavior of the group on this occasion seems remarkably restrained under the circumstances and is evidence of an improvement over earlier games. What are likely to be the learnings from such an experience? Is the inner harmony evident here related to the opportunity for turning their hostility outward on the opposing team?

After the game the club went on a trip to the radio station.

"Up the elevator to station XBN went the Pirates. They arrived too late to see the performance then going on but were advised by the attendant to remain in the waiting room until eleven o'clock when the Jewish program of the weekly nationality broadcasts would go on the air. The Leader asked the Pirates whether they chose to stay or try another station but when they learned that in the hour that they would have to wait the Lucky Strike orchestra was broadcasting they all sank into soft chairs and waited. Henry and Joe lit up cigarettes which they had snatched up on the street en route. Leonard was awkward in lighting his and everybody laughed at him a little nervously. Only Blackie had a whole cigarette and a respectable package to draw it from. For a while they sat there grinning at each other. Once Bert turned to the Leader and said, 'Look at Henry. Watch him when he laughs. He looks like them little rats in the movie fables.' The Leader chuckled at this. After a while even the soft armchairs became too hard for the Pirates and they wandered around, some going downstairs to buy candy, others just to wander.

"The attendant arrived at this time and volunteered to take the Pirates through the studios. He led them from one to another, explaining the various microphones, instruments and methods of procedure. The boys did not fail to test carefully every set of ear phones, every microphone, every group of chimes; but they comported themselves very decently. In one room they were told, 'There's Tom Buck. He broadcasts sports.' They all stopped and looked at him curiously. In turn he looked up at them and said, 'What outfit is this?' Thus emboldened, Henry stepped into the room. He said nothing about just having taken a licking at Talbot House. Instead he answered, 'Pirates. Nearly champions of St. John's League. Flashy East Side Team,' which made Tom Buck laugh and say, 'Why don't you ever win a game?' 'We need two more to win the cup,' said Henry. 'Well,' said Buck, 'you win that cup and let me know and I'll put you on the air.' The boys departed with audible remarks of incredulity, notably, 'Bologney.' Later, however, the Leader found a few of them back in Buck's office and this time when they emerged they were talking about how all the other kids on the block and in the league would be looking out the windows at them after they had gone on the air.

"Now the Pirates were led into the broadcasting room for the Nationality Hour and here they stayed sleepily through a half hour, not even stirring, so eager were they to follow the injunctions of the attendant not to disturb the program."

The Leader comments:

"Conduct at the radio station was amusing but pleasing to the Leader. The boys were very much impressed by the high ceilings and the splendor of the rooms. They tried to hide their feelings by puffing away jauntily at cigarettes, some of these the very same butts they had pounced upon in the street some minutes before. But even here their excitement betrayed them and they giggled nervously at each other's attempts to smoke nonchalantly."

The Leader comments at this time:

"Next week the Pirates will have a regular meeting. The season is nearing its end and perhaps the Pirates will want to finish it up with a party. John, Charles, Blackie, Carl and Fred have heard from the Leader about the junior volunteer group for next year and they are good prospects. They have expressed a wish to become club leaders."

April 5, 1932

The next meeting was short and significant chiefly for the announcement that the Pirates had won the championship at St. John's. They were awarded a plaque—"one of them boards you hang on the wall"—Henry put it.

April 12, 1932

This was the last meeting of the year. A controversy arose over the Pirates' playing in the baseball league for the clubs of their age in the Community House. The difficulty arose largely because Henry had failed to appear at a meeting of managers of teams announced for a previous week and so the Pirates had been excluded. They felt that the staff member responsible for the league was protecting his own team of "gully rats," the Scientifics, who were long standing rivals of the Pirates.

"'Do you know,' said the Leader quietly after the argument

had raged a while, 'you got yourself into all this mess?' Several
started to reply but Henry shouted them down. 'Listen to Mr. T.,
you kids.' They listened. 'It's all because you weren't organized,'
continued the Leader. 'When the basket ball season started, you
all got together, chose a captain and a manager, sent them down
to enter you in the tournament and as a result you played every
game in your best form and you won that tournament. Again,
when we went out camping, everyone of you pitched in and did
his job. I had never seen a bunch work together so smoothly and
as a result we had a most enjoyable time. But when the baseball
season came, what happened? You were told time and again to
get together, appoint a captain and a manager, send them down
to the Playshop and enter the tournament with exactly the same
advantages that all the other teams had. About this, however, you
failed to do anything. Not one of you led the others in getting
organized. Now that is your own fault, isn't it? Look at it hon-
estly. You can't blame the "gully rats." They haven't ever protested you. You just think they may. You can't blame me. I
reminded you time and again. It's nobody's fault but your own.
You neglected to attend the meeting. All right, take your medicine
like men.'

"After this long speech, there was a silence, broken eventually
by John who said, 'Maybe if we go back and see Mr. M. now he
can fix up some way for us to play.' John's tone was a good deal
more restrained now. Joined by Carl, Fred and Bert, he went to
see Mr. M."

The Leader comments:

"Tonight's dispute is the first one of any importance that the
Pirates have had this year. Somehow they had got the idea that,
being basket ball champions of their class, they deserved a bit of
extra consideration in everything else.

"What has interested the Leader has been the gradual lessening
of Henry's leadership in the club. The negligence of the Pirates in
not sending representatives to the meeting of baseball captains and
managers was a clear sign that nobody was at the helm. Evidently,
Henry does not consider himself leader of the Pirates any more.
On the other hand, the Pirates have not got to the point of organizing themselves without a leader. It is a good thing that Henry's
leadership is failing. It never was constructive leadership. None
of the Pirates ever said, 'Henry is our leader.' They would say,
'Henry is getting the team up.' Henry is himself a truant, selfish,
self-centered and not one to lead for the club's good. Perhaps with

time Charles or John will assume leadership; either of these would make a good leader."

Note: The Leader does not tell us how this dispute was finally settled. Certainly the club learned something about the necessity for taking its part with other groups, and possibly it helped them to gauge Henry's leadership better.

Since this was the Leader's last meeting he made a farewell address to the club:

" 'This is our last regular meeting as you know,' he said, 'we've been together for two years; we've had a lot of fun together and now our partnership ends. I don't know whom you'll be meeting with next year but I think your leader will find he is leading an interesting bunch of fellows, fellows he'll like. Four or five of you may be permitted to enter the junior volunteers' training class next year. That will be a great step forward for you.' Nobody made any comments on the Leader's words; nobody evinced any concern over them."

He interprets this as follows:

"The indifference which met the Leader's farewell address was no sign that there exists no bond between the Pirates and himself. Six times a day the Leader sees the Pirates as he walks to and from meals and each time they stop him to tell him of their plans. Their indifference was partly the result of their emotional excitement over the dispute this evening and partially the result of a natural stolidity. Were the Leader assailed in word or deed, they would undoubtedly come to his aid but as for expressing emotion over parting from him, that is not like them."

ANNUAL SUMMARY 1931-32

The Leader estimates the assets of the club as follows:

"The Pirates have a strong group tie and stand together at all points in spite of differences in age and nationality. Good cooperation has been developed in several undertakings and the club has proved itself capable of planning and carrying through common projects of various kinds. The business meeting has been growing in importance and this provides some training in group control. They are quite skilled in athletics as witnessed by their winning the championship of the church league in which they played. The Leader feels that, although their interests originally centered only on basket ball, they are gradually widening so that they now see the club as including other types of program.

"Five of the older boys have indicated an interest in assuming responsibility next year as leaders of younger clubs. There are some other indications in evidence of a new sense of responsibility and greater maturity on the part of some of the older members.

"The interest in girls is increasingly manifested this year and is in some ways forcing a transformation in the character of the club. They are still hesitant and inexperienced but this year was the period of transition for them from the prejudice and dislike of the little boy for girls to the absorbing concern of adolescence.

"On the other hand, the group has many shortcomings. In spite of a good deal of unity there is a split between the more serious boys and the clique of mischievous, irresponsible youngsters. This difference in interests constantly causes friction and disrupts programs.

"Their conception of leadership is still the gang concept of following a dictator implicitly. They have not yet learned to select the leader with much consideration or to expect him to use democratic procedures. Their selection of Henry and their willingness to follow him is some indication of what they consider acceptable in regard to stealing and lying. The experience with Henry may be one of the ways in which they are learning the requisites for good leadership. The Leader feels that they lack initiative and that many of them are slow in learning. They are still restless, disorderly, uncontrolled and irresponsible. He sums it up by saying they are still more of a gang than a club."

The reader may wish to ask the following questions about this year's record:

1. Does the Leader establish an effective relation with his group? What positive contribution does he make to its activities? Does he exert control where needed and in constructive ways? Does he successfully represent the values of the agency in ways likely to be convincing to these boys?

2. Does he have valuable contacts with individuals? Should he attempt to make any individual contact with Henry? What is his responsibility for individual behavior problems which emerge in such group contacts?

3. Does the group provide through its social interactions for developing experiences? Do the inevitable hostilities find harmless or useful outlets? Is a strong enough bond developed to provide

the security needed by the individuals? Does the program give sufficient scope for individual interests.

4. How much does the group learn about self-government from this experience? Do they assume increasing responsibility for their behavior? What do they learn about the functions of leadership from Henry's methods?

5. Is the program adequate for their interests? Does it provide sufficiently for the new interest in girls? Does it give scope for the growing interests of the older group?

6. Is the esprit de corps of the club maintained throughout? What part in this is played by the jackets? by the club treasury? by the basket ball championship?

7. Are these boys learning anything about their community from this experience? What opportunities are there here for learning from inter-group contacts? Can the new interest in politics evident at one point be developed? What effect, if any, does such group experience have on their developing socially desirable attitudes toward honesty or other community values?

VI

THE CONCORDIA CLUB: A STUDY IN HILARITY
AND CONFLICT

THE Concordia Club has a history of seven years. The records here given deal with the fourth year and a part of the fifth when it was well established and in its prime. The club has a membership of twenty-nine women. All of them are mothers and some of them are grandmothers. Their ages range between thirty and sixty with a majority of the women in the late thirties or early forties. In nationality the club is thoroughly mixed. Twenty-two were born in America, two in England, one in Wales, one in Germany, one in Italy and two in Poland. Of the twenty-two born here seven are of Polish descent and closely associated with the Polish community. These members added to the two actually born in Poland and the presence of a large Polish community in the neighborhood create a strong Polish subgroup which colors the relationships and the activities of the club.

The economic status of the group is, of course, affected by the depression. No information is available as to the exact amount of unemployment of the husbands but there is evidence throughout the record of the struggles of the various families with unemployment, part-time work and illness. Several of the families are on relief. The husbands of these women are employed in various occupations: one as attorney, one as manager of a small plant, one as a railroad engineer, two as pattern makers and two as small store owners. The majority are in the semi-skilled or unskilled occupations as truck drivers, laborers or helpers.

Several of the women also have occasional jobs. These include machine sewing in the garment industry, occasional tailoring and sewing, taking in washing, day work in homes and work as janitress and waitress. Several of them have worked before marriage. They are on the whole, a group of housekeepers, with children in the adolescent years or older, whose main occupation is homemaking and whose interests are centered in their homes.

The club began in January 1927, with an enrollment of nine. It has been noted throughout its history for its fine group spirit, its intelligent interest in the Community House as a whole and the good times it has afforded its members.

During this year the group has a student leader, Miss F., considerably younger than most of the women. Miss L., one of the staff members of the agency who had previously been their leader continues as a member and takes an active part in their affairs. This provides at many points the more mature leadership which the student cannot give.

This record is of interest to the group worker at several points. It provides in the first place a picture of the recreation interests and needs of mature women and the way in which these are met through their program. The dominant interest in their homes supplies the foundation for much of the program, but some interest in wider community concerns is also apparent. The place of hilarious entertainment in such a program is clearly evident.

In addition, the record reveals a conflict not unusual in such groups in which are involved certain personal hostilities combined with nationality loyalties. The leadership of the very able president in handling this conflict and the final outcome of it raise questions as to how such conflicts can be dealt with effectively.

DRAMATIS PERSONAE

Mrs. Knowles—the president of the club, a woman of about forty, of American descent and the wife of a highly skilled worker; able, tactful, quick at grasping ideas, outspoken but good-humored, somewhat more refined than some of the members, a resourceful, responsible leader.

Mrs. Ritchie—a pink-cheeked English woman, the wife of a railroad engineer; possessed of boundless energy and enthusiasm, public spirited and interested in the Community House, tactful, loyal, respected by the group.

Mrs. Korsybski—a woman of Czecko-Slovak parentage, about sixty years old, the wife of a small store keeper; ungainly and sometimes unkempt, sharp-tongued but sensitive, affectionate, generous, humorous and energetic.

Mrs. Taylor—a woman of American parentage and proud of it, the wife of a manager of a small business with a higher income and a better house than the others; distinguished for her stylish clothes, her plucked eyebrows and her frequent "facials," suspected by some of smoking and drinking cocktails, outspoken to the verge of rudeness in asserting her superiority to the Polish contingent.

Mrs. Ramsay—a friend and follower of Mrs. Taylor, also of American parentage, a person who craves publicity, glib but without comprehension, fond of horseplay.

Mrs. Pasklowski—a dignified woman of Polish descent, between fifty and sixty years of age, extremely neat in appearance, forceful, outspoken, enthusiastic and dependable.

Mrs. Christie—one of the older members of Polish descent, generous, humorous, friendly, loyal to the club, often too ill to attend but always an outstanding member.

Mrs. D'Antonio—an Italian woman of about thirty, large, complacent, loyal and responsible, not much interested in educational program.

Mrs. Slavek—a woman of Slovak descent, wife of an attorney and local politician, a stenographer before her marriage, conscious of her slightly higher social position, usually cooperative, an ardent supporter of her husband.

Exact information on the age and nationality of these women is not available in all cases.

Mrs. Rowan—a Welsh woman, friend of Mrs. D'Antonio, large, white-haired, dignified.

Mrs. Grofek—a quiet woman of Polish descent, friendly, loyal and pleasant, unassuming and unwilling to accept responsibility.

Mrs. Dudansky—a German woman, faithful but slow, jolly and interested in active games.

Mrs. Achtel—a large woman, alert, intelligent and humorous, generous and frank, a loyal and steady member of the group.

Mrs. Horonek—a rather complaining woman, considered a trouble maker and stingy.

Mrs. Krewski—a stout Polish woman, blunt in her speech, occasionally a supporter of Mrs. Taylor.

Mrs. Kimble—a quiet, rather weak woman, less responsible in the group.

Mrs. Liphitz—a large, slow-moving woman who occupies herself largely with the refreshments, steady, loyal and reliable.

Mrs. Milkowski—a tall, thin woman, even tempered and reserved; a leader in a very quiet but effective way.

Mrs. Tomaszewski—a younger woman, very quiet, steady but too shy to assume any responsibility.

Mrs. Ringel—an anaemic looking woman; a great talker.

Other minor characters appear at various times but not sufficiently to require characterization.

FIRST YEAR

The first year here recorded is the fourth of the life of the group. The usual program of the club consists of two meetings a month spent on handcraft of various kinds, one party and one "special event," usually a speech or a trip of some kind.

October 9, 1930

At the first meeting of the Concordias, only fourteen members arrived. This small attendance dampened the spirits of those present but in spite of that plans were made for a bunco party to raise money for a pledge which the club had made to the House.

"The first item of business was to appoint a committee to plan for this party. Mrs. Korsybski when asked said, 'Let some of the young ones do it. I'm no good as a committee member.' A murmur of protest arose. Mrs. Korsybski answered, 'Well, I'm no good.' At that they all objected and Mrs. Knowles said, 'Now we won't hear that again.' Mrs. Korsybski still refused to serve, stating that she thought that the reason why so few members had returned this year was that the others felt that they were not asked to do enough. The older members always plan everything. Mrs. Ritchie retorted, 'But if they don't come, how can they be asked to serve?' When Mrs. Knowles asked Mrs. Ritchie to serve she said that perhaps it would be better to let some of the new ones do it. At that Mrs. Horonek said, 'But there can't be all new ones. We wouldn't know what to do.' After the discussion had run a little while, Mrs. Knowles rapped on the table and instructed the secretary to take down the following for the committee: Mrs. Korsybski, Mrs. Horonek, Mrs. Ritchie and Mrs. Pasklowski."

In accordance with the usual program of handcraft, jars to be painted were produced by the Leader. This suggestion had been presented at a previous meeting and the jars had been ordered by five of the women. Seven more ordered them this evening and several others brought bottles of their own to paint. The question of a play to be given by the club was raised. After the handcraft period refreshments were served.

This was the first meeting for which the new student leader was responsible. She comments on her position with the group as follows:

"The Leader's situation is a bit peculiar. The club is very loath to give up their former leader, Miss L. Mrs. Knowles thought it might be especially bad now at the beginning, since the attendance has dropped. She thought it best to have the Leader come to the meetings without being recognized as such by the other women. Meanwhile the former leader will visit from time to time. Mrs. Knowles believes this gradual transition will not be harmful to the club. Nothing was said at this meeting about their Leader, perhaps because the small attendance and the bunco party absorbed their thoughts."

Note: Is this a wise decision? How can the Leader establish an effective relationship on this basis?

October 16, 1930

This was the occasion of the bunco party planned the previous week. Sixty people including nineteen members of the club attended.

"As the guests arrived, Miss L., their former leader, and Mrs. Knowles placed them at tables of bridge, bunco or pinochle. Soon the hum of voices rose loud as everyone became interested in the games. At nine-thirty doughnuts and coffee were served. The guests continued to play after lunch until nearly eleven when some of the members started to fold up the tables and chairs of those who had gone early!"

October 22, 1930

This meeting was one of the special events to which an outside speaker had been asked by the committee of the club responsible for these events. The following gives a picture of this occasion:

"Mesdames Christie, Ramsay and Taylor arrived, followed soon by Mrs. Knowles and Mrs. Ritchie. Since there was to be a speaker, the subject of politics came up and the discussion centered around Wets and Drys. The women agreed that prohibition was bad; that bootleggers were spending thousands of dollars to prevent the destruction of prohibition; that dry agents 'grabbed the booze, took it home and drank it up!' (This last according to Mrs. Christie.) Mrs. Ramsay finished with a loud exclamation, 'I'll tell youse, if you're eligible, go and vote for Conover. He's wet.'

"Just then Mrs. Jackson of the Bar Association arrived to speak on the judicial candidates. She stressed the importance of the offices, of women's votes, the non-partisan aspect of the Association. She appealed to the women as mothers to take more responsibility. She passed out cards with the Bar Association choices, calling attention to the fact that she had accidentally picked up the one with her husband's name on the back. She called in her husband to meet these 'fine women.' He reminisced about his boyhood in Newburgh district. The women clapped when he left and were loath to have him stop. Mrs. Slavek intercepted him in the hall and introduced herself as 'Frankie Slavek's wife.' A light of recognition dawned in Judge Jackson's eyes. Mrs. Slavek said in the Leader's ear, 'I belong to this gang too.'

"As lunch was being served, Mrs. Pasklowski said to the Leader, 'He's nice but I wouldn't be doing right as a Pole to vote against my own Judge Plewacki.' She then went on to tell of her acquaintance with him as a boy at St. John's School, emphasizing his cleanliness."

> **Note:** This description conveys the atmosphere of the discussion of public questions which sometimes occurs in the group. Is there anything here either in the discussion of prohibition or of the speech which offers leads for further program? What could the Leader do in following up Mrs. Pasklowski's remark on her Polish loyalty?

October 30, 1930

This is the occasion of the annual Hallowe'en Masquerade which is one of the traditions of the club.

"Mrs. Taylor arrived early to finish some details of decorating. While she was working, the Leader slipped into the room, fully masked in an Indian Costume. As the other women came, Mrs. Taylor decorated those not in costume with crêpe paper pumpkins and cats. When Mrs. Christie came dressed as a bowery tough, Mrs. Taylor gave her a cigarette and also lit one for herself. Some of the women looked astonished but Mrs. Taylor loudly asserted that 'everybody in society smokes these days.'

"There was a commotion in the hall and in pranced an Indian figure who danced around the room to the beat of a toy drum. After a moment, she sank exhausted into a chair, snatched off her mask and exclaimed, 'I've all the family's bath robes on.' It was Mrs. Slavek.

"Mrs. Ramsay arrived dressed as a Negro man, wearing extremely tight knee length trousers. For the next fifteen minutes or so she and Mrs. Taylor entertained the women with vulgar 'horse play.' Mrs. Taylor's remarks referring to Mrs. Ramsay's costume and previous activities were obscene. The other women laughed but took no active part.

"The judging of costumes was postponed until the arrival of Mrs. Ritchie. When she came the procession started. Miss B., a staff member was to judge the costumes but Mesdames Knowles, Christie and Taylor discussed the decisions with her. Mesdames Dudansky, Grofek, Korsybski and Ramsay were awarded prizes. There was some question about Mrs. Slavek. Mrs. Christie settled the matter with, 'It isn't whether we ought to give her one; we've got to.' So she was added to the list.

"Mrs. Taylor started games. The first two, 'Butts Up' and a trick of sitting on a crock and writing one's name again resulted in vulgar byplay. Next came contests of suspended apples, marshmallows on a string and other Hallowe'en games.

"When lunch was served, the women squealed and jostled one another in order to get a place near their choice of pie. Even so, many of them ate a large piece of both pumpkin and apple in addition to many sandwiches. Mrs. Slavek apologetically said she 'hated to make a hog of herself' but was not deterred by such scruples from eating a great deal!"

Note: This hilarity is typical of the Concordias and the fun they get from these occasions is one of the chief appeals of the club. Certainly in light of the hard work of their daily lives such parties offer much needed release and recreation. Does this party raise any questions?

The Leader comments as follows:

"The smoking was probably the first occurrence of women's smoking at the Community House. Strange that the Concordia Club should have been the ones to introduce it! It undoubtedly resulted from the general release from restraint so evident in Mrs. Taylor's behavior the whole evening.

"The vulgarity led by Mesdames Taylor and Ramsay was a problem. Had the party been planned by the Leader or had the Leader assisted in the plans it might have been avoided. Perhaps the Leader should have stepped in but her mask presented a difficulty. Mrs. Knowles was the only one who knew her so the women were not conscious of the presence of any House representative. The Leader was not certain about the attitude of the other women. Although they laughed they did not participate to any great extent. The problem seemed to rest entirely with Mesdames Taylor and Ramsay."

Note: What should the Leader have done here? How could she fulfill her responsibility as a representative of the House under these circumstances?

The Leader also discussed the club program with Mrs. Knowles and suggested a talk about Mexico by a Mexican student who was available, and a trip to the Police Women's Bureau.

November 6, 1930

This was the night for a special event and Miss Herrera, a Mexican student, had been secured to speak on Mexico.

"Miss Herrera began her talk after a brief introduction by the Leader. She gave the background of Mexican history first and then talked about Mexican customs. She said that the Catholic Church in Mexico was one factor which had prevented freedom and so retarded advancement of the country. However, she said the Catholic Church there was different from what it was here, being more rigid in its censorship of the people's acts and work. The women gradually became more interested in her talk and finally they were nodding their heads and even voicing their agreement when she reached the subject of the status of women in Mexico. When she told of her own embarrassment in wearing a bathing suit in public, Mrs. Christie threw up her hands and shouted, 'Oh, we don't think nothing of that here.' Miss Herrera went on to say that the general temperament of the Mexican people was sad in contrast to the gayety of life in America. She said she had been surprised to see people having such good times in America and had missed them when she had returned to Mexico.

"At that Mrs. Ramsay burst out, 'You should have seen me at the Hallowe'en party last week!' The other women voiced their agreement and advised her to have a good time while she was here. They invited her to their next party at Christmas time. She finished her talk with a poem by a Mexican poet. She suggested that perhaps she should not read it since they would not understand it but they protested and said they would like to hear the sound of it anyway. There was quite a hush when she finished. Then Mrs. D'Antonio said softly, 'That sounds like Italian.' Miss Herrera then sang two Mexican songs, after which the women clapped lustily. Mrs. Dudansky then asked Miss Herrera if she were Catholic. When she answered 'no' Mrs. Dudansky said, 'Well, that's all right. It doesn't make so much difference.' Mrs. Christie burst in with, 'No, Pollacks, Bohemians, Dutch, Irish, Eyetalians, we're all one in this club.' The women laughed heartily and joked about their diversity of nationality. The speaker had to leave them so the women bade her good-by, reiterating their invitation to their parties and their advice about having a good time in America."

Note: This occasion seems to have been very successful in arousing interest and the closing remark of Mrs. Christie shows that she connected it in some way with the attitudes toward various nationalities in the club. A question might be raised, however, as to whether this type of subject unrelated to their experience is of as great value to such a group as one in which it is possible for them to assimilate what they learn into their own lives. What is the place in adult education of such introduction of new and alien material?

"Club program was next discussed and since the next meeting was to be devoted to handcraft, the president asked for suggestions. Some of them wanted to make lamp shades and others quilts. Mrs. Pasklowski offered to teach them how to make lamp shades. Mrs. Korsybski suggested making some with small beads but several of the women informed her that they were no longer stylish. Mrs. Knowles said, 'Let me tell you this. No one will be allowed to start new things until their crocks are finished. Some of the club members have criticized the club for starting things and never finishing them. We're not going to do that.' At that point five more women ordered crocks for next time."

Note: This is quite representative of the type of interest in handcraft prevalent in this group. Nearly all the articles planned and made are small household furnishings or personal belongings. They seldom have much artistic value but they provide opportunity for sociability, for a certain limited amount of creativeness and for an improved social status. What is the value educationally of such activities? Should any attempt be made to direct interest into activities providing more scope for the creative or so-called "higher" levels of taste?

November 13, 1930

This evening was devoted to the painting of crocks.

November 20, 1930

On this occasion the first sign of conflict appears:

"While the women were playing games, Mrs. Knowles called the Leader into the kitchen and gave her a note which proved to be from Mrs. Achtel, stating that she wished to resign from her position as club reporter for the Community House newspaper and as a member of the club. Mrs. Knowles explained that at a club meeting (not the Concordia Club) at which she and Mesdames Ramsay, Taylor and Achtel were present during the week, Mrs. Taylor in her cutting way had hurt Mrs. Achtel by telling her that she had not been any good as club reporter to the Community House newspaper. Mrs. Achtel was very much hurt. Mrs. Knowles said, 'That's what comes of taking up club business outside of meeting. If there are any complaints, they ought to be made right here. Mrs. Taylor ought to be more careful of what she says. Her tongue is too sharp.'

"At this same club meeting already referred to Mesdames Ramsay and Taylor had disapproved of having a nominating committee. Mrs. Knowles remarked, 'I know why that is. They want to push Mrs. Korsybski through for president. Well, it should be as the club wants but personally I don't think she would be a very good president. Neither does Mrs. Ritchie. She thinks a club president should never have a sharp temper. I'm stepping out of office for certain but I'm going to see that there is a nominating committee.' "

The Leader comments on these incidents:

"None of the women knew why Mrs. Taylor was absent. Mrs. Knowles shrugged her shoulders and said it may have been because of the trouble with Mrs. Achtel. Mrs. Achtel is extremely sensitive, while Mrs. Taylor is coarse and thoughtless. She often hurts people with her sharp tongue. It is interesting that Mrs. Taylor wants Mrs. Korsybski for president of the club since they were very unfriendly at the beginning of last year. Although Mrs. Korsybski does lack the poise and tact which go to make a good president, it no doubt would be very good for her to have the responsibility. Given the opportunity, she might develop some of those characteristics which are lacking now. The Leader is not aware of any particular reason why Mrs. Knowles should object to her so strenuously except that she is not as outstanding as some of the other women in the club. Mrs. Knowles' concern that the club have good leadership indicates her genuine feeling of responsibility."

Note: The record is full of accounts of small bickerings and misunderstandings between the members. Mrs. Taylor especially seems to be a storm center and becomes increasingly so. Many of the women are sharp-tongued or sensitive or often both. If group work claims to provide any valuable experience in social adjustment this type of interaction certainly demands attention. What could the Leader do to reduce unnecessary friction or to encourage more cooperative attitudes? Is this desirable? Do such petty quarrels provide a necessary outlet for hostilities which are inevitable and must be expected? What should the Leader aim to do in these situations?

December 4, 1930

This meeting was occupied chiefly with the election of officers. "The business meeting progressed to the election of officers. Mrs. Knowles presented the situation: the club had elected officers last year by voting on candidates chosen by a nominating committee. However, since there had been considerable dissatisfaction in the club about this, she felt that there should be a discussion of the subject. Mrs. Ritchie was decidedly against having a nominating committee saying, 'It's all right when the group is large but I don't think it's necessary in a small club like this where we all know each other.' Mrs. Slavek said that in all the large groups like the P. T. A. they always had a nominating committee. Miss L. pointed out that nominations might also be made from the floor to add to the candidates selected by the committee and this made it a fair method. At that Mrs. Pasklowski rose to her feet and said heatedly, 'But it has caused hard feelings in our club. There are some women who say that the committee selects the wrong ones and they get the offices.' She bobbed her head at Miss L. as she spoke and sat down with an air of finality at the end of her speech. Miss L. then pointed out that if they wished to vote directly they would have to amend the constitution, since they had changed it last year to provide for a nominating committee. At Mrs. Knowles' request Mrs. Ramsay looked up the

constitution and laboriously read the clause on making an amendment. This read that a proposed amendment could not be voted
upon until the following week. Miss L. did a good deal of explaining to show that the officers could not be elected until the
following week in any case. The air was tense and when Mrs.
Knowles asked what they wished to do, a dead silence resulted.
Miss L. then moved that the constitution be amended so that
officers could be elected directly. The motion was defeated by a
close vote. Then followed more explanation on the part of Miss
L. and Mrs. Knowles to point out that a nominating committee
must then be selected according to the constitution. Mrs. Ramsay had a difficult time comprehending this.

"Each member voted for her first, second and third choices
for the nominating committee. Mesdames Christie, Slavek, Pasklowski and Knowles received the highest number of votes. When
the results were announced, Mrs. Slavek wrinkled her forehead,
looked worried and said that she would have to decline. Miss L.
said, 'Now, I don't think anyone has a right to decline a thing
like that. It will only mean one short meeting.' Mrs. Slavek on
the verge of tears said, 'I can't do it. I have to cut out everything
extra. My health won't stand it—not even for one meeting. I'm
so tied up at home. He's out every evening. If you have a meeting you have to get the house all cleaned up—' Mrs. Pasklowski
broke in quietly with, 'You can have the meeting at my house,
Mrs. Slavek.' Mrs. Christie said placidly, 'Sure and any time
that is all right for you. When can you come?' Mrs. Slavek
looked a bit ashamed so Mrs. Knowles settled it by saying, 'All
right, you three get together afterwards and decide when you'll
meet.' At that point Mrs. Knowles said, 'Whew,' wiped her face
with her handkerchief and laughed. The rest of the women followed her example and the tenseness broke into a rustle as the
women shifted positions, sighed and laughed or talked.

"During the last informal part of the meeting the nominating
committee had gone into a side room and after ejecting Mrs.
Knowles chose the following nominees:

"For President Mrs. Ritchie
                    Mrs. Knowles
"For Vice President Mrs. Tomaszewski
                    Mrs. Rowan
"For Secretary Mrs. Ramsay
                    Mrs. Christie

"For Treasurer Mrs. Krewski
              Mrs. Korsybski

"They announced these to Miss L., explaining, 'Mrs. Ritchie will decline so Mrs. Knowles will get the presidency. We have a Polish woman up for each office.' "

Note: Note the attention to the Polish contingent evident in the nominations. Some consciousness of the presence of the subgroup is evident here but the result seems to indicate an active attempt at fairness in the distribution of honors. Is representation by such subgroups the best way of handling situations of this kind or should individuals be nominated for their ability regardless of the representative character of the result?

"Later Mrs. Pasklowski said to Miss L. (in private) 'I was getting sick of this club. Now that we've had a good fight I like it again.' Miss L. then said, 'You were angry at me weren't you?' Mrs. Pasklowski replied, 'Yes, I was. But now that we've had the fight it's all right.' "

The Leader comments on this issue:

"Previous to last year the elections in the club had been a farce. The women carelessly put up anyone for office. In order that they exercise more thought in the process, Miss L. persuaded them to select a nominating committee to choose the candidates. Many of the women were not convinced of its value and they repeated their objections this year. The Leader is not sure why they voted down the amendment to the constitution which would have done away with the committee. In the heated discussion which preceded the motion, the Leader thought the feeling was decidedly for a direct election. Either they did not understand the implications of the motion or else they were stubbornly refusing to vote for anything. It was a mixture of these two no doubt."

Note: The pleasures of controversy are well illustrated in Mrs. Pasklowski's remark. Is there any difference in this situation either in the issue (an impersonal matter of the constitution) or in the way it was handled by the president and Miss L. which makes this conflict more constructive than the personal bickerings noted above. Miss L.'s method of handling the hostility directed at her is noteworthy here. What effect would it have on her future relationship to the group?

The Leader comments:
"The women were intensely interested in the conflict and en-

joyed it. In many respects the Leader believes this conflict to have been of value because:

"1. It promoted a sense of club structure and unity.

"2. The value and use of a club constitution was apparent.

"3. The importance of club elections was brought out. Surely an issue which would cause such disagreement must be important.

"4. The women were all vitally interested and apparently enjoyed the arguments."

The Leader comments after this meeting on her own position in the club.

"The Leader's technique in view of her youth has been to participate in the women's club activities avoiding, however, any strong suggestions to the club as a whole. Rather, she has talked over affairs with Mrs. Knowles before meetings. Mrs. Knowles' energy and quick grasp of ideas have resulted in her taking over any of the Leader's suggestions which seem agreeable and presenting them to the club along with her own. The Leader feels that she is gradually being accepted by the group."

Note: Is this the best technique she could have adopted under the circumstances?

December 11, 1930

This meeting consisted of a Christmas Bazaar planned at a previous meeting.

"Mrs. Taylor arrived very early with a basketful of Christmas trimmings and two towels for the sale. She said that Mrs. Ritchie had asked her to decorate the tables. The other women began to arrive bringing with them cookies, cup cakes, towels and other things for the sale. There was much discussion about prices and they were set extremely low. Some sat around in groups and chatted while others arranged and rearranged the goods to be sold. Mrs. Ramsay was absent because of illness. Mrs. Christie exclaimed at this news, 'Why didn't she tell us now or else send her cake? She was supposed to serve refreshments to-night.' Mrs. Achtel sent two handmade string holders for the sale and offered to take orders for more. The Leader asked Mrs. Knowles about Mrs. Achtel's feeling toward the club. Mrs. Knowles answered that when she had last seen her she still felt that she would not come back to the club for a while but might a little later on. Mesdames Tomaszewski, Christie and Knowles were gathered in

the hall. One of them remarked that Mr. Achtel was not working.
Mrs. Knowles said, 'That's too bad because Mrs. Achtel is used to
quite a bit. Sometimes he made seventy-five and eighty dollars
a week.' Mrs. Christie threw up her hands and cried, 'My God,
woman! She oughta have money. Me, if my husband brings
home seventy-five every two weeks I think I'm lucky.' Mrs. Liphitz shook her head and said mournfully, 'Yes, and how would
she like to have it like I got. For eleven years now two days a
week!' Mrs. Knowles then said, 'Well, we haven't had steady work
either for a year.'

"All during this time the women had been buying their own
things. Very few outsiders came to the sale, just nine including
the children and people from the Community House.

"After the sale the president called a business meeting. Before
calling it to order, Mrs. Knowles said to the Leader: 'In a few
minutes I'm going to make an announcement so I better tell you
because you might be surprised. Someone in the club said that
you and I were too dumb to tell the club that you are their Leader.
I'm going to make an announcement to-night and tell them that
you are their Leader.' This she did a little later."

Note: This reaction may indicate that the plan of letting the
Leader attend unannounced was not a good one. What should
be done in such situations?

December 21, 1930

The following describes the Christmas party:
"When they had all assembled Mrs. Knowles said, 'Come on,
let's do something.' The Leader suggested two games. Mrs.
Knowles led the women in 'Spooning' the one which she thought
the better of the two the Leader had suggested. Much hilarious
laughter ensued during the game. Mrs. Knowles was then called
into the kitchen. The Leader suggested playing 'The Girl is Slowly
Walking' but there was not much response. When Mrs. Knowles
came in she insisted that the women play it. Again there was much
laughing and giggling. Tea, coffee and nut rolls were then served.
Mrs. Taylor had decided that nut rolls were not good without
butter so she went across the street and bought some butter. When
Mrs. Knowles inquired if she had bought the butter, Mrs. Taylor
answered, 'Yes, for myself.' She took it to a table on her plate
and later shared it with some of the other women. The women

grouped themselves around little tables for lunch. Those from one of the tables wanted sugar so the Leader asked if she might borrow that from another table. Mrs. Dudansky answered irritably, 'Why no, we haven't used it yet. I'm not at all satisfied with this party. Here we've waited all night for the sugar and now she wants to take it away from us.' Mrs. Korsybski chimed in in the same tone, 'Oh, my husband gets nut rolls that have pecans all the way through them instead of just on top—the way these are.' Mrs. Christie said in a soothing tone, 'Now, Mrs. Dudansky, you don't mind that. You wait until the party's over before you complain.'

"After refreshments the women stood in a circle and the gifts were passed around one at a time to music. When the music stopped, the person who then had the gift kept it. They enjoyed this immensely and shrieks of laughter resulted each time the music stopped. The Leader had been playing the piano but the women sent out Mrs. Rowan to play as soon as she had a gift so that the Leader could take her place in the circle. Besides the regular ten-cent gift they also gave the Leader another package which proved to be two pairs of silk hose. There was much excitement when the women unwrapped their gifts, everybody exclaiming over her own."

Note: Here there appear again the childish complaints of some of the women. Could the Leader or Mrs. Knowles have handled this any more successfully?

January 8, 1931

This was the occasion for the election of officers. Before the meeting Mrs. Knowles told the Leader the following incident:

"At Peterson School on Wednesday night Mrs. Ramsay had told Mrs. Knowles, 'I don't like the people they have nominated at all.' Mrs. Knowles asked her how she knew, since the names were not to be divulged until the report was given at the meeting. Mrs. Ramsay answered, 'Why I have them in the minutes.' Mrs. Knowles told her that they were not to be read in the minutes for that was not the business of the previous meeting. The club members should not have known who the nominees were until the report was given by the chairman of the committee. Mrs. Ramsay then told Mrs. Knowles that she could tell *her* how to do a few things, too, as president of the club. Mrs. Knowles told the Leader that she was determined not to run because of this undercurrent of opposition. She said that Mrs. Taylor probably felt the same way as Mrs. Ramsay. She had intimated that Mesdames Knowles and Ritchie do too much and try to run things at the House. Mrs. Knowles said, 'But we put other people on the committees and then they don't do the work.' The Leader said that she was sorry since this feeling existed on the part of such a small percentage of the club and that the club really needed a strong president to hold the various factions together. However, Mrs. Knowles still insisted that she would not run for office.

"When the group had assembled the president called upon Mrs. Slavek to give the report of the nominating committee. After the report, Mrs. Knowles said in a determined voice, 'Well, ladies, I decline the nomination.' Mrs. Ritchie spoke up abruptly, 'Well then, I'll decline it too.' There was a dead silence, broken after a few seconds by Mrs. Pasklowski who pushed to the edge of her chair and started to talk, bobbing her head in rhythm with the words, 'Now, Mrs. Knowles we want you to be our president. Why do you decline?' Mrs. Knowles answered, 'Well, I've had it for a year and there are probably some in the club who don't like the way things have been done, so I think somebody else should have the honor.' Mrs. Pasklowski answered still bobbing, 'But we want you to be our president. I don't think anybody should be president for just one term. You've only learned what there is to do. It would not help the club if you refused to take the office for another year, to take advantage of what you've already learned.' Mesdames Slavek, Grofek, Christie and Korsybski nodded approval to her statement. However, Mrs. Taylor spoke out in a sharp voice, 'Well, I think we ought to respect what Mrs. Knowles says. I nominate Mrs. Korsybski.' A high, crackly laugh came from Mrs. Korsybski and she said, 'Sure, I'll run if you all vote for Mrs. Knowles.' Mrs. Ritchie then nominated Mrs. Taylor but she declined, saying that she was too hot-headed for that job. Mrs. Knowles finally accepted the nomination and was elected.

"Mrs. Ramsay declined the nomination of secretary and no amount of persuasion would make her reconsider it. Mrs. Christie was nominated and elected. Mrs. Rowan was elected vice-president and Mrs. Korsybski treasurer. Mrs. Knowles as new president then appointed Mrs. Pasklowski as House Council representative. Mrs. Pasklowski declined vigorously but the women used the same argument which she had used with Mrs. Knowles, namely, that she had just had enough experience to make her useful and that it was her duty to continue in office. Then the president proceeded to select chairmen for the club committees and these chairmen selected two people to serve with them.

"In choosing these committees, Mrs. Taylor who was chairman of the social committee was the cause of much merriment when she said bluntly, 'I'll have that D'Antonio, you know, that big fat woman. She's one of the steadiest women in our club and she's never on any committee.'"

Note: Elections are often the occasion when latent hostilities come into the open in the struggle for dominance. Mrs. Ramsay as a former president probably feels her dethronement. Was Mrs. Knowles right in attempting to withdraw and then finally accepting? Could anything further be done by her or the Leader to lessen the conflict which is appearing?

The club also discussed its program for the year:
"Then followed a more or less informal discussion of plans for the coming year. It was the general opinion that there should be more handcraft. Mrs. Pasklowski said, 'I wouldn't come if they didn't have some good handcraft sometimes.' The complaint was made that there was not enough time to accomplish much in handcraft. This was answered by the comment that if people would be prompt in coming there would be time. Mrs. Taylor pointed out that usually the business meetings were too long and that probably the business could be confined to one meeting a month. This was agreed upon, the plan being to have one important business meeting supplemented by necessary announcements at the other meetings.

"Plans for a play were also discussed. Mrs. Taylor agreed to take responsibility for finding a play."

January 15, 1931

After a short business meeting the club turned to handcraft.
"Mrs. Christie showed the women quilt blocks of a simple pattern and explained the scheme whereby two or three people would make blocks for each other until they each had a whole quilt. Mrs. Knowles thought this was a good idea and wanted to try it but the rest of the women were not especially enthusiastic.

"The Leader had brought some paper for the making of lamp

shades and was prepared to teach the group how to make them. The project did not go very well and created little enthusiasm."

The Leader comments on this project:

"The mottled paper lamp shades were a total flop in spite of the fact that the Leader had spent a great deal of time and thought in preparing paints and samples and organizing the materials that they might be easily used. For one thing the lamp shades that the women brought required too large a piece of paper for the size of the pan holding the water; also, the Leader's presentation might have been better. She might have demonstrated making the mottled paper in club meeting rather than showing samples which she had made before. This might have aroused their interest so that the women would have been ready to make the shades. Part of the difficulty might have been due also to the fact that the Leader herself is not enthusiastic about club meetings where handcraft is the program. It is so difficult to attend to the demands of all the women if they are all working; if they are not working, it is difficult to arouse their enthusiasm though individually some of the women are very fond of handwork. Perhaps it would be a good thing to make the handcraft program more of an individual affair, rather than trying to induce all the women to make the same thing."

Note: What type of handcraft would be best fitted to the interests and abilities of the group? What was wrong with this project? What should be expected of a handcraft program in such a group?

Some time was spent in discussing a possible play to be given by the group. They were very anxious to have it funny but the humor of several plays suggested did not appeal to them. The Leader introduced a new idea.

"When there was a lull in conversation the Leader brought in pictures of the Guelph Treasure which is on exhibit at the Art Museum. She told the women the story of how it had come to be in the church for eight hundred years and now was being exhibited in only four cities in the world. The women listened intently and broke in with comments and nods of the head. The Leader then suggested that the club visit the Art Museum for their next meeting. It was finally decided to have the regular social night on Thursday and go to the Art Museum on Friday evening, thus not breaking into the schedule of the club meeting."

January 23, 1931

Six women went on the trip to the Art Museum:

"When the group arrived at the Art Museum the other three women were waiting. Miss Forman of the Museum Staff conducted the trip. As she talked about the various objects large crowds would gather but she was always careful to see that the club women were close to her. The women were very much interested and occasionally strayed from the group and lingered before the cases in which the objects were exhibited. Toward the end of the trip several of them remarked enthusiastically about Miss Forman. 'My, she's a good speaker.' 'Isn't she interesting!' After the women had seen all of the Treasure, Mesdames Slavek, Krewski and their friends started to go back to the place where their coats were checked. Mesdames Korsybski, Dudansky and Grofek, however, preferred to see the rest of the Museum, remarking, 'We might as well see it all while we're here.' The Leader with Mrs. Korsybski went through one of the rooms which held the International Exhibit. On seeing three or four nudes Mrs. Korsybski dropped her eyes, put her hand over her mouth, nudged the Leader and giggled, 'Ain't that awful, Miss F.!' The Leader merely smiled. By that time the women who had gone on had disappeared. Since the other three showed no signs of wanting to leave, the Leader arranged with them to stay on while she went on to meet the other women. She found them at the check room about to get their wraps. They were enthusiastic about the trip. Mrs. Krewski said, 'Now, I'll have something to tell the family about to-night at supper time. My, I think it was wonderful.' The Leader tried to impress the women with the fact that they could come to the Art Museum at any time and that Wednesday, Saturday and Sunday were free. Mrs. Slavek said that she had come frequently."

Note: The comparatively small response to this trip may indicate that this suggestion had little relation to the group's interest. Its success for those who went, however, suggests the value of such opportunities in developing new interests. Should this kind of program be attempted again?

January 29, 1931

After a short business session, this meeting was devoted to handcraft in the form of painting glass jars by dipping them into

paints spread on the surface of water. This had been initiated by
Mrs. Christie and was taught by her to the other women. The
play committee met to discuss the play and the women not otherwise occupied played cards.

"Toward the end of the evening the cast for the play was announced. There are to be two one-act plays 'Sparkin' and 'A
Warm Reception.' Mesdames Rowan, Christie, Slavek, Pasklowski, Korsybski, Horonek and Knowles have been selected for
the parts. There was some protest from the characters about being
too busy. Mrs. Korsybski commented, 'Well, if none of youse
want to take part, why do we give a play?' The Leader said she
was sure it would be a lot of fun and that it would be fine if the
Concordia Club could start a precedent of giving a really good
dramatic performance. It was arranged that the group meet at
the Playshop on Wednesday evening at seven-thirty for the first
rehearsal."

The Leader comments on this:

"The Leader thinks the selection of characters for the plays is
good in that they are the faithful members who will surely stick
by the project. However, she feels there might have been a better
representation whereby some of the newer women might have
been drawn in. The Leader suggested this to Mrs. Christie but
she said, 'If we do that they won't come and we won't have a
play.' This is another aspect of a problem that has recurred during
the year. The newer women feel that a certain little group consisting of Mesdames Knowles, Ritchie, Slavek, Pasklowski,
Christie and Korsybski do all the club activities while the other
women are not included. The other women always defend themselves by saying that these women have been given a chance to
serve on committees but have not been faithful in fulfilling their
responsibilities. The Leader believes the newer women should be
given more opportunity for activity.

"Since Mrs. Taylor was taking such an interest in the play and
apparently handled the women so well she seemed the best person
to be director. The Leader thought it advisable, however, to wait
until after the first rehearsal before it was decided to do this. It
is strange that Mrs. Taylor with all her hot-headed speeches is
able to get the women to do things for her.

"The Leader is uncertain why the women all refused to take
their parts at first. She suspects it is part of their habit of thinking
it is polite and necessary to refuse everything when it is first

offered or suggested. In reality she believes they were really eager to take part."

February 4, 1931

Preparations for the play were immediately started:

"The first play rehearsal occurred Wednesday night with everyone present except Mrs. Horonek. Mrs. Ramsay was not especially pleased with her part as a younger sister in 'The Warm Reception.' Mrs. Taylor asked what would be done if Mrs. Horonek would not come to take her part as a bashful country lover in 'Sparkin'. Without waiting for an answer she suggested that Mrs. Ramsay might take it. Mrs. Ramsay said, 'But what would I do about the part in "The Warm Reception"? Oh well, I guess I could do them both.' The Leader said that although she probably could do it it would also be a good idea to draw in some of the other women of the club. She emphasized how well Mrs. Ramsay's hair could be arranged to suggest a young girl. She then proposed that the matter be dropped until it could be determined whether or not Mrs. Horonek was coming.

"During the rehearsal Mrs. Taylor took a good bit of the responsibility to start activities. Mrs. Ritchie came in to visit. Mrs. Taylor objected to this and made this announcement: 'Now ladies, there's one thing that we can't have and that is visitors. None of the other women can see the play until it's finished.' There was a little confusion while she said this and apparently Mrs. Ritchie did not hear. Mrs. Taylor said no more about the matter but the Leader suggested that she appoint Mrs. Ritchie as chairman of the committee on properties and costumes. Mrs. Taylor did nothing about this suggestion."

The Leader comments on this:

"The Leader believes it would be extremely bad for Mrs. Ramsay to take a man's part in the play. She is too large to wear men's clothes. Besides, it seems to have a bad effect on her. However, she and Mrs. Taylor are very friendly and Mrs. Taylor will want to please her. The Leader has temporarily prevented her being chosen for a man's part. Mrs. Taylor as chairman of the play committee has taken the whole affair in her own hands. This is good as long as she does not lose her head and say sarcastic things. She appears to have some dramatic sense. The Leader will have to be at hand for rehearsals to guide her."

February 7, 1931

This meeting was one of the special events for which the committee had secured a speaker on unemployment insurance.

"When the group had quieted, Mrs. Knowles introduced Miss Harlan of the Consumers' League who spoke on Unemployment Insurance. She gave a brief background and then asked for questions. Mesdames Ramsay, Ritchie, Christie, Rowan and Knowles asked questions having to do with the amount of the premium and the length of time at work necessary to get it. There was no one who was against the bill and so the discussion was quite mild. Miss Harlan gave the women stationery and suggested that they write letters to their representatives if they were in favor of the bill. The women took this very seriously, fourteen of them writing letters. Mrs. Krewski, after finishing one for herself, wrote one for Mrs. Simowski since she could not write in English. Mesdames Slavek, D'Antonio, Ringel, Tomaszewski and Liphitz took stationery home, planning to write them there."

Note: This presentation and discussion was evidently well received and effective in promoting actual participation in community affairs. How much value has this kind of subject for groups of women like this?

Some difficulties seemed to have arisen in connection with the play. Mrs. Taylor felt that Mrs. Christie should not be allowed to be in it unless she paid up certain back dues. This has caused bad feeling.

February 12, 1931

This meeting was in charge of Mrs. Taylor and had been planned as a hardtimes party in which the women were asked to masquerade. The following description gives a picture of the occasion:

"When the Leader arrived, six or eight women had gathered, three of them dressed in all manner of ragged dresses, fancy flower-bedecked hats and torn hose. The unmasked ones talked in low tones while the others sat silent and immobile. As others came in shrieks of laughter greeted those in costume. If, however, they were not masked, Mrs. Christie would announce, 'You'll have to pay ten cents.' She became more gleeful as the evening went on and the ten cent fines amounted to over a dollar. She herself was dressed in a quaint old-fashioned dress and hat. Mrs. Hilgendorff, the guest of Mrs. Taylor for the last two meetings, announced that Mrs. Taylor would not be present tonight since she was ill. A masked figure whom the Leader recognized as Mrs. Ramsay affirmed this statement. The Leader became concerned at this news and went upstairs to look up some games since Mrs. Taylor was to have planned them. By eight-thirty about twenty women had arrived and the Leader realizing things were getting dull, asked Mrs. Christie if she knew about the plans for the evening. She gave the Leader a sly look and said, 'Sure, that's Mrs. Taylor over there,' and she pointed to a dumpy figure in the corner whose head was completely covered with a black cloth. The Leader said she thought it was about time to start things because the women were getting restless. Mrs. Christie then went over and whispered to the black masked figure. After a few moments' conference she proclaimed grandly, 'All right ladies, now youse can unmask.'

"Amid screams of laughter Mesdames D'Antonio, Dudansky, Grofek, Korsybski, Knowles, Ramsay and Taylor tore off their masks and a general hubbub ensued during which Mrs. Taylor announced, 'Ladies, I swallowed my tooth,' and she pointed with her little finger to a vacant place in her mouth. More screams greeted this remark. After a moment the 'party' began. Mesdames Liphitz, Christie, Grofek and Dudanski retired to the kitchen to prepare the refreshments. Mrs. Taylor divided the rest of the women into three groups and gave each an envelope which contained a jumble of letters. The contest was to see which group could first form from their letters the title of a well-known song. Mrs. Taylor presented each member of the winning group with a tiny red box of hearts, explaining as she did so that there were not going to be big prizes for this party. She then announced that somewhere in the room was hidden a chocolate heart and that the women were to stay in their respective groups, link arms and search for it. Any group unlinking arms would be out of the contest. Mrs. Krewski was in the midst of the line in which the Leader was. She became impatient, broke the line and dashed hither and yon trying to find the prize. Finally Mrs. Tomaszewski found the heart in the hem of one of the curtains and boxes of hearts were duly awarded to each member of the winning side.

"Mrs. Taylor then told the Leader that she would have to go to the kitchen to help Mrs. Christie tag the valentines which the women had brought and asked the Leader to put on a game. She also said that Mrs. Korsybski had planned an initiation stunt for Mrs. Hilgendorff, since this was her third attendance and this would be ready in a few minutes. The Leader with the help of Mrs. Knowles got the women arranged in a circle and started a game. Just then Miss L., their former leader, and a guest came in. Hilarious shouts greeted her and she was invited to join the game which she did after introducing her guest. As the game was about to continue, Mrs. Korsybski opened the door from the kitchen and with a grand flourish announced, 'Make way for the Queen of Sheba. She is approaching in her royal carriage.' Silence fell and in came Mrs. Hilgendorff dressed in queenly garb, seated on a wheelbarrow, with Mrs. Kimble wielding a huge fan. Mrs. Korsybski wheeled her around the room, announcing that she had come all the way from Africa. The queen then shook hands with all the members of the club and thus ended the ceremony. Mrs. Christie, who was standing beside the Leader, jostled her as she fairly jiggled up and down, saying, 'Oh boy, and my family said I shouldn't come tonight. Am I glad I did!'

"Refreshments were then served. They looked very pretty, each plate containing a Polish rosette, heart-shaped cookies with pink frosting, heart-shaped pieces of bread spread with red jelly topped with whipped cream and a cherry and sandwiches. While the women were eating, Mrs. Ramsay who had been quiet up to this time stepped out into the middle of the room and began to show off. She had on a very tight skirt which had become split in the middle of the back during the evening's activities. To show this off she strutted around in a most exaggerated posture. Mrs. Christie cut short her antics by announcing a valentine hunt."

The Leader comments:

"The Leader was very much pleased at the general tone of the party. The games were quite successful and the refreshments very dainty and attractive. Only once was the note of obscenity so prevalent at the Hallowe'en party present. The Leader believes this was due partly to the fact that Mesdames Taylor and Ramsay were in women's costumes. Mrs. Taylor was anxious to conceal her identity and hence could not talk. The Leader purposely came unmasked since she thought that perhaps the obscenity at the Hallowe'en party might have been due to the fact that they did not realize that a staff member was present. The Leader was particularly pleased with the result since she had gone to the party in fear and trembling. Mrs. Korsybski had been at the Community House as a dinner guest and confided to the Leader that everybody was set to have a good time."

Note: Here again we get an illustration of the hilarity and release which these women find in the club. The effect of the presence of the Leader, young as she is, on the crude horse play of Mrs. Taylor and Mrs. Ramsay is an interesting commentary on their conception of the Community House and its standards. As in so many other relationships these two women show an immaturity in their behavior which is noticeably different from the attitude of other members of the group.

At the short business meeting, plans were made for making crocheted rugs, and orders taken for the materials.

February 19, 1931

All this evening the club engaged in handcraft either painting vases or crocheting rugs. The rehearsals of the plays had not been going well. The women did not come regularly and personal difficulties have made their appearance. The following is a typical incident:

"The Leader could not attend the rehearsal of the play tonight except for the last few minutes. At that time Mrs. Korsybski said, 'Come here, Miss F. You're the Leader of our club and you ought to know. Something's the matter with Mrs. Pasklowski. She won't be in the play. It's something about the Community Center Frolic at the school. All the committee should have been invited but the Pasklowskis weren't. Mrs. Pasklowski says Mary Ritchie just went ahead and asked the ones she wanted. Now Mrs. Pasklowski says she won't take part in club activities. Mrs. Ritchie wants to run things as she pleases. I talked to her for a long time but she just wouldn't listen.' After a few minutes more the Leader promised to call on her and talk to her. 'Yes, Miss F., you do that but don't let her know that you know about this.' The Leader assured her that she would not.

"That evening Mrs. Pasklowski came to the House for another meeting. She was early so the Leader talked to her a few minutes about casual things and then Mrs. Pasklowski said, 'I'm not going to be in the play, Miss F. I've decided not to take part in anything outside the club meetings. You do a lot of work and the other people choose the ones they want.' The Leader encouraged her to elaborate so she told about the Community Center Frolic. The

Leader weakly suggested that there might have been a mistake but Mrs. Pasklowski denied this. 'No, Mary Ritchie chose the ones she wanted!' The Leader then pointed out that there was no real connection between the Community Center and the Community House. 'Oh, I don't mean the House, Miss F., they are all right. It's Ritchies. Let Mrs. Ritchie be in the play. Ask Mrs. Slavek about them. They were awful to Mr. Slavek when he ran for councilman.'

"Mrs. Pasklowski talked on much longer, repeating in essence the above statements. The Leader was at a loss to explain the situation. Mrs. Pasklowski is temperamental. Naturally she was hurt by the slight. Mrs. Pasklowski is Polish while the Ritchies are English. The old animosity between the older and newer nationality groups may be involved.

"Mrs. Knowles in talking with the Leader about the affair on Tuesday said that it was the Slaveks who were at the root of the trouble. The Ritchies and Slaveks do not get along well. It was Mrs. Slavek who told Mrs. Pasklowski that it was Mary Ritchie who had slighted her."

Note: The combination of personal and nationality factors evident in this conflict is not unusual in such circumstances. The fact that Mrs. Slavek, while of foreign background is herself more Americanized, better educated and an aspirant for a higher social status may influence her feeling toward the Ritchies who are English and well established in the community. This blending of the strands of feeling in such conflicts makes them very complicated to handle. What could the Leader do in this situation?

February 24, 1931

Because of the absence of Mrs. Ramsay and Mrs. Taylor at the next rehearsal nothing was accomplished except an aroused animosity against them and charges that they were not doing their part in carrying through the plays. The Leader comments on this:

"The Leader is not sure as to the cause for Mesdames Ramsay's and Taylor's lack of interest in the play. It may be due to the Leader's efforts to prevent Mrs. Ramsay from taking a man's part, though no open opposition has been shown. The Leader is not surprised that the other women are discouraged. If these two women do not come to the next rehearsal the Leader will take definite steps to change the cast of the play. Even at the club meeting the Leader detected antagonism in Mrs. Taylor's actions. The Leader is not sure of the cause of this."

February 26, 1931

Most of this evening was taken up with the crocheting of rugs about which the women were very enthusiastic.

March 4, 1931

Again Mrs. Ramsay did not appear for rehearsal and when called asked to have a substitute put in her place. Some question was raised about giving up the play but a substitute was found and the rehearsal continued.

March 5, 1931

In the course of the business meeting the following incident occurred:

"Mrs. Knowles called for a report from the social committee. Mrs. Taylor began with sharp remarks about the lack of interest in the play rehearsals. Looking at Mrs. Ramsay, she said, 'You say you want to be in the play and you don't come to rehearsals. Do you want to be in it?' Mrs. Ramsay replied, 'No, or that is, I want to but it's hard for me to come so far.' At this point the Leader was called out of the room and when she returned Miss L. was urging the women to continue the play and Mrs. Ramsay had promised to come. Mrs. Taylor then briefly sketched the idea of the play followed by a card party as a scheme by which to earn the rest of the money for the club pledge to the House.

"The business meeting was followed by a talk on sex education by Mr. Frey, a member of the University faculty. Mr. Frey began by stating some newer principles in sex education, emphasizing the fact that children are essentially good in their approach, while adults are hampered by a warped viewpoint. Thus it is the task of the adults to learn from the children in a good many cases. He then sketched some of the newer ideas prevalent in progressive schools where there is no separation of the sexes in any of their activities. He also discussed some of the problems of adolescents in preparation for marriage. The women gave very close attention. Their facial expressions showed that they were interested. Occasionally they would giggle at some humorous part. Mrs. Dudansky, who was sitting beside the Leader, jabbed her in the ribs and chuckled when she was particularly pleased.

"After he had talked for about forty-five minutes, Mr. Frey asked for questions. The women were a bit restrained but finally Mrs. Christie said, 'I have a book at home that tells all about it. It starts in with the flowers.' Mr. Frey said that though this had some advantages, children were really more satisfied with the direct reply. It is also true that they sometimes fail to make the transition from flowers to human beings. Mrs. Christie, however, clung tenaciously to her idea. Mrs. Grofek brought up the importance of a physical examination before marriage. Mr. Frey heartily agreed with her. Mrs. Ramsay then said that her boy, fifteen, is not curious about sex matters. 'But I made a break the other day. Our dog is going to have puppies and I said something about it in front of him. When he asked me what was the matter with the dog I remembered and just told him she was sick. I found a picture of some girls without any clothes on in his drawer the other day—you know— actresses. I asked him what he was doing with them and he said they were pretty. Well, I threw them out.' Several of the women had been smiling and Mrs. Christie burst out with, 'See, you're just like he said—old-fashioned. You're afraid to tell him the truth.' Mrs. Ramsay, however, refused to change her opinion. After a little more discussion, Miss L. asked Mr. Frey if sex education should be done individually or with groups of youngsters. Mr. Frey said that either very small groups or individuals were best. Mrs. Slavek spoke up with, 'Yes, a deaconess told us in our Sunday School Class. She used the lily—you know—the symbol of purity.' Mr. Frey then told the women about Mary Ware Dennett's pamphlet on 'The Sex Side of Life' and suggested that any of the women who would like to buy it could leave orders with the Leader."

Note: While it is clear that not all of this talk was understood, it seems to have aroused a great deal of interest. It is probably the first time that these women have heard this subject discussed frankly and seriously. Is this a valuable subject for such a group? Should more be done to follow up the interest shown?

March 10, 1931

More difficulties developed about the play. Several women did not attend rehearsal and a personal quarrel between Mrs. Taylor and Mrs. Ramsay resulted in Mrs. Ramsay's withdrawing in disgust.

In the meantime, another source of trouble had appeared.

"The Leader walked home with Mesdames Kimble and Korsybski. When she arrived at the House Mrs. Knowles was waiting to talk to the Leader. She greeted her with, 'We have some trouble on our hands. Mrs. Korsybski found a mistake in the books.' She then showed the Leader the books and pointed to Mrs. Christie's entry of 'paints—one dollar' under club expenses. 'And at the meeting Thursday Mrs. Christie took a dollar in payment of the paints. Of course Mrs. Christie didn't do it on purpose. She's just careless and made a mistake. But what will we do about it? It would disrupt the whole club if they ever found out about it. Mrs. Korsybski and I talked it over and decided that maybe Miss L. or somebody could talk to Mrs. Christie.' The Leader answered that she did not think this was such a wise scheme because it would put too much emphasis on the affair in Mrs. Christie's eyes. On the other hand, Mrs. Korsybski as the present treasurer could show the books to Mrs. Christie and tell her that she wanted to check up the books and had not been able to understand this item. Mrs. Knowles answered, 'Yes, that's true. We don't want Mrs. Christie to think that everybody knows it. The only trouble is Mrs. Korsybski says it's hard for her to be tactful and she's afraid she'll hurt Mrs. Christie's feelings.' The Leader answered that if Mrs. Korsybski were convinced that this was only a mistake on Mrs. Christie's part, there would be no cause to worry."

March 16, 1931

"Then the Leader called on Mrs. Knowles and found her talking with Mrs. Korsybski. The Leader asked what had been done about the mistake in the books. Mrs. Korsybski replied, 'That's what I came here for. I went to see her and she saw the mistake right away and laughed about it. She said, "My God, they'll think I'll be buying a fur coat with the money." But she did not offer to pay the dollar. She erased the word "paints" and put in "supplies."' Mrs. Knowles said, 'I think we ought to forget about it. She just doesn't understand that she owes the club a dollar.' Mrs. Korsybski put in, 'Yes, and maybe some day it will come to her in a flash and she'll pay it. If ever the club would know it they'd call us all a bunch of robbers but this way they'll never know. You won't tell anyone, will you, Miss F.?' The Leader assured her that she would not tell and also expressed approval of the plan, stating that the amount of money was small compared to the good will of the women in the club."

Note: The amicable way in which this was settled for the sake of the good will of the group shows Mrs. Knowles' methods and Mrs. Korsybski's attitude in sharp contrast to that of some of the other members.

March 17, 1931

The plans for the play were thrown into confusion by the discovery that another club was planning to give one of the same plays. This club had previously rehearsed the play and then had given it up. They had now decided to put it on.

March 19, 1931

At the business meeting on this date the play situation reached its climax.

"Mrs. Knowles called a business meeting at about eight-fifteen. After the minutes were read, Mrs. Knowles asked Mrs. Taylor for a report from the social committee. Before she was started, Mrs. Korsybski burst out with, 'I'm disgusted with the ladies in this club. Here we try to put on a play with just four characters and no one turns up.' Mrs. Ramsay exclaimed, 'Well, Mrs. Korsybski, I'd like to know why you weren't there. I was at the Playshop on Tuesday and there wasn't anybody there. I know my lines by heart. I had an awful cold too. It costs me money to come way down here like that.' Mrs. Taylor, turning to Mrs. Ramsay, burst out with, "Well, you said at your bridge party that you didn't care about my old play and that you were going to quit.' 'Yes, and I'd like to know why you didn't come to that bridge party,' retaliated Mrs. Ramsay quickly. By this time these two women were fairly shrieking at each other. The Leader started to talk quietly and the two stopped to listen. The Leader explained what had finally happened about the play, stating that in January a group had started rehearsals but had discontinued them. Recently they had resumed rehearsals and were going to present 'Sparkin' Thursday night. Since the women on the committee did not think it wise to repeat the play, they advised that the club drop the project. Before the Leader's last words were out, Mrs. Ramsay raised her hoarse voice and said, 'Why didn't they tell us so that we could have chosen another play?' The Leader explained that she had mentioned it to the women at the very first rehearsal and that she thought the Concordia Club would appeal to an entirely different audience. Mrs. Pasklowski then said in a concerned tone, 'But they should have talked to us before letting that other play go ahead.'

"Mrs. Knowles said, 'Well, ladies, I think that's right but we certainly don't want our whole club to break up just because of the play. I think somebody ought to move that we give up dramatics for the rest of the year.' Someone so moved and the motion was seconded. It carried unanimously. This all happened vehemently and in a very short period of time."

Note: It would certainly seem that the Concordias had some justification for feeling that the other group should not have been allowed to revive their play when theirs was in process of rehearsal. Under the circumstances what could the Leader have done? Considering the other difficulties encountered in putting on the play was this perhaps a fortunate way out?

The Leader comments that Mrs. Taylor and Mrs. Ramsay seemed to enjoy their fight thoroughly.

Note: What should a Leader do under such circumstances? Are such conflicts to be expected occasionally? Is there any way in which they might be handled more constructively?

March 26, 1931

The women continued with crocheting rugs. Further conflict was precipitated by Mrs. Taylor at the next meeting:

"Mrs. Knowles then suggested that, since it was customary to use money in the treasury for the spring picnic, an attempt be made to make an extra amount for the pledge to the House in order that there might be money left over for the picnic. Mrs. Taylor again spoke out in a loud voice, asking where all the club money was anyway and stating that the club never used to be so poor. She intimated that several other women had been wondering why this was so. Mrs. Korsybski said sharply, 'Here, do you want to see the book? It's all in there.' Mrs. Knowles silenced Mrs. Korsybski with a look and then with assistance from Mesdames Christie, Pasklowski and Slavek she explained that the club had pledged twenty-five dollars to the House for maintenance expenses in addition to the twenty-five dollar pledge of last year. Mrs. Taylor prolonged the discussion by doggedly asking questions which the above three answered. The discussion finally ended when Mrs. Taylor said, 'Well, I didn't know and I'm sure there are lots of other women who didn't know that our club has given fifty dollars in the last two years. I'm glad they have. I just wanted to know where the money went because I've heard remarks here and there.' "

The Leader comments:

"If Mrs. Taylor would suggest the same things with a different attitude, she would be a good influence in the club. She pursues things to the bitter end and brings out matters for discussion which, if allowed to remain under the surface might rankle. However, she does all this with a decided gleam in her eye and in a tone of voice which shows delight in stirring up trouble. She is ruthlessly frank in making remarks which bear directly on the actions of club members. Her behavior in January meetings indicates that she feels a personal antagonism for Mrs. Knowles. It impresses the Leader that she does a good bit of 'disturbing' to put Mrs. Knowles in a bad situation. Mrs. Knowles usually manages to bring the discussion to some satisfactory solution through her tactful frankness and facing of the situations which arise."

April 4, 1931

On this occasion Mrs. Knowles tried to deal with Mrs. Taylor in the meeting.

"After several other women had arrived, Mrs. Knowles called the meeting to order. As she did so, Mesdames Slavek and Taylor changed places so that Mrs. Taylor could sit beside Mrs. Ramsay. Meanwhile they were talking together in loud whispers. Mrs. Knowles looked at them and said, 'You'd better change back.' Mrs. Ramsay looked up and answered, 'But she's just telling me about her cat.' Mrs. Knowles laughed but said firmly, 'This is a business meeting. I think it's awful the way you talk right through the meeting.' Mrs. Taylor promised that she would be quiet. Mrs. Hilgendorff entered, sat down on one side of the room and then seeing an empty chair beside Mrs. Taylor, crossed the room and seated herself there. She immediately began to whisper to Mrs. Taylor. Mrs. Knowles called for the reading of the minutes and everyone became quiet."

The rest of the evening was spent in planning a party to make money for their pledge and in playing games.

The following incident shows the reactions of the women to the material on sex education:

"The Leader then distributed the pamphlets, 'The Sex Side of Life,' which the women had ordered from Mr. Frey. Mesdames Ramsay, Taylor and Hilgendorff made a great disturbance in one corner reading it and giggling about the pictures. They made various comments in loud whispers. Mrs. Christie called from across the room, 'What youse up to over there? Shame on you.' The three women only giggled all the more. The rest of the women appeared not to notice them. Mrs. Milkowski did not have the money to pay for hers and arranged to have the Leader give it to a neighbor's daughter who came to club on Friday. After reading Mrs. Krewski's, Mrs. Milkowski said to the Leader, 'Say, don't give that book to her on Friday. I don't want her to read it.' The Leader said she would keep it for the next meeting. Mrs. Ramsay did not pay for hers, saying that she wanted to look at one first. However, she took a pamphlet and the Leader forgot to ask her for the money."

Note: This type of immature reaction can be counted on from certain members of groups of this type. Does this mean that this material should not be injected into the program? Is there any way in which this could have been better handled?

May 21, 1931

The four succeeding meetings were occupied with a spring party, a trip to an electrical exhibit and two evenings devoted to crocheting of rugs, Mexican drawn work and folk dancing. The picnic had been planned for this date. It brought out only five women. The following account gives a picture of the occasion:

"The five women met the Leader and set out for Bedford on the ten-thirty car. All the way out the women commented on the small attendance and tried to explain it. The weather, housework and lack of interest were some of the reasons suggested. After arriving at the park they spent an hour or so exploring. During this time the Leader, assisted by Mrs. Ritchie, laid a trail for a treasure hunt. The notes were written in a simple code, a figure standing for each letter of the alphabet. When the Leader returned to the group, the women were ready to eat. They took their lunches to the picnic grove and spread them on a table. Each woman brought her own lunch but they insisted on exchanging things with each other. Two cups of coffee apiece were purchased with the club money. At the end of the lunch Mrs. Knowles presented the Leader with a package, explaining that the club wanted to give her a gift since she would be leaving soon. The package contained three pairs of sport stockings. Mrs. Knowles explained that they wanted to buy something which the Leader could use at camp. The Leader thanked them for their thoughtfulness.

"After lunch the women tried the play apparatus including the swings, slide and merry-go-round. Much gayety resulted. When they tired of this, the Leader suggested that they go down into the glens for games and the treasure hunt. They enjoyed the walk down, commenting frequently about the beauty of the place. When they arrived at the bottom of the hill, the Leader divided them into two teams and started relays. They enjoyed them immensely. A match box relay, carrying beans on a knife, rope relay, running in couples, back to back with arms locked were the relays used. The Leader then suggested playing a form of baseball with the soccer ball which she had brought, kicking the ball instead of batting. This proved disastrous, for twice the ball went into the tree. Mrs. Christie suggested that they just play catch. They did so but instead of throwing it they would kick it from one to the other. After a little while Mrs. Christie suggested playing 'Up Jenkins.' This proved to be very entertaining and was changed at the suggestion of Mrs. Ritchie to 'Going on a Picnic.' At four o'clock the Leader suggested that it was time to follow the treasure trail. They puzzled long over the first note. Mrs. Korsybski was the first to decipher the code and the only one to follow the trail to the end. The others said it was too much work. She was very much pleased when she found the box of marshmallows at the end. After this the women returned to the picnic grove and bought sundaes with the club money. Mrs. Knowles said, 'I'll probably get killed for this. We're spending an awful lot of money; but then it's the others' fault if they don't come out.' "

May 28, 1931

The last meeting of the year was attended by thirteen women. Mrs. Knowles was absent because of a sprained ankle. The evening was devoted to bunco and pinochle. Toward the end of the evening, the following incident precipitated the conflict over Mrs. Taylor and Mrs. Ramsay.

"In a few minutes Mrs. Taylor told the Leader that she and Mrs. Ramsay had business to attend to and would have to leave. They went through the kitchen and Mrs. Taylor seeing a good looking cake on the table said, 'Gee, I'd like a piece of that!' She proceeded to cut a slice for Mrs. Ramsay and herself. Mrs. Christie called out, 'No, sir, not until it is served.' Mrs. Taylor continued to eat. Mrs. Christie repeated the statement in a louder voice and Mrs. Pasklowski reiterated the statement. Mrs. Taylor threw down the piece left and said, 'You can have your old cake. We've got to go,' and the two women hurried out.

"A tirade followed their exit in which Mesdames Christie and Pasklowski took the leading part. They continued their pinochle game as they talked but they excitedly slammed the cards on the table. Mrs. Christie said, 'They don't bring nothing themselves but they want to eat everybody else's. Mrs. Ramsay brought a fifteen cent jelly roll to-night—bakery!' Mrs. Pasklowski went on, 'Yes, and both you and I told her specially to bring home bake because it's Miss F.'s last time.' With one thought they both ran to the kitchen. The tirade continued; Mrs. Ramsay had taken her fifteen cent jelly roll with her! They finally calmed down but the dying phrases were still biting: 'Talk about ignorance. They think they know so much. *They're hungry.* They gad about all the time and don't even cook themselves.'

"The other women had been listening but not talking. Finally Mrs. Liphitz burst out with, 'Shut up, will you?' The two women quieted but in a minute Mrs. Pasklowski declared that she would not come to club next year if they were members. The Leader waited a minute, not knowing what to say. Mrs. Korsybski answered, 'Don't be a fool, Pasklowski. Quit the club just because you don't like everybody in it! Think what you'd miss. I've had my nose dirtied by them too.' Mrs. Pasklowski answered, 'Well, I can't enjoy it if they're here.' "

The Leader comments on this:

"The actions of Mesdames Ramsay and Taylor made for a 'typical' club meeting for the Leader's last impression. The Leader is not sure whether or not Mrs. Pasklowski will live up to her vow not to return to the club if the other two come back. This difficulty will be solved if Mesdames Ramsay and Taylor do not return. If they do, they should be talked to about their behavior at this meeting. The Leader will talk to Mrs. Knowles about it.

She is the logical person to treat the situation. It was interesting to hear Mrs. Korsybski, the sharp-tongued, reason with Mrs. Pasklowski. This is indicative of what Mrs. Korsybski has learned. Her speaking in this fashion is a thing which seldom happens in children's groups. It shows the ability of the club to solve its own difficulties."

Note: This conflict has now reached the point where it is likely to disrupt the club unless some answer can be found. There seems no way of keeping Mrs. Taylor and Mrs. Ramsay without ruining the club for the others. What can be done in such situations?

The following comment on the Leader is significant as to her place in the group.

"Mrs. Slavek then said, 'Who are we going to have for a leader next year?' Miss Q., the girls' worker at the agency was present and asked if they had any ideas. Mrs. Ritchie said that she thought Miss F. a 'very nice girl.' Miss Q. explained that her schedule was already crowded and that she had been wondering if the women might not like a new first year student who could be with them two years. Mrs. Slavek said, 'Why yes, that would be good. You know, Miss Q., we hadn't been so sure about having Miss F. this year. We thought she was so young for a bunch of old ladies like us. We don't think so any more. One thing, Miss F., you didn't let the ladies mother you and tell you what to do. You held your own.' "

Annual Summary, 1930-1931

The Leader in summarizing the work of the club describes its strong and weak points as she sees them.

During this year the Concordias have shown a strong sense of unity and an extremely low turnover in membership. They have displayed a marked readiness to develop new ideas and to accept those proposed by others. They are able to solve many of their conflicts by open discussion. They are responsible in their own group and have a wider loyalty to the Community House as a whole. One of their chief accomplishments is the progress made in the overcoming of the nationality animosities which are common in the neighborhood.

They have, however, had certain defects. These were chiefly concerned with their failure to carry out plans made and the inefficiency of several of the committees. They have been disturbed this year by several minor controversies and a major conflict in which Mrs. Taylor and Mrs. Ramsay were the leaders. This has now reached a crisis which must be dealt with if the club is to survive. Mrs. Taylor and Mrs. Ramsay have threatened to resign and if they do so the Leader feels they should not be urged to return. The Leader feels their most urgent need for the coming year is to settle in some way the controversy over Mrs. Taylor and to strengthen some of the committees.

SECOND YEAR

The controversy precipitated by Mrs. Taylor reappeared the following fall. Mrs. Taylor had assured the Leader during the summer that she did not want to return and had in fact sent in her resignation. Some members of the club, however, had urged her to come back. At the first meetings in October the Polish women did not appear and the Leader thought this was due to Mrs. Taylor's attitude toward them.

October 22, 1931

On this occasion the controversy reached a crisis.

"During the meeting the women were working on the mats and talking, when who should walk in 'dressed up to kill' but Mrs. Taylor, Mrs. Hilgendorff and a friend. The expression on the women's faces was one of amazement—and the Leader was perturbed to say the least. The Leader was sitting beside Mrs. Knowles at the time and was informed quietly that 'we are in for trouble now.'

"After the speaker of the evening had left the Leader came back and, lo and behold, Mrs. Taylor and Mrs. Hilgendorff had paid their dues and gone breezing out the door, heads high and confident that they had really done something. The women were rather quiet after this exit, until Mrs. Korsybski said, 'I certainly should have told Mrs. Taylor how she looked in that hat; she looked exactly like Annie Rooney.' At this the women howled and things were in a better mood.

"As Mesdames Slavek and Rowan were expected later, the women kept on sewing for a while and then when they did not come, Mrs. Knowles called a meeting. She evidently saw that the subject of Mrs. Taylor would have to be faced so she brought it up immediately. She said that the resignation of Mrs. Taylor had not been voted on and that it should be done but that there should be more members present because it must be a representative vote. Mrs. Ramsay felt that she had evidently changed her mind and that the club ought to overlook it but Mrs. Knowles insisted that it was a matter of form and did not apply only to Mrs. Taylor but to any resignation that was handed in. This irked Mrs. Ramsay and she said, 'Well, many exceptions have been made at this club and I think that here is a place that we can make one but maybe you don't want Mrs. Taylor to come back.'

"With this opening, Mrs. Pasklowski stepped into the speaker's box and said, 'Well, you know I have always believed in "trashing" a thing out here at club and since you bring me to this point, Mrs. Ramsay (this with a toss of the head) I will tell you frankly that I do not want Mrs. Taylor to come back and furthermore if I had known that she was going to be here tonight, I would not have come.' Mrs. Ramsay came back with, 'Mrs. Pasklowski, I certainly wouldn't make such frank and broad statements in the club. There are people here I don't like but I don't stay away because of it.' 'Then trash it out here, it's much better to do that than to talk about it afterwards,' replied Mrs. Pasklowski.

"And so the battle raged until Mrs. Grofek said, 'Why do we have to argue this way? We come to this club for recreation and fun, not to fight.' Mrs. Knowles asked Mrs. Ritchie what she thought and she said that she felt that Mrs. Taylor had been a good worker and had evidently changed her mind so should be allowed to come back into the club. Mrs. D'Antonio seconded that thought, saying, 'Oh, she's all right. I suppose we ought to let her be in the club. It's all right with me.' Mrs. Horonek said that since she had paid her dues, she evidently had decided to come back but that the club must go through the form to make it 'at least look square.' 'But,' said Mrs. Korsybski, referring to her books, 'she did not pay clear up, she only paid two months and that means that she hasn't paid for October yet.' Mrs. Knowles at this point asked the Leader if Miss L. were coming so the Leader tried to get in touch with her and succeeded in getting some advice on the subject but when she had returned to the room, the subject had been dropped and referred to a time when there would be more members present. Feeling that there was no point in bringing up this touchy subject again, the Leader said nothing in the meeting but talked to Mrs. Knowles later."

The Leader comments on this:

"The event of the evening was the entrance and exit of Mrs. Taylor and her friends. The expressions on the faces of the women were significant in themselves, showing surprise and disappointment. While Mrs. Pasklowski's decided views on the subject seem to reflect how most of the Polish women feel about the matter, she is about the only one who is willing to come out and say so. The Leader feels that if Mrs. Taylor should come back, the Polish women would drop out and that the club would become disorganized and ineffective. Because it would keep out many women to whom the club means a great deal, the Leader feels that some drastic, definite and rapid steps should be made to get a thorough understanding with Mrs. Taylor and to make her stick to her resignation if possible."

Note: The unwillingness of the group to oust Mrs. Taylor is an interesting feature of this discussion. What should the Leader do in this situation? Could a solution be worked out if she remained?

This incident agitated the club for several weeks until it was settled on November 5, 1931. On this occasion:
"Mrs. Knowles read a letter from Mrs. Taylor in which she stated that the club need not take action on her resignation, that she 'did not wish to belong to a club which talked about people behind their backs.' This evidently referred to Mrs. Korsybski's remark about her hat which had been repeated to her by Mrs. Ramsay. This registered Mrs. Taylor's final departure from the club. Mrs. Knowles summarized the situation by saying, 'So I guess we don't have to bother any more about that.' A committee was appointed to see why Mrs. Ramsay was not coming."

Note: Was this the best solution for this conflict under the circumstances?

After Mrs. Taylor's final withdrawal the group continued on its way with a noticeable improvement in the relationships between individuals and between the various nationality groups.

This record raises many questions. The reader may wish to ask:
1. Does the Leader, in spite of her difference in age, establish an effective relationship with the group? Is she apparently accepted by them as a leader? Can she fulfill her function as a representative of the standards of the House? What definite contribution does she make to their program?
2. Has the Leader effective relationships with individuals? What is her rôle in relation to a capable president like Mrs. Knowles? Should she attempt to get better acquainted with Mrs. Taylor or Mrs. Ramsay?
3. Are the conflicts within the group handled wisely? What if anything can be done about the minor bickering between the

women? Could the major conflict have been solved in any other way than by elimination?

4. Is the program adapted to their needs? Does it meet their interests and provide for growth? Does it provide adequate handling of the subjects considered?

5. Does the group encourage wider contacts and more intelligent participation in the community? Could more have been done to promote this? What effect does the group have on breaking down or building up the feeling between nationality groups?

APPENDIX

RECORD KEEPING

The records used here were written according to forms furnished the students in the School of Applied Social Sciences, for the purpose. Some modification of the forms has occurred since these records were written. The record forms used include the following:

1. Group record of Historical Information (Form A)
2. Current Face Sheet for group (Form B)
3. Outline for group record of each meeting (Form C)
4. A semi-annual group analysis form is also used at the School. It is not included here because it is primarily a teaching device and can be used satisfactorily only in connection with the course in which it was developed.
5. Individual Record including Face Sheet, Historical Summary, Chronological Record (Form D)

In addition to these, a roster sheet and an attendance blank of the usual sort are used.

FORM A

HISTORICAL INFORMATION

1. Date of original enrollment
2. Stated purpose of group at time of enrollment
3. Type of group (check) at original enrollment

Natural	Discussion
Formed	Other
Closed	Male
Open	Female
Club	Mixed
Class or Interest	

4. Make-up of Group at original enrollment:

Age Classification	Sex		Relig. Affiliation				Occupation				Country of Birth			Race		If foreign parents or for. born, list by mother tongue of parents				TOTALS
	Male	Female	R.C.	Prot.	G.O.	J.	Pub. School	Par. School	Work	Unemployed	Native Born of Native Parents	Native Born of Foreign Parents	Foreign Born	White	Negro	Italian	Polish			
2–5																				
6–9																				
10–11																				
12–14																				
15–17																				
18–20																				
21–23																				
24–26																				
27–29																				
30–39																				
40–over																				
TOTALS																				

5. Names of Leaders   Addresses   Date of Service
6. Names of Supervisors   Addresses   Date of Service

FORM B

CURRENT FACE SHEET

1. Name of Group   Closed
2. Agency   Open
Place of Meeting   Club
Day and time of   Class or Interest
meeting   Discussion
3. Type of Group (Check)   Other
    Natural   Male
    Formed   Female
                                    Mixed

4. Present Make-up of Group:

Age Classification	Sex		Relig. Affiliation				Occupation									Country of birth			Race		If foreign parents or for. born, list by mother tongue of parents					TOTALS
	Male	Female	R. C.	Prot.	G. O.	J.	Pub. School	Par. School	Industrial	Merchantile	Clerical	Managerial	Professional	Other	Unemployed	Native Born of Native Parents	Nat. Born of Foreign Parents	Foreign Born	White	Negro	Italian	Polish				
2–5																										
6–9																										
10–11																										
12–14																										
15–17																										
18–20																										
21–23																										
24–26																										
27–29																										
30–39																										
40–over																										
TOTALS																										

5. Name of Leader   Address   Telephone   Date assuming charge
6. Name of Supervisor   Date assuming charge
7. Officers: Names   Title   Address   Telephone
8. Formal relationships to other groups (check, give name)
    Membership in intergroup council of agency
    Membership in outside intergroup body
    Membership (as group) in other agencies
9. Representatives to other bodies:
    Name of Body   Name of Representative

OUTLINE FOR GROUP RECORD FOR EACH MEETING

I. Regular meeting   Name of Group:
         Leader: Date:

A. *Statistical*

     1. Number present (includes members enrolled, visitors)
_____

     2. Number members present————Names of members present————

     3. Number visitors present————Names (not including staff)
_____

     4. Total enrollment to date————(Last meeting's figure plus new members minus members dropped)

     5. Old members dropped (number and names)

     6. New members added (number and names)

     7. Supervisors or observers present (staff and faculty) (Names)

B. *Narrative*

Chronological narrative account of group and individual behavior observed at regular meetings. This includes such information as:

     1. Manner of assembly; who arrives with whom.

     2. Conscious efforts or techniques of L (leader).

     3. What was done, said, giving names and quotations if possible.

Keep in mind such things as what is proposed and by whom, what the responses to proposals are (give names), activities engaged in, duration of activities, when and how terminated, participation (i.e. response to activity itself), sub-groupings, expressions revealing attitudes toward persons or groups outside this particular group such as parents, teachers, home, friends, job, neighborhood, community, other groups, agency, etc.; conflict situations including persons involved, type, issues, controls, results.

Note: Use specific terms, that is, overt acts or words. Quote exactly wherever possible, including what L says. Note gestures, expressions, tone. Pay attention to withdrawing, submissive behaviors as well as aggressive, dominant, leadership behaviors. Note conditioning factors such as facilities, equipment, temperature, etc.

C. *Interpretation*

This section should contain L's interpretation of observations recorded above and should include:

     1. L's interpretation of individual backgrounds, capacities, attitudes, scale of values, needs, skills, etc.

2. L's interpretation of what happened and why.
3. L's interpretation and evaluation of choice and application of his techniques.
4. L's estimates of group status of individuals and of L, and possible reasons for changes in status.
5. L's estimate of individuals' acceptance of the group.
6. L's estimate of the group's relationship with other groups.
7. L's estimate of individual relationship with other groups.
8. L's interpretation of general esprit de corps.
9. L's interpretation of possible learnings.

II. *Plan of Procedure*

1. Plans for next meeting. Give details and reasons.
2. Plans for special or committee meetings.
3. Plans for outside contacts.
4. Plans for work with individuals.
5. Plans for future meetings or contacts.

III. *Outside Contacts* (*outside regular meeting*)

Chronological record of all outside contacts such as home visits, casual meetings or conversation with individuals, subgroups or group, school teachers, special or committee meetings. (Separate narrative and interpretation.) Record of contacts with other interested agencies, etc.

IV. *Conferences with Supervisor*

Account of conference, problems discussed and suggestions made by supervisor.

INDIVIDUAL RECORD OUTLINE
Form D

I. FACE SHEET

A. Identifying data (individual)
  1. Name
  2. Address
  3. Date and place of birth
  4. Sibling
  5. Occupation or school, name, grade
  6. Member of what other groups?

B. Identifying data (family)
  Father
          name
          nativity
          trade or occupation
  Mother
          name

nativity

trade or occupation

Others in home

II. HISTORICAL SUMMARY

A. Individual make-up

Description of individual's make-up, physical characteristics, dress, mannerisms, etc.

Mental data   I.Q. or P.L.R., etc.

Physical and medical history—specific data from examination; handicaps, etc.

Psychiatric history (if any)

B. Family background

Economic status

Religious affiliation

Parents (step), boarders or relatives living in home

Early home atmosphere, training, etc.

Family problems—agency, clearances

C. Other background material (of individual)

Schools

Church

Institutional

Work

Social agency

Community

Other former group background and experience

D. When and how introduced to this group? By whom?

Did member ever drop out of this group? When? Why?

Did member ever rejoin? When?

Was member referred to other group? Give details.

Was member referred to other agency? Give details.

Was member referred from other agencies? Give details.

III. CHRONOLOGICAL RECORD of the individual's activities, other than in this group, including,

Family group

School group

Work group

Other groups

Activities not in groups

Contacts with L outside regular group meetings*

(This is a running account, dated, initialed by worker)

* If individual records are not being kept, record of outside contacts, calls, etc. are recorded as part of Part III "Outside Contacts" of group record.